Senior Physical Education
An Integrated Approach

Second Edition

D1315084

David Kirk, PhD
Loughborough University

Robin Burgess-Limerick, PhD
The University of Queensland

Michael Kiss, BHMS (Ed)
Avoca State School

Janine Lahey, BEd
Sunshine Beach State High School

Dawn Penney, PhD
Edith Cowan University

Human Kinetics

Library of Congress Cataloging-in-Publication Data

Senior physical education / an integrated approach / David Kirk . . . [et al.].--2nd ed.
      p. cm.
Includes bibliographical references (p.   ) and index.
  ISBN 0-7360-5208-9 (pbk.)
  1. Physical education and training--Study and teaching
(Secondary)--Australia.   I. Kirk, David, 1958-
    GV361.S42 2004
    613.7'071'294--dc22   2003015564

ISBN: 0-7360-5208-9

The Web addresses cited in this text were current as of August 2003, unless otherwise noted.

Acquisitions Editor: Bonnie Pettifor; **Developmental Editor:** Jennifer L. Walker; **Assistant Editors:** Derek Campbell, Susan C. Hagan, Ragen E. Sanner; **Copyeditor:** Kathy Knight Calder; **Proofreader:** Jim Burns; **Indexer:** Bobbi Swanson; **Permission Manager:** Dalene Reeder; **Graphic Designer:** Fred Starbird; **Graphic Artist:** Yvonne Griffith; **Photo Manager:** Kareema McLendon; **Cover Designer:** Andrea Souflée; **Photographer (cover):** © Sport The Library; **Photographer (interior):** Chapter-opening photos © Sport The Library (pp. 2-3, 20-21, 40-41, 54-55, 76-77, 90-91, 106-107, 118-119, 132-133, 150-151, and 168-169); **Art Manager:** Kelly Hendren; **Illustrators:** Denise Lowry and Jennifer Delmotte (graphs), Roberto Sabas (illustrations), Roger Phillips (medical), Mic Greenberg (color); **Printer:** Hyde Park

10   9   8   7   6   5   4   3   2   1

Human Kinetics
Web site: www.HumanKinetics.com

United States: Human Kinetics, P.O. Box 5076, Champaign, IL 61825-5076
800-747-4457
e-mail: humank@hkusa.com

Canada: Human Kinetics, 475 Devonshire Road Unit 100, Windsor, ON N8Y 2L5
800-465-7301 (in Canada only)
e-mail: orders@hkcanada.com

Europe: Human Kinetics, 107 Bradford Road, Stanningley, Leeds LS28 6AT, United Kingdom
+44 (0) 113 255 5665
e-mail: hk@hkeurope.com

Australia: Human Kinetics, 57A Price Avenue, Lower Mitcham, South Australia 5062
08 8277 1555
e-mail: liaw@hkaustralia.com

New Zealand: Human Kinetics, Division of Sports Distributors NZ Ltd.,
P.O. Box 300 226 Albany, North Shore City, Auckland
0064 9 448 1207
e-mail: blairc@hknewz.com

Contents

Preface

This book draws on the latest developments in the research and practice of human movement studies and physical education. It presents a balanced view of physical education, informed by biophysical, psychological and socio-cultural knowledge integrated with a wide range of physical activities.

Initially, we wrote this book to support students participating in Senior Physical Education programs in Queensland. For this reason, it reflects the major divisions of subject matter that appear in the current Queensland Studies Authority Physical Education Syllabus. The book also reflects and supports the philosophical underpinnings of the Senior Physical Education Syllabus and the version of physical education that it outlines. However, we need to make clear that the book is solely our work and in no way reflects any official position of the Queensland Studies Authority, nor is it endorsed by the Board.

Although we wrote the book to support a specific version of physical education, it has developed into a useful resource for all students studying physical education in other Australian states. It has also been useful to tertiary-level students who are taking introductory subjects in the fields of human movement studies, sport studies and exercise science.

In this new edition, we have updated every chapter with the latest research and practice in movement studies and physical education. We have reorganised sections of the text, based on teacher and student feedback, to make the book more accessible to readers. In addition, each chapter now provides detailed learning outcomes so that you can monitor your learning as you work through the material. We have retained our emphasis on making the book as practical and useful to you as possible, particularly in relation to integrating theoretical knowledge and practical physical activities.

We hope that you will find this revised text useful in preparing you to complete your studies of physical education successfully.

Acknowledgements

M any people have been involved in the production of *Senior Physical Education: An Integrated Approach*. We wish to thank our colleague, Trish Gorely, for providing most of the material for chapter 2. Senior physical education teachers David Brown, Gavin Gagen, Colin Walker and Naree Wittwer provided generous advice at various stages of the book's conception and writing. The department of human movement studies at the University of Queensland, and in particular Debbie Noon, provided invaluable assistance with the production of the text. We wish to thank all members of the Human Kinetics team, both in Adelaide and Champaign, for their very hard work in getting this project up and running in the first place, and then helping us see it through to a timely conclusion. Finally, we particularly wish to thank our families, friends and colleagues for their ongoing forbearance and support.

Introduction

Physical education is a challenging and demanding subject to study. It covers a broad range of physical activities and subject matter. The combination of physical activities and subject matter is what makes the subject challenging and demanding for you as a learner. Few individuals can become experts in each individual component of physical education. In any case, this is not what physical education aims to do. You may be a good netball or basketball player, or you may be interested in the physiology of sport. Expertise in isolated aspects of physical education, however, is not the same thing as developing expertise in physical education.

Exploring the range of physical activities offered in physical education programs is the medium for learning *in* the physical domain. Studying the academic subdisciplines of sport, such as biomechanics and sociology, facilitates learning *about* physical activity. As you engage in physical activities and study the academic side of physical education, you learn *through* physical activity social values such as teamwork and fair play.

What makes physical education a unique field of study is that it integrates physical activity, academic knowledge and social values. This integration makes the field both demanding and educationally comprehensive.

Physical education and the teaching of physical education have evolved dramatically over the past 50 years. This introduction provides a road map for you to follow as you begin to explore the past, present and future of physical education in Australia in the pages of this book.

THE BEGINNINGS OF PHYSICAL EDUCATION

The term *physical education* did not come into widespread use in Australian schools until the 1950s. Before the end of World War II in 1945, government schools more commonly used the term *physical training* to describe their physical activity programs. Physical training consisted mainly of callisthenics (a systematic form of exercise performed in unison by large classes of students), marching and drilling.

By the beginning of the 1950s the term *new physical education* was growing in popularity. This type of physical education had two distinguishing features whose influence still characterises many of our school physical education programs today. The first feature was playing games—particularly the major competitive team games such as cricket, football, netball and hockey. The second feature was learning the physical skills that were the components of these games. This form of physical education sought to develop physical skills but tended to neglect the cognitive skills that are required of a physically educated person. These skills include the ability to use strategies in game play, the capacity to use theoretical knowledge to improve performance and the expertise to place physical activity in its social context.

In the 1970s, exercises specifically designed to have a health-related outcome were added to physical education. Also during the 1970s, some Australian state education systems began to develop physical education as a subject for study in the senior secondary schools and counted the subject toward university entrance. In Queensland, for example, the first syllabus for senior health and physical education was made available to all secondary schools in the state in 1978. These early senior school versions of physical education proved to be very popular and attracted large numbers of students.

Over time, however, teachers and students began to criticise these courses. Three criticisms were common. The first was that the subject was too similar to the university field of human movement studies and therefore was, in some respects, inappropriate at high school level. The second was that an imbalance existed between biophysical scientific subject matter, such as physiology and biomechanics, and sociocultural knowledge—with the biophysical knowledge side taking the largest share of available time. The third common criticism was that the subject was too theoretical, not because there was insufficient time given to practical physical activity, but because the relationship between academic subject matter (such as physiology and sociology) and physical activities (such as tennis or swimming) was unclear. These three criticisms stimulated the development of new forms of physical education, which we see today.

PHYSICAL EDUCATION TODAY

Physical education currently is based on a progressive curriculum that is informed by three major principles—integration, personalisation, and social justice and equity.

Integration

The first principle is integration. Integration refers to connecting academic matter such as physiology or history with learning physical activities. This principle is informed by the work of several educational philosophers who describe physical education as a process of learning in, about and through movement.

Learning physical activities requires a range of cognitive skills as well as movement competencies. You can better understand and enhance your performance of physical activities when you integrate three aspects of the activity:

- Academic information about movement (such as the physiological, psychological and biomechanical information contained in chapters 2 to 7)
- Knowledge of the sociological and historical context of the activity (such as that found in chapters 9 to 11)
- Theoretical and practical experience of the activity

You can also learn a whole range of social values and competencies through movement, such as responsibility for your actions and caring for others.

Recently, physical educators in Australia have looked for ways of applying the principle of integration to school programs. They have achieved their goal by developing learning experiences that provide students with opportunities to connect academic content like sociology or biomechanics with physical activities like basketball or aquatics. The sample learning experiences found in the chapters of this book link some of the key theoretical concepts of the chapter with a physical activity, through a carefully designed learning experience.

Personalisation

The second principle is personalisation. Personalisation refers to making new information meaningful to a learner. The type of learning that results in both understanding theoretical principles and increasing physical proficiency is largely dependent on the extent to which physical education is personalised. Recent advances in the fields of educational learning theory, motor control and the psychology of sport and exercise, discussed in chapters 1 and 2, have further developed the concept of personalisation.

Personalisation is not simply a matter of finding an aspect of the new information that is recognisable, familiar or comfortable for the learner. The process also involves

- finding the links between what we already know or already can do and the new information and physical challenges we encounter;
- working out which pieces of information within a range of new knowledge are most important and then attending to them;
- becoming more aware of how we learn and better able to learn from experience;
- understanding the relationships between local, national and global environments and adapting that information to suit the local, national and global contexts in which we live; and
- learning through critical reflection on our own experience and the experiences of others.

As you read through this textbook, you will come across a number of sections in each chapter called focus activities. These sections contain a series of tasks that implement the notion of personalisation in this book. Focus activities provide you with opportunities to relate new information encountered in the text to both your personal experience and the experience of others in your class, family, school or community. The tasks are intended to help you make sense of new information by encouraging you to apply the information to situations that you are familiar with or to real-life examples besides those provided in the book.

Each chapter contains an extension activity. The exercises in this section provide you with another opportunity to apply what you have learnt and personalise the chapter information. They integrate the key points of the chapter into one exercise.

Social Justice and Equity

The third principle is composed of social justice and equity. Social justice and equity derive from the democratic movements in Australian society that attempt to ensure that all people are treated equally and fairly, that people are supported in fulfilling their responsibilities as members of society and that human dignity is respected. In physical education, the principles of social justice and equity are essential to identifying the ways in which sport, exercise and physical education can play a part in enhancing the quality of life for people, for local communities and for Australian society as a whole.

The application of these principles to the development of new forms of physical education has also been crucial, because it has shown that sport has sometimes been used to discriminate unfairly against individuals and groups of people. Examples of how organised physical activities such as sport, exercise and physical recreation can be used to treat people unjustly and inequitably are explained in chapter 8 and then developed in chapters 9 to 11.

People sometimes assume that social justice and equity issues in sport relate only to discrimination against girls and women. Although it is true that girls and women have been treated unfairly in sport, chapter 8 shows that all kinds of individuals and groups have been treated unjustly and inequitably because of their disability, ethnicity, age, area of residence or sexual preference. However, the new forms of physical education that have been informed by this principle actively promote social justice and equity. They do so by empowering students with the skills and information to make critical assessments and constructive responses to unfair situations in sport, exercise and physical recreation.

PHYSICAL EDUCATION IN THE FUTURE

The way in which physical education as a field of study has been described in this book represents only one version of the subject. Using historical and sociological methods, you will discover other versions of physical education that were popular at different times in history, in both Australia and different parts of the world. Physical education as a subject has been constructed according to the social class interests and gender interests of particular groups of people. For example, gender considerations have strongly influenced physical education throughout its recent history.

The version of physical education described in this textbook is a social construction. This means that it places in the foreground particular values, such as a preference for integrating academic knowledge with practical knowledge, an emphasis on personalising new information and a commitment to equity and inclusion.

Acknowledging physical education as a social construction does not mean, however, that anything goes. Teachers, curriculum developers and researchers have worked out the version of physical education you are studying based on years of experience. The form that this field of study takes currently is considered the best, latest and most appropriate version for programs of study at senior level. However, because it is a social construction, physical education can also be changed when the present form is no longer considered appropriate to the needs and interests of new generations of students. Since you are a student of the subject in the present, you will have a vital role to play in the development of physical education in the future.

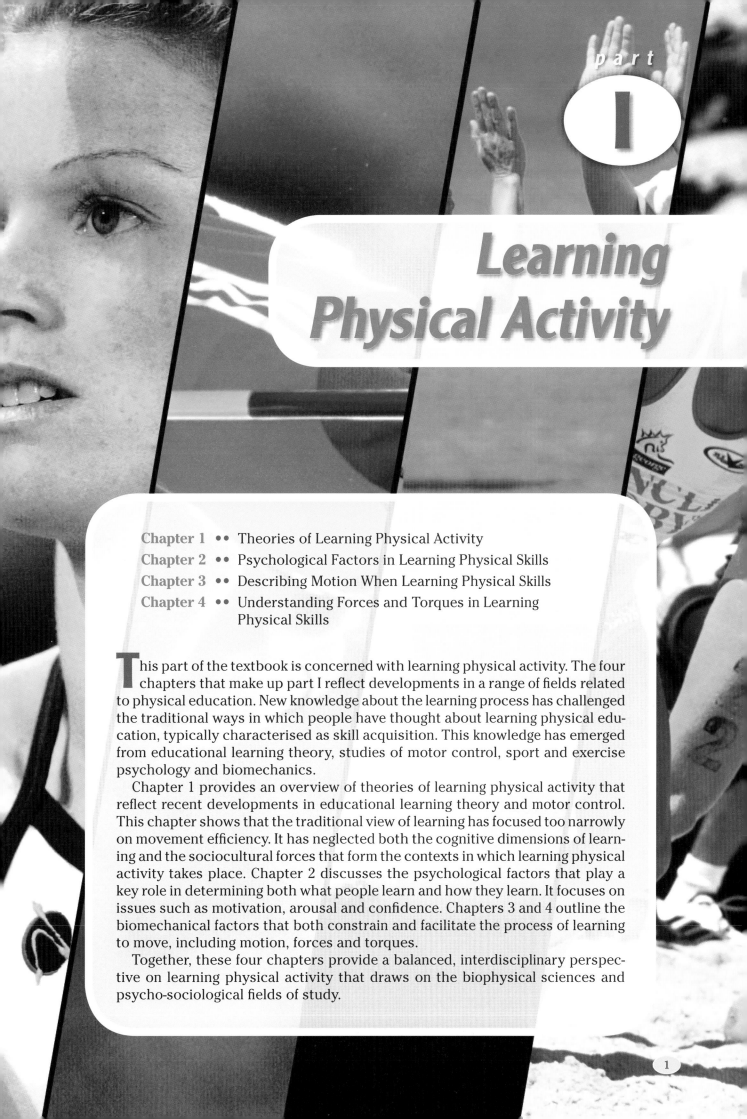

Learning Physical Activity

This part of the textbook is concerned with learning physical activity. The four chapters that make up part I reflect developments in a range of fields related to physical education. New knowledge about the learning process has challenged the traditional ways in which people have thought about learning physical education, typically characterised as skill acquisition. This knowledge has emerged from educational learning theory, studies of motor control, sport and exercise psychology and biomechanics.

Chapter 1 provides an overview of theories of learning physical activity that reflect recent developments in educational learning theory and motor control. This chapter shows that the traditional view of learning has focused too narrowly on movement efficiency. It has neglected both the cognitive dimensions of learning and the sociocultural forces that form the contexts in which learning physical activity takes place. Chapter 2 discusses the psychological factors that play a key role in determining both what people learn and how they learn. It focuses on issues such as motivation, arousal and confidence. Chapters 3 and 4 outline the biomechanical factors that both constrain and facilitate the process of learning to move, including motion, forces and torques.

Together, these four chapters provide a balanced, interdisciplinary perspective on learning physical activity that draws on the biophysical sciences and psycho-sociological fields of study.

chapter

1

Theories of Learning Physical Activity

Chapter Overview

- Traditional Approaches to Motor Learning and Skill Acquisition
- Information-Processing Approach
- Focus Activity: The Three Phases of Information Processing
- Sample Learning Experience: Kinaesthetic Feedback and Canoeing
- Constructivist Approaches to Learning
- Focus Activity: Learning As an Active Process
- The Teacher or Coach As a Facilitator of Learning
- Focus Activity: Explicit and Hidden Learning of Physical Skills
- Focus Activity: Different Teaching Styles
- Extension Activity: Active Learning and Acquisition of Skills
- Test Yourself

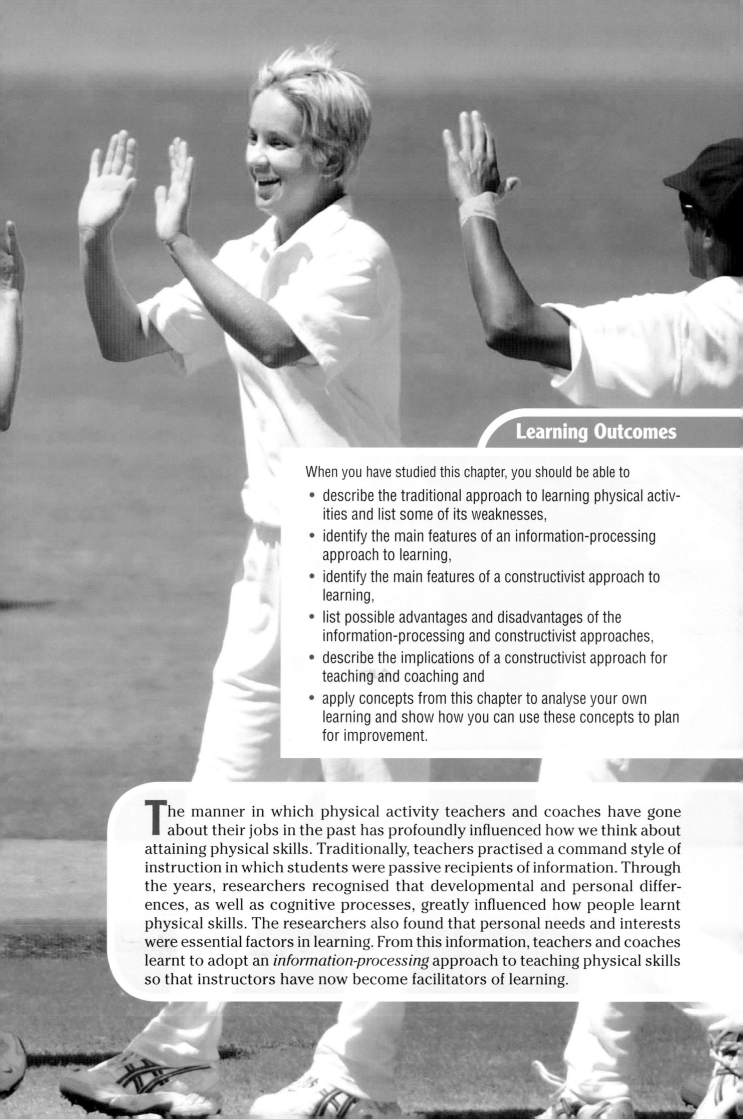

When you have studied this chapter, you should be able to

- describe the traditional approach to learning physical activities and list some of its weaknesses,
- identify the main features of an information-processing approach to learning,
- identify the main features of a constructivist approach to learning,
- list possible advantages and disadvantages of the information-processing and constructivist approaches,
- describe the implications of a constructivist approach for teaching and coaching and
- apply concepts from this chapter to analyse your own learning and show how you can use these concepts to plan for improvement.

The manner in which physical activity teachers and coaches have gone about their jobs in the past has profoundly influenced how we think about attaining physical skills. Traditionally, teachers practised a command style of instruction in which students were passive recipients of information. Through the years, researchers recognised that developmental and personal differences, as well as cognitive processes, greatly influenced how people learnt physical skills. The researchers also found that personal needs and interests were essential factors in learning. From this information, teachers and coaches learnt to adopt an *information-processing* approach to teaching physical skills so that instructors have now become facilitators of learning.

TRADITIONAL APPROACHES TO MOTOR LEARNING AND SKILL ACQUISITION

callisthenics:
A systematic method of exercise performed in unison by large classes, commonly used in schools between the 1910s and 1940s.

From the 1880s to the 1950s, militaristic forms of instruction dominated physical education in schools. Children who attended government schools participated in a system of drilling and exercising known as Dano-Swedish gymnastics—also called **callisthenics.** In this form of physical education, the teacher shouted commands and demonstrated movements for students to imitate. The teacher stood in front of the class and expected students to move in unison. Instructors provided no leeway for different abilities or interest levels among children. This method understandably proved to be an unpopular form of physical education.

Through the 1950s, games and sports gradually began to replace drills and exercises as the primary content of physical education programs in schools. Although this innovation provided teachers with opportunities to change their instruction methods, the old militaristic, or command, style continued to influence key aspects of their teaching. Information still moved in one direction only, from the teacher to the student. It was the student's job to follow the teacher's instructions as closely as possible. Teachers assumed that learning had occurred when a student could reproduce the skills in a form that closely resembled the teacher's instructions and demonstrations.

The assumption that the teacher was the most important factor in the learning equation was not limited to physical education. Other school subjects used similar analogies for learning. The empty bucket model of learning described a passive student whose empty head was ready to be filled with information. The sponge analogy depicted the student absorbing information as a sponge soaks up water. As appealing as these analogies seemed to some people, they failed to explain how learning actually took place and provided no guidelines to help students improve their physical skills.

Today most educators acknowledge that the traditional model for learning physical skills fails to appreciate the importance of the cognitive processes involved. Traditional thinking assumes that acquiring physical skills is simply a matter of getting the movements right and demands little cognitive activity from the learner. Because this approach does not recognise that acquiring skills employs cognitive processes, it does not explain how people learn to apply physical skills creatively or adapt to novel situations effectively. Nor is it able to account for the critical evaluation of game play that enables a player to apply strategies and tactics. Recognition of the importance of cognitive processes laid the groundwork for the information-processing approach to motor learning.

INFORMATION-PROCESSING APPROACH

information-processing:
An approach to learning skills that suggests humans learn in a manner similar to how computers process information.

The **information-processing** approach to teaching physical skills explains how people produce controlled and coordinated movements in all aspects of their daily lives. To produce even the simplest of body movements, a person must vary the forces that numerous muscles produce, while timing these adjustments appropriately.

To get an idea of how difficult even simple movements are, watch a young baby try to grasp a toy with her hand. Her arm jerks about, and her hand has little chance of reaching its destination (at least initially). This inability exists not because of a physical limitation that prevents the baby from grasping the toy, but because she has not yet mastered the complexity of her neuromuscular system.

How do adults manage to produce controlled and coordinated movements, apparently without conscious thought? The information-processing model offers a simple way for teachers and coaches to conceptualise motor learning and skill acquisition. It compares the neural process involved in such learning to a software program that controls the operations of a computer system. Think of a human being as a system that receives input through its senses, as a computer receives input from a keyboard or other device. The person's central nervous system then processes the information, just as a computer's central processing unit does. Finally, the central nervous system sends a message to the muscles in the form of neural commands, in the same way that a computer sends output to a printer. In this model, motor learning is equivalent to a computer program—it translates neural impulses into a desired and specific muscle movement pattern.

The information-processing approach to learning stresses the importance of perception and decision making. It concentrates on how people learn to interpret information in their environments and then decide on effective movements. This approach assumes that there are three sequential phases in skilful performance—perceiving, deciding and acting.

Perceiving

During the perceiving phase, you determine what is happening and identify which information is relevant to a particular set of circumstances. For example, you are a basketball player who has just received the ball. You must interpret a variety of information in your immediate environment—your position on the court, the position of other players, the distance to the goal, the stage of the game, the score, players' levels of fatigue and so on. The ability to sift through information and determine the important bits quickly and accurately is a key quality of expert players.

Deciding

Next comes the deciding stage, when you choose the best course of action. As mentioned previously, you have just received the ball and perceived a variety of information. You must now decide whether to pass, dribble or shoot, and then select the most appropriate kind of pass, dribble or shot to make. Expert players decide on plays more quickly and efficiently than novice players do, because experience has taught them how to adapt their actions to a variety of game conditions.

Acting

During the acting phase, a series of neural impulses recruit muscles to carry out your chosen movements with appropriate timing, coordination and force.

You act based on your perception of the situation and your decision on a response. Movement execution is a vital part of skilful physical performance, but it is not necessarily the most important part.

The three steps of perceiving, deciding and acting are interdependent and often, in the case of skilled performers, happen very rapidly. Beginners to an activity take in information more slowly, and they usually have difficulty recognising what factors are most relevant to their performance. Expert performers decide on movements more rapidly and effectively than novices. They have the advantage of experience—experts already know how effective their actions can be, based on previous similar occasions.

The information-processing approach to learning clearly shows, in contrast to the traditional approach, that executing movements is only one component of learning physical skills. It also demonstrates the significance of two cognitive processes, perceiving and deciding.

The information-processing model provides the basis for the game-sense approach to learning in games. This approach develops players' understanding of strategies and improves their decision making at the same time that it develops their physical skills. Such recent versions of information processing suggest that there is no single best way to execute a movement. Much depends on the circumstances under which a player performs the movement and on the player's perception and decision-making capabilities.

Processing Feedback

feedback:
Information received from a variety of senses about the outcome of one's movements.

An integral part of an information-processing model is a **feedback** loop. A feedback loop means that in order to execute a movement successfully, one must continually process information about that movement obtained through the senses. Information is available from a variety of sources, one of which is vision. Vision provides information about how you are moving through your environment and about the location of your arms and legs (if you can see them).

kinaesthetic information:
The ability of the body, through the use of proprioceptors, to know where body parts are positioned in relation to each other.

Whenever you move, receptors located in your muscles, tendons, ligaments and skin transmit neural impulses. The neural impulses provide information to your brain about the position and velocity of your arms and legs. This feedback is called **kinaesthetic information.** You can think of kinaesthetic information as how a movement feels. Other types of kinaesthetic information include the orientation and movement of the head (gathered by the vestibular receptors in the ears) and auditory information.

Every movement one makes provides feedback. All these pieces of information, taken together, make up the perceptual consequences of movement. Learning what the perceptual consequences of successful movement look, feel and sound like is perhaps the most critical part of learning to execute a movement.

A coach or teacher can also provide information about how you perform a movement. The coach might give you oral feedback or show you a videotape of the movement. Information about the outcome of the movement, such as where the ball went after it was hit or how long it took to run the 100 metres, is also useful.

Acquiring a skill takes practice, but practice alone does not guarantee improvement. You must vary the way you perform a movement during practice and then decide whether the change is an improvement. For instance, your coach may have you practice your jump shot while a defensive player guards you closely. This way your coach facilitates learning by placing you in

••• Focus Activity —

THE THREE PHASES OF INFORMATION PROCESSING

Purpose

To understand the relationship between cognition and performance when performing physical skills.

Equipment

One watch or stopwatch and one whistle.

Procedure

1. Select a physical activity that you are currently studying. Ask a teacher or volunteer to let you and others participate in your chosen physical activity for 2 minutes.

2. After the teacher blows the whistle to signal the end of the 2 minutes, get your notebook and pencil and sit in a group with the other participants.

3. Reflect together on the last 2 minutes of exercise. Then take 5 to 10 minutes to consider the following task and respond to it in writing.

Written Task

Using the definitions of the perceiving, deciding and acting phases of information processing, write a comprehensive example of when you were engaged in each of these phases in the last 2 minutes of exercise. Your written response should clearly explain what particular aspect of the activity matched it with one of the three phases. You must provide reasons to justify your decision.

Repeat Task

Repeat the exercise interval, reflection and writing time two or three more times. On each consecutive occasion, focus on different examples to demonstrate your understanding of the concepts.

a situation where you are likely to experience the perceptual consequences of successful movement.

Your coach might also provide you with additional information about the movement and its results, such as, 'Your shoulders are bunched up when a defensive player challenges you. That is why you overshoot the ball'. Your coach can help you change the movement to make it more effective. A demonstration or some other visual cue is one way for the coach to sketch out such alterations successfully so that you can understand and act on them.

SAMPLE LEARNING EXPERIENCE

Kinaesthetic Feedback and Canoeing

Stephen was studying skill acquisition in conjunction with canoeing. He and his classmates were in canoes on the river, and the teacher was about to begin a session on how feedback enhances the learning and performance of physical skills. The task the teacher set for the class helped Stephen understand how vital kinaesthetic feedback is to learning a physical skill such as canoeing.

The first part of the task was to paddle a two-person canoe through a figure of eight with a partner. After completing the figure of eight, Stephen and his partner had a brief discussion about their experiences. Both students were carrying a notebook and pen in a plastic pocket and made notes about the feedback they collected to monitor their performance. They agreed that their main source of information during the figure of eight was visual. By using vision, they could monitor exactly where they were on the course during and after each paddle stroke. Another source of information was their hearing. Stephen and his partner could tell how efficient their paddle strokes were by the sound they made in the water. During the figure of eight, Stephen and his partner talked to each other constantly about their course, position in the water and the kind of strokes required to make the turns.

After each canoe team had completed the exercise and recorded their reflections, the instructor explained the concept of kinaesthetic feedback. He told the students about the role of semicircular canals in the skull, which provide information on balance. He then explained how proprioceptors in the muscles give feedback about where parts of the body are in relation to each other and where the body is in space. To illustrate the significance of these sources of information, the teacher asked the paddling teams to repeat the same figure of eight, but this time performing the manoeuvre blindfolded and with the aid of verbal directions from the teacher. The teacher limited the directions to comments such as 'keep turning right' or 'turn left'. The paddlers decided the stroke combinations.

After some initial fumbling, and a few mistimed strokes during which they almost capsized, Stephen and his partner were actually able to perform the task reasonably well. They did so despite operating without what they earlier agreed to be the most important kind of feedback—vision. After further practice, they found that they were able to perform the task well without even the verbal directions.

Explanation

Visual feedback is important during most skill learning. However, as the canoeing task demonstrated to Stephen's class, it is not the only form of useful feedback. Kinaesthetic feedback is crucial to the development of body awareness and to the skilful performance of physical activities. One can obtain it only through actually participating in a physical activity, because kinaesthetic information consists of how a movement feels to the person doing it.

Stephen and his partner were able to complete their task without the luxury of visual feedback, because proprioceptors in their muscles and joints were providing kinaesthetic feedback. They sensed where their body parts were in relation to one another, so they were able to perform paddling strokes without actually seeing what they were doing. Kinaesthetic feedback provided data on performance while the strokes were taking place. The semicircular canals in the skull provided information about balance that allowed Stephen and his partner to maintain a stable position on the water and avoid capsizing. The paddlers received more feedback from touch and pressure receptors in their muscles and skin.

After practicing with the blindfold, Stephen and his partner were able to perform the task more easily, with no verbal directions, because their kinaesthetic and tactile senses were becoming more attuned to the task. Just as vision provided them with information on what correct physical performance looked like, kinaesthetic feedback developed their sense of what correct physical performance felt like. As a result, when they repeated the figure of eight without the blindfold, their performance improved.

Kinaesthetic feedback explains how visually impaired athletes can attain high levels of performance. Many instructors fail to appreciate it as a source of information essential to learning physical skills.

Performing Without Feedback— Motor Programs and Schema Theory

Researchers have proposed various theories to account for a person's ability to execute rapid movements without feedback. The motor program theory suggests that to execute a movement, the brain selects and implements a pre-existing set of neural commands—a motor program. The problem for such a theory is that it does not explain how the infinite number of programs needed could be determined.

Schema theory proposes that the brain adjusts a set of generalised motor programs to suit the specific details of each situation by altering the parameters of a motor program. For example, some researchers suggest that a single generalised motor program (or schema) exists for walking. To walk faster or slower, the brain adjusts both the temporal parameters of the motor program and the required neural commands. Running, on the other hand, is a qualitatively different pattern of movement, which the body carries out by using a different motor program.

Schema theory led to a number of other proposals, such as the invariant relative timing hypothesis. This theory suggests that if a single generalised motor program controls a set of movements, such as walking at different speeds, then the different phases of the movement should remain in constant temporal proportion when speeded up or slowed down. Although this hypothesis received support for a time, it is has subsequently become clear that the theory is not true in general and cannot account for movement control as a whole.

CONSTRUCTIVIST APPROACHES TO LEARNING

Recent developments in learning theory in academic subjects such as science and mathematics have inspired fresh approaches for physical education. Constructivist approaches to learning emphasise that learning is an active process, in which a person seeks out information about both the task and the current circumstances. The person then tests out her own capabilities within the context of the task and the environment.

constructivism:
An approach to learning skills that views learning as an active, developmental, and multi-dimensional process.

Constructivism further develops the information-processing approach by maintaining that learning is also a developmental process, in two senses:

- There are identifiable phases to learning physical skills.
- Learning changes over time as individuals become more experienced.

Researchers now believe that learning, in addition to being an active and developmental process, is multi-dimensional; people typically learn more than one thing at a time. These three aspects of learning—active, developmental and multi-dimensional—are common features of the broad range of constructivist approaches to learning.

Learning Is an Active Process

The idea that learning is an active process challenges the traditional approach to teaching physical activity. Constructivist researchers claim that people actively attempt to make sense of specific tasks in two ways—within a set of environmental conditions, and in relation to what they know they can already do. An example is learning to use the lay-up shot in basketball. A player brings to the task a range of prior experiences that influence the ability to learn this move. The task is the lay-up shot, which typically has a high percentage of success, since it involves the player shooting from close to the basket. The circumstances that call for a lay-up shot vary, but players normally use it when there is a reasonably clear path to the basket.

Performing a lay-up combines a sequence of physical acts—dribbling the ball, performing the pick-up, stepping and jumping, and taking the shot itself. However, it is common for players to be able to perform the actions of the lay-up shot in an unopposed practice but then never to use it during a game, because they do not know how to recognise when this shot is the best option. A player must consider the status of the game and the positions of other players on court, then decide that a lay-up shot is appropriate. Therefore, this active attempt to make sense of the task is consistent with the information-processing theory; it involves the three phases of perceiving, deciding and acting.

The interdependence of the person's abilities, the task's demands and the environmental conditions is evident in learning to perform a basketball lay-up. These three features apply to other physical skills that are part of everyday life, as well as to games and sports. People are continually required to make judgements about what they can already do in relation to what the task is asking them to do, and in relation to particular sets of circumstances. Therefore, learning physical skills requires a cognitive process—you must make judgements about what you can already do in relation to the task and to the environmental conditions. You improve your performance of a lay-up shot when you become quicker and more accurate at picking out the environmental cues that tell you that the shot is on. Your physical actions become smoother at the same time, and you become capable of introducing subtle variations. With experience, you are more likely than a novice is to use the lay-up shot effectively in scoring baskets.

The notion that learning is an active process also takes into account your motivation and readiness to learn. A constructivist approach acknowledges that you have feelings and emotions that influence your ability to work hard, to accept failure without becoming discouraged, to experience discomfort and to feel elated when you succeed. The constructivist approach also considers the fact that people have preferences for how they like to learn. Some people prefer to watch, listen and experiment, whereas others prefer to try an activity first and refine their learning through feedback. Their preferences also may change, depending on the nature of the task and their prior experiences.

• • • *Focus Activity* —

LEARNING AS AN ACTIVE PROCESS

Purpose

To understand that learning a physical skill is an active process in which a person interacts with the environment to identify information that is relevant to the task at hand. What the person perceives as important in the environment will affect how and what he learns from the experience.

Equipment

One videotape of a person performing the physical activity that you are currently studying. If you have access to a video camera, you may have someone film you doing the activity. For the following task, swap your recording with that of another student whose video you have not observed.

Procedure

1. Play the videotape and pause the action at a point when the person is about to perform a skill. For example, in tennis it might be when the person is about to return the ball across the net.

2. Try to predict what will happen next by analysing the task, the abilities that the athlete must possess to accomplish the task and the factors in the performance environment that will influence the player's decision to act in a particular way.

Written Tasks

- Write down your predictions. Perform this task for at least three different situations.

- Write a brief discussion in which you evaluate the task's demands, the necessary abilities and the environmental conditions to determine which of these factors will have the greatest effect on the rate of and quality of learning physical skills. Can you separate the three factors, or are they interdependent as the text suggests? Use examples from your own learning experiences in the physical activity you are currently studying to justify your position.

Learning Is Developmental

The way you learn changes as you progress from being a beginner to being an expert. An experienced basketball player can adapt to new or different circumstances more easily than a beginner can. As we learnt previously in this chapter, one of the ways to distinguish between an expert and a novice is the speed and ease with which the expert adapts to changing circumstances.

Before reaching physical maturity, a person's changing size and strength have a pronounced effect on learning. Children may be clumsy as they struggle to match their existing skills and their expectations of competence with their changing bodies. As people grow older, physical deterioration alters their learning experiences. This ongoing process of growth, development and maturation across one's life span means that learning is always adapting to new conditions.

The stages you typically pass through as you learn physical skills also exhibit a process of development. Some researchers suggest that there are three distinct phases to developing skills: the cognitive phase, the practice or associative phase and the autonomous phase. These phases describe a learner's journey from novice to skilled performer.

In the cognitive phase, a person grasps the demands of the task and discovers the circumstances under which she should perform it. Some researchers claim that the cognitive phase can last from a few minutes to several hours. The actual duration of this phase depends on the nature of the task, the complexity of the environmental factors and the prior experiences of the person. It is likely that the cognitive phase never ends, since even experts must adapt their skills to varying circumstances. A novice's grasp of a skill is likely to be simplistic—her understanding deepens with greater experience.

A person enters the practice or associative phase as, through practice and experience, he gradually improves his ability to cope with more information about the task and the circumstances. The components of a skill, such as judging whether a lay-up is on or deciding which tennis shot to play, typically begin to require less conscious effort. The person performs the skill more smoothly and gradually pays less attention to it. Eventually the person can take in other information from his surroundings while executing the physical acts proficiently.

One can view the autonomous phase as an extension of the associative phase. It signals an ending point in learning a physical skill. Performing the actions that make up the skill becomes so automatic that a player does not need to pay conscious attention to them. Some doubt that this is a useful way to describe expert performance. The expert player's execution of a skill may seem effortless when compared to that of a novice, but such proficiency does not imply that the expert player is no longer capable of thinking, learning and improving.

Researchers who support the idea of an autonomous phase assume that it applies mainly at the level of dexterity in performing a skill. After these physical acts become automatic, the person is free to attend to the circumstances in which they perform the skill. This assumption is, however, inconsistent with the notion of an active learner described previously. Learning skills requires learning the relationships among necessary abilities, task demands and environmental circumstances. Skilful performances depend on how a person links perceiving, deciding and acting. The active learner juggles with these relationships all of the time, not just after meeting the physical demands of the task.

If the autonomous phase is to remain a useful descriptor within the developmental process of learning, perhaps it must be modified. It can refer to people who have achieved such a high level of proficiency in most aspects of an activity that their performance is automatic, efficient and successful. Entering the autonomous phase need not mean that a highly proficient performer cannot go on learning, although increasingly subtle refinements of a skill might become difficult for observers to detect.

Learning Is Multi-Dimensional

A third premise of constructivist approaches is that learning is multi-dimensional. A person typically learns more than one thing at a time. Again, consider the lay-up shot in basketball. You might try very hard to learn how to perform this shot successfully. While working on the lay-up, you might also learn that you like or dislike basketball and that your friends, Leanne and Tony, are enjoyable to work with in the basketball team, but another friend, Michael, is too selfish with the ball and doesn't give others a fair go. You might learn what your coach means when she gives advice in a certain manner, when she is serious and when she is only joking. The whole time, all of you in the basketball team are learning about appropriate behaviour in this setting and about appropriate ways of being feminine or masculine.

Even though you might concentrate on one task, you learn other things at the same time. You do not acquire all of this information through a conscious effort. You can attend to only a limited amount of information at any given time. Much of the learning that goes on while you are acquiring, applying and evaluating your physical skills is reflexive. Reflexive learning means that you learn one thing as part of learning something else. In the basketball example, reflexive learning occurs when, while practicing the lay-up shot, you find that you enjoy (or dislike) playing basketball.

Recognising that learning is multi-dimensional highlights the complexity of acquiring even the most basic of physical skills. Broader aspects of life, such as the social construction of gender, take place as we learn physical skills. For example, in the process of learning various skills in physical education classes, you are also reflexively learning such things as

- what is expected of you as a female or male student in this particular teacher's class and in this school,
- how to work with friends and classmates and
- whether you are any good at these activities.

If someone breaks an unspoken rule, such as keeping quiet when the teacher is talking or always trying hard, the things students learn reflexively while they practice physical skills become more apparent. Researchers refer to the multi-dimensional character of learning as the hidden curriculum, since this learning often is neither apparent nor clearly stated as a part of the explicit curriculum.

THE TEACHER OR COACH AS A FACILITATOR OF LEARNING

In the traditional approach to learning physical skills, the teacher or coach occupied centre stage in the learning process and often adopted a directive or **command style** of instruction. Verbal feedback played a prominent role. Current theories view learning as an active, developmental and multi-dimensional process. Each of these characteristics has important implications

command style: A teacher-centred approach in which teachers direct student learning and are not active participants.

for the role of the teacher or coach as well as the learner. Teachers and coaches are facilitators of learning, and the learner is an active participant in the learning process.

As a facilitator of learning, the teacher or coach does not merely give the learner information. Teachers create opportunities for students to learn physical skills. The learners may have different prior experiences of a task and may learn at different rates. They may have diverse learning styles and respond to different kinds of feedback, including visual, auditory and kinaesthetic information.

The idea that learning is an active process does not mean that the instructor becomes passive. It does mean that the teacher or coach must use a wider range of instructional strategies than they commonly did within the traditional approach. It also means that the instructor must make effective and appropriate use of the various forms of feedback.

One educational researcher named Muska Mosston has developed a spectrum of instructional styles that acknowledges people as active learners. As figure 1.1 shows, active and independent learning becomes more obvious as the teacher moves from a directing role to a facilitating role.

task-based learning:
An approach to teaching that provides students with some control over the process of learning.

Task-based learning is an approach that provides people with more independence and responsibility for their own learning than is typical within the traditional approach. Circuit training, in which learners use task cards and move from station to station, is a good example of task-based learning.

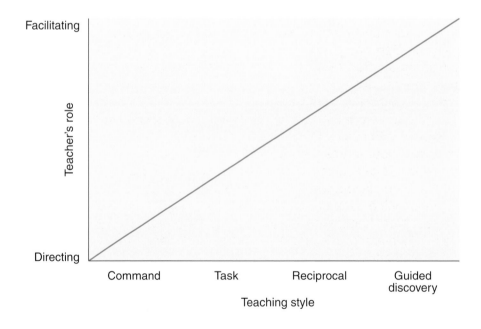

Figure 1.1 Mosston's spectrum of teaching styles.
Reprinted from D. Kirk et al. 1996, *The sociocultural foundations of human movement* (South Melbourne, Australia: Macmillan), 69.

EXPLICIT AND HIDDEN LEARNING OF PHYSICAL SKILLS

Purpose

To understand the multi-dimensional nature of learning physical skills by identifying explicit and hidden learning that takes place when engaging in physical activity.

Procedure

Read the following story:

It is 4.30 on a sunny Tuesday afternoon, and North-South United's practice session for the soccer team (ages 9 and under) is just getting under way. Bob is the coach and the father of one of the players. He calls the 14 children in and tells them to sprint to the goalpost, run round it twice and sprint back to him. The children run off, and in the process of running round the goalposts, there are two heavy collisions. One player in particular is obviously winded and trails back slowly after the rest.

'Ten push-ups!' shouts Bob, as the players return. Some children are still arriving from their sprint as some of the faster players finish the push-ups. 'Ten sit-ups!' yells Bob. 'When you've finished, another sprint to the goalpost and back. Go, go, go!' Some of the players who are lagging behind on the exercises cut short their routine.

When the players return from the sprint, Bob singles out the laggards. He orders them to do the 10 repetitions of push-ups and sit-ups again, while the other players stand around laughing and offering unwanted advice. Two of the players, Ben and Gayle, cannot manage all of the push-ups. 'Come on, Muscles,' shouts Bob. 'Just leave it, you two—we can't waste the whole session waiting for you!'

Bob then gathers the players round. 'Our tackling was hopeless last week, so that's what we will practice today. I want to see you go in hard at the ball, and if you miss the ball, at least make sure you get the man. Right! Steve and Michael, pick your teams—you've got first pick, Michael.'

The two boys call out the names of their players. The last players picked are two of the three players who had to do the extra exercises. The players line up in two lines facing each other and begin the tackling practice. 'What did I say, Ben—go in hard! Look, even the girls are tackling harder than you.' The tackling practice continues for 10 minutes in the same format, and Bob spends most of that time chatting with another parent.

'Are we going to play a game today?' asks one of the boys. Bob then organises the players into boxed areas and sets up a pass-and-move drill that requires the players to make an accurate pass and then move into a space within the box. Michael, Steve and Wendy find this drill too easy and look bored and a little frustrated. Quite a few of the players have trouble passing accurately. Four of them, including Ben and Gayle, obviously have not grasped the concept of the drill. Bob offers his usual motivational remarks, and ends the practice after about 5 minutes.

The training session ends in a game of 7-vs-7, with Bob refereeing. The players seem to have fun, although Michael and occasionally other players continue to give Ben a hard time. Bob says nothing to them about this. The children play the game very seriously, although both the players and Bob seem to have forgotten their practice of tackling and pass-and-move.

Written Task

Identify and write down anything that you think any child or group of children has learnt during the practice session described in the story. Think beyond the obvious physical skills to consider the hidden messages, social constructions and reinforcements of stereotyping that these children have learnt from this training session.

Observation Task

Work with your class and teacher so that half of the class engages in the physical activity you are currently studying, while the rest of the class performs an observation and note-taking task. After 15 minutes of activity, exchange the two groups so that everyone has a chance to both observe and perform.

Your task is to watch closely and to identify anything that the students might learn during the period of exercise. Observe not only physical skills and tactics, but also relationships, power and authority, hierarchical structures, stereotyping and other social phenomena.

reciprocal learning:
An approach to instruction that involves peer teaching, in which students work together and provide each other with feedback.

guided discovery:
A style of teaching in which the teacher guides rather than directs the learner through a series of tasks.

Reciprocal learning is another example of treating people as active and independent learners. This approach usually involves working with a partner and providing feedback as both learners work at a task.

Guided discovery is another approach, in which the teacher guides the learner through a series of tasks instead of giving commands. The goal of the guided discovery approach is for learners to explore the environment and discover information or develop a skill through their own abilities.

Instructors may use the command, task-based, reciprocal, guided discovery and other approaches to learning by themselves or in combination. The choice of which approach or approaches to use depends on

- the physical skills to be learnt;
- the ages and stages of the learners;
- the knowledge, interests and goals of the teacher or coach; and
- a range of other factors and circumstances, such as available time, facilities, equipment and so on.

As discussed earlier in this chapter, constructivist approaches to learning physical skills emphasise the interdependence of individual abilities, the task and the environment. When teachers and coaches adopt the role of a facilitator of learning, their main task is to organise learning experiences so that you are able to explore the relationships between your own abilities, the task and the environment. The main job of the teacher or coach is to maximise learning through creating suitable tasks and environments. The instructor has a responsibility to design learning tasks and structure the learning environment in ways that are appropriate to the range of individual abilities within a group.

• • • *Focus Activity —*

DIFFERENT TEACHING STYLES

Purpose

To understand that people respond in different ways to various teaching and coaching styles. For example, some people may learn at a faster or slower rate than others do. Another difference may be that some forms of teaching enhance a person's cognition and perception better than other styles do.

Procedure

1. With a partner, choose one of the teaching styles outlined in Mosston's spectrum of teaching styles (see figure 1.1).

2. Choose a skill or tactic from the physical activity that you are currently studying and use the chosen teaching style to design a mini-lesson that you can teach to other members of your class. The mini-lesson should last for 5 to 10 minutes. Other students in the class can adopt other teaching styles. Try to cover all of the styles.

3. After each of the mini-lessons, sit down for 2 to 3 minutes to make notes on what you like and dislike about each style of teaching adopted by the various groups of students. Be sure that your comments relate to the teaching style and not to the competency or personalities of other students.

Written Tasks

- Evaluate in writing each of the teaching styles according to their effectiveness at teaching skills in the physical activity you are currently studying.

- Are there any environmental conditions peculiar to the performance of this physical activity that make one teaching style more or less effective than any other? What styles does your teacher employ to teach this physical activity?

EXTENSION ACTIVITY

ACTIVE LEARNING AND ACQUISITION OF SKILLS

Consider This

Consider the physical activity that you are currently studying. Make a list of a number of individual skills or actions that are common in this activity.

Try This

- Close your eyes (or blindfold yourself) and attempt to complete each of these actions relying only on the kinaesthetic and tactile feedback that you receive from the interaction of your body senses and the performance environment. It will be difficult to hit a ball or interact with another player easily; the intention is to replicate the body actions during specific movements.

- If you have access to video equipment, have a peer help you make a videotape of your performance—first under normal circumstances, then while you are blindfolded. If you do not have access to video equipment, ask a peer to watch and make notes about your performance under normal circumstances and when blindfolded.

Think and Write

To what extent does your body depend on feedback from the various senses in your body? Provide written examples of how, when you're participating in your chosen physical activity, your senses (including kinaesthetic and balance senses) provide both knowledge of performance (feedback you receive during an action) and knowledge of results (feedback you receive at the end of an action). Draw conclusions as to which senses provide the most crucial feedback.

Compare and Contrast

Look for the similarities and differences between the techniques you demonstrated in both scenarios. Look closely at both the gross motor skill components and the fine motor control aspects of the skills.

1. Why do traditional theories of learning physical activity fail to explain fully how learning takes place?

2. Apply the three stages of information processing to the physical activity you are currently studying, to a new activity or to an activity that is difficult for you to perform.

3. What sources provide you with information for the feedback loop for effective learning in your current physical activity?

4. Reflecting on your current physical activity, how would kinaesthetic feedback enhance your performance?

5. What perspectives is the schema theory, outdated though it is, based on?

6. A constructivist approach to learning physical skills further develops the information-processing approach. What three additional features does it include?

7. Outline the process of active learning for a skill you have recently been developing.

8. What effect will your developmental changes as a teenager have on the learning of skills?

9. Outline the three distinct phases of learning as applied to a skill from your current physical activity, describing yourself as a learner progressing from a beginner to an experienced player.

10. Apply the concerns raised about the use of the term *automatic* to describe the expert performance of an athlete, in relation to the concept that all learning is active.

11. How can one understand the perception of the autonomous learner to include active learning?

12. Why is it important to recognise that all learning is multi-dimensional?

13. What role does your teacher or coach play as a facilitator of learning, and why?

14. What benefits do students or players gain as the teacher or coach moves from a directing approach to a facilitating role? Can you give examples from your experience?

Psychological Factors in Learning Physical Skills

Trish Gorely*

Chapter Overview

*Trish Gorely, PhD, lectures in the School of Sport and Exercise Sciences at Loughborough University.

When you have studied this chapter, you should be able to

- identify your own optimal mental climate associated with your best performances;
- evaluate how participation motives, definitions of success and attributions influence motivation;
- explain, using theories and models, how arousal and anxiety affect performance;
- explain the link between confidence and performance;
- identify the components of effective concentration;
- explain the role and influence of cohesion in performance; and
- identify and explain strategies to manipulate or manage the psychological components of performance.

It is now widely accepted that performance is influenced by psychological factors. Some sports people credit up to 95 per cent of their performance on any given day to their mental state. Motivation, anxiety, confidence and concentration can all affect the quality of our performance as individuals. How we relate to each other in team games can affect team performance. This chapter introduces some of the psychological influences on performance and highlights some strategies that reflective performers can use to maximise their psychological readiness before and during performance.

DEFINING A GOOD PERFORMANCE

For a long time it was thought that personality was a key psychological factor in sports performance. During the 1960s and 1970s a large part of the sport psychology research effort examined the role of personality in sport and physical activity participation and performance. From this work it became obvious that there are few personality differences between athletes and nonathletes.

What is interesting, however, is that some differences were found between successful and less successful athletes. The more successful athletes tended to possess a variety of psychological skills that assist good performance. These skills included well-developed mental preparation plans, skills to maintain confidence and focus and skills to cope with anxiety.

The most important lesson to learn from the personality research is that everyone is different and is going to respond differently in the same situation. For example, Mary may approach a competition with confidence and excitement, whereas John approaches the same competition with extreme nervousness. It is not these personality differences that determine performance but the skills people have to control their motivation, confidence, concentration and anxiety effectively, regardless of the situation.

Knowing this, to maximise our performance we have to develop better self-awareness. We also need to know how we react in different situations. With this understanding we can develop strategies and skills to perform at our best more often.

interactionist perspective:
The view that behaviour is influenced by both the person and the situation they are in.

The idea that both the person and situation are important when looking at a person's behaviour is called the **interactionist perspective.** This perspective is common throughout psychology. You should keep the interactionist perspective in mind as you complete all the tasks in this chapter.

In performance psychology it is now understood that an individual's ability to consistently create the mental climate associated with their good performances helps to iron out the differences between good days and bad days. Although this doesn't guarantee winning, a positive mental climate raises the standard of performance overall. You can provide a platform on which your physical training and skills are more consistently displayed by becoming aware of your own **optimal mental climate** and working to re-create it before each performance.

optimal mental climate:
The combination of psychological factors associated with an individual's best performances.

The optimal mental climate for good performances is different for every person. For Abdul, a good performance happens when he feels calm and confident in his preparation, when he knows the opposition's game plan, and when he feels he really wants to be there. Abdul feels successful when he plays to his potential and manages to include some new skills he has been learning in practice.

For Grace, a good performance happens when she feels excited and a little bit apprehensive about the event. The nerves seem to wake her up and get her focused on the task. Grace feels successful when she beats others, although she takes some pride from playing well even if she loses.

Throughout this chapter you will be asked to reflect on your own performances, good and bad, and try to work out how different levels of motivation, arousal, anxiety, confidence, concentration and teamwork influence your optimal mental climate and performance.

••• Focus Activity —

FINDING THE OPTIMAL MENTAL CLIMATE

Purpose

To determine a person's optimal mental climate.

Procedure

1. Based on what you've learned so far, design a brief questionnaire to find out someone's optimal mental climate.
2. Think of a best-ever performance and try it on yourself first, then the rest of your group.

Written Task

Write down five situations in sport when your optimal mental climate might be challenged (e.g., performing in front of a large audience).

MOTIVATION AND PERFORMANCE

Motivation is central to all that we do. When we talk about motivation, we are talking about why people do what they do. We look at factors such as what they choose to participate in, how much effort they put in and how long they persist with an activity, especially when things aren't going well. Sometimes you will hear people say, 'Oh, Jo just has no motivation'. Strictly speaking, this is rarely true. People always have some level of motivation, although it just may be for some other activity.

Think about an activity that you do that you really like. Now ask yourself, 'What are my reasons for taking part in this activity?' You will probably come up with several different reasons. For example, you play tennis because you enjoy it; you meet new people; it helps keep you fit; and you like the competition. As long as these different reasons are being met, your motivation is likely to remain high. So if we are looking to change someone's motivation, one thing we need to know is what are his or her reasons for participating.

Consider also that motivation levels are influenced by the person and the situation they are put in. For example, Sam likes running and is pretty good at it. At the school cross-country event he is keen and enthusiastic and puts in a lot of effort. However, at the school sports day on the track, he has to be convinced to participate and puts in very little effort, saying: 'I hate the track. It's so boring going round and round.' The basic activity, running, hasn't changed, but the situation has resulted in a decrease in motivation. So to influence motivation levels we have to consider the characteristics of the person and the situation. This is an example of the interactionist perspective.

motivation:
The effort and persistence people put into the activities they choose to do.

• • • *Focus Activity* —

MOTIVATION

Purpose

To understand your motivations and the motivations of others for participating in activities.

Procedure

1. Take two activities you have chosen to study in Senior physical education. What are your reasons (motives) for choosing these sports? Write them down.

2. Compare your reasons with others in your class. Note similarities and differences.

3. Think of an activity that you have been involved in for several years. Have your motives for participating changed? Make a note.

Written Task

In your own words define motivation. Write down the definition.

Goal Orientations: Task and Ego

task orientation:
Focusing on learning new skills and on comparing performance with personal standards.

Another important factor in understanding motivation is to understand how individuals define success. This way of looking at motivation is referred to as goal orientation. When someone defines success in terms of mastering a new skill or demonstrating skill, this is called a **task orientation.** People with a task orientation are interested in how well they perform a particular task and compare their performance with their own previous performances (figure 2.1a).

When someone defines success in terms of winning, this is called an **ego orientation.** People with an ego orientation focus on social comparison and how they compare to others (figure 2.1b).

ego orientation:
Focusing on defeating others and comparing one's performance against that of other people.

Usually a person will have a mix of these two orientations. Sport psychologists believe that a high task orientation in combination with either high or low ego orientation is good for motivation. A strong focus on an ego orientation with a low task orientation is viewed as undesirable—motivationally maladaptive.

High task orientation is good because it provides greater personal control. You are focusing on what you do and how well you do it and not on how well someone else does. For example, a basketball team may have been working on a new attacking move. In the first game where the team tries the new move it works superbly. However, the opposition play better than all expectations and win by three points. Regardless of orientation, you are likely to be disappointed by this result. But with a task orientation you are more likely to look back at the game and feel satisfied that you played well and were successful with the new move.

With an ego orientation, you are more likely to continue to feel like a loser and think that the new move, and maybe the team, is no good. Individuals with high task orientation are likely to work harder and persist longer in difficult situations. Individuals with high ego orientation are likely to give up or make excuses when things aren't going their way.

WINNING VERSUS MASTERING A SKILL

Purpose

To understand how players feel when they focus on different outcomes in a match.

Procedure

1. Set up a practice match in one of your chosen activities where one team is focusing on winning as the only important outcome, and the other team is focusing on mastering a set move or a newly learned skill.

2. Afterwards discuss how the members of the two teams felt during the match. How would they feel if the outcome had been reversed?

Written Task

After the practice match, make notes about how the players felt during the match and write down a summary of the discussion.

Figure 2.1 *(a)* An ego-oriented golf player might be thinking, 'My partner's drive was 180 metres. This time, my drive will be 200 metres.' *(b)* A task-oriented golf player might be thinking, 'My last drive swung to the left. I'll change my grip to send my drive straight.'

Attributions

Motivation is also influenced by the **attributions** (reasons) people give for their performances. For example, a tenpin bowler, Chris, who is not playing well, might attribute her poor performance to lack of practice, to poor technique or to not being any good. The sorts of attributions people make affect their motivation. If Chris attributes her poor performances to lack of practice, she might get motivated to do something about it and practice. Likewise, if the attribution is to poor technique, she might ask a coach for help. However, if the attribution is 'I'm just no good', she may just give up.

Think of a successful performance you've had in a sport. Why were you successful? What was the main reason for your success? Now think of a poor or unsuccessful performance in that sport. Why were you unsuccessful? What was the main reason for your lack of success? Probably the reasons you will give fall under one of the following four headings.

- Luck (e.g., chance events such as weather, the ref was on their side, and getting lucky)
- Ability (e.g., you were the better player; your team was no good)
- Effort (e.g., you worked really hard all of the game)
- Task difficulty (e.g., the opponents were more experienced; you had the best grasp of tactics)

TABLE 2.1   Four Common Attributions for Success or Failure

	Stable	Unstable
Internal	Ability	Effort
External	Task difficulty	Luck

Although most attributions fall under these four headings, sport psychologist Bob Weiner suggests that what is more important is where these attributions fit along two dimensions. These dimensions are locus of causality and stability. Locus of causality relates to whether the cause is due to something inside or internal to the person, or something outside the person or external. Stability relates to whether the cause is likely to occur again in the future, in which case it is stable; or not, in which case it is unstable. The four common attributions can be placed in Weiner's dimensions as shown in table 2.1.

Internal and external attributions influence how a person feels about a performance. If you attribute success to internal factors, you experience greater pride and satisfaction than if you attribute success to external factors. If you attribute failure to internal factors, you experience greater shame than if you attribute failure to external factors. So it is best if you attribute success to internal factors and failure to external factors because this maximises feelings of pride and satisfaction and minimises feelings of shame.

The stability dimension influences our perceptions of whether success or failure is likely to occur again. If Jamie attributes success to a stable dimension, he will expect success to occur again. If he attributes failure to stable causes, he will expect to fail again in the future. These expectations of future success and failure influence a person's confidence and enthusiasm for future participation. When considering motivation it is important that we examine the attributions that we typically give and try to maximise their motivating power.

GOAL SETTING:
A STRATEGY FOR INCREASING MOTIVATION

We can use goal setting to increase motivation, task orientation and appropriate attributions. This is a process where someone decides what they want to achieve and plans how they are going to get there. People tend to set goals spontaneously—'I want to get on the school netball team', 'My aim is to be a doctor', 'My goal is to get fitter'. You can set goals in many different areas:

- Physical (e.g., to get fitter)

- Mental (e.g., to improve concentration)

- Skill (e.g., to learn to do breaststroke)

- Tactical (e.g., to learn a new defensive pattern)

However, not all goals are equally effective in helping you to do your best. But by following seven guidelines we can increase their effectiveness.

Guideline 1: Set Specific Goals

Clearly worded specific goals enhance motivation more than general goals. The idea of 'do your best' doesn't highlight what to work on. Likewise, a goal such as 'I want to be a fast rugby player' is broad and imprecise compared with 'Because I am a winger, I need speed and power. I want to reduce my time for a 50-metre sprint by one second'. This last goal sets out exactly what you want to do and why.

Guideline 2: Set Challenging Goals

Goals are most motivating when they extend you from where you are. If goals are too easy, you are not likely to take them seriously. On the other hand, if they are too difficult a person may feel that they are impossible to reach and won't try. The trick with goal setting is to set goals that are challenging but at the same time make the goals realistic enough that, with some effort on your part, you will achieve them.

Guideline 3: Set Long-Term and Short-Term Goals

Often our ultimate goal is a long way away. For example, at the start of the season the finals are a long way off. At the beginning of a new school year, final exams seem to be a long way off. Although these ultimate goals are very important, motivation is best served if you break the big goal down into a series of smaller, short-term goals. As you reach each of these smaller goals you feel you are moving closer to your ultimate goal. You can then re-evaluate what you need to do next to keep you moving in the right direction.

Guideline 4: Set Performance Goals

Performance goals focus on what action you have to take to do your best. They contrast with outcome goals that focus on winning or doing better than others. You should be able to see the similarity between performance and outcome goals and task and ego orientation. For the same reasons that task orientation is thought to be better than ego orientation, performance goals are thought to be better for motivation than outcome goals. Performance goals increase your control of your performance so that you only need to concentrate to perform well. In addition, performance goals can help reduce anxiety and improve concentration because they assist you to focus on the task at hand rather than the outcome.

Guideline 5:
Identify Strategies That Will Help You Achieve Your Goal

One of the biggest mistakes people make when they set goals is forgetting to work out what they need to do to achieve the goal. Many people set goals that meet guidelines 1 to 4. But, unless you also work out what you need to do to reach the goal, the goal-setting process will not be effective. As an example, I have set a goal of increasing my percentage of successful shots from the free throw line in basketball from 60 per cent to 75 per cent. My next step would be to chose some exercises or drills to help me do this. I might decide that I am going to do 3 sets of 10 free throws each lunchtime for the next 2 weeks and record the number I score. I am also going to keep a record of the percentage I score in games. I might also decide to talk to my coach about my technique and check that it is correct and work on any exercises the coach suggests. By setting these strategies it is more motivating, because I now know exactly what I am going to do to achieve my goal.

Guideline 6: Write Down Your Goals

Writing down goals prevents you from changing your mind when the going gets tough. If it's written down, you've got no option but to say, 'Yeah, that's what I was aiming for'. Also writing down goals is effective because it means you can then display the goal somewhere prominent and constantly remind yourself of what you are trying to achieve.

Guideline 7: Evaluate Your Goals Regularly

Are you reaching your goals? Are they motivating you? You may need to readjust or reset your goals so that they remain challenging. If you are reaching your goals, regular evaluation allows you take pride in your improvements.

• • • Focus Activity —

SHORT- AND LONG-TERM GOALS

Purpose

To learn how to set short-term goals and how to determine if they are met in order to reach a long-term goal.

Procedure

1. Give an example of a long-term goal for a sporting situation you are involved in.

2. Identify five relevant short-term goals that help move you towards your long-term goal—remember all the different areas you can set goals in.

3. Taking one of these short-term goals, complete the goal-setting process by addressing the following issues: My goal is . . . Date set . . . Date to be achieved by . . . What do I need to do to achieve my goal? Who can help me and how? How will I know I have achieved my goal?

4. Check that you have followed guidelines 1 to 7.

5. Switch with a friend and check that each of you has met the guidelines. Can you tell exactly what the person is going to do to achieve their goal?

Written Task

Create an acronym to remind you of the seven goal-setting guidelines.

Why Does Goal Setting Work?

There are many reasons why goal setting is effective in enhancing or maintaining motivation. By progressively achieving small goals on the way to a larger goal you can see where you have come from; you can see the improvements you are making towards your ultimate goal. This helps motivation remain high. By setting goals, you can also identify your strengths and weaknesses. You can then target key areas where improvements will lead to improved performance. Goals also help provide you with a sense of purpose and direction because they help you to determine what is important to work on now and why. Finally, goals help you look for new strategies to learn a skill.

● ● ● *Focus Activity* —

GOAL SETTING

Purpose

To use goal setting in physical education.

Procedure

Think about how you could use goal setting to help you study for your Senior physical education course.

Written Task

Write down some goals that could help you study for your Senior physical education course.

ANXIETY, AROUSAL AND PERFORMANCE

Imagine yourself before an important event such as a race, an exam or a job interview. How are you feeling? The chances are you might have a few butterflies in the stomach, perhaps your heart is racing and your palms are sweaty, maybe you feel excited or worried, or your mind is full of thoughts about how you are going to perform.

Most of us have experienced some of these changes in arousal and anxiety before a performance. **Arousal** refers to changes in activation from deep sleep to high excitement. Arousal is associated with good events, such as doing well in your exams, and not-so-good events, such as falling off your bike. **Anxiety** is a negative response to these changes in arousal. Negative responses may relate to cognitive events (such as feelings of worry) or physiological occurrences (such as feelings of muscle tension).

How Do Arousal and Anxiety Affect Performance?

Many people assume that increases in arousal and anxiety lead to decreases in performance. This is not necessarily so. Most of us need an increase in arousal to perform at our best. In exams, for example, it helps to be awake, alert and interested. Even anxiety may not decrease performance. It is generally thought that **cognitive anxiety** is detrimental to performance. However, **physiological anxiety** can be a positive sign as long as we interpret it as meaning we are ready to perform at our best.

The Inverted-U Hypothesis

Several models and theories have been proposed to explain the relationship between arousal states and performance. One of the most widely cited is the inverted-U hypothesis (see figure 2.2). This hypothesis suggests that as arousal increases there will be an increase in performance up to a point where further increases in arousal lead to decreases in performance. This approach suggests that there is an optimal level of arousal that is associated with best performances. Any deviation from this optimal level will result in poorer performance.

It is likely that the optimal level of arousal will be different for different people. You can probably think of someone who seems to perform their best when they appear to be very calm and relaxed, and others who need to be

arousal:
The level of psychological and physiological activation, ranging from deep sleep to high excitement.

anxiety:
A feeling of uneasiness that stems from a negative interpretation of changes in arousal.

cognitive anxiety:
A mental state which arises from feelings of nervousness and worry associated with changes in arousal.

physiological anxiety:
A condition associated with heightened arousal, revealed in physiological responses such as increased heart rate and sweaty palms.

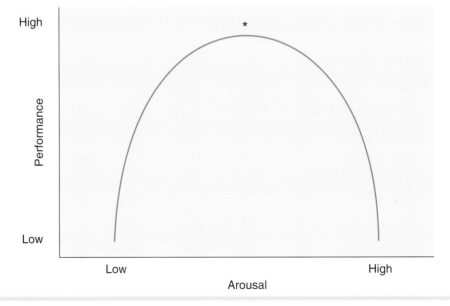

Figure 2.2   Model of the inverted-U hypothesis.

really jumping out of their skin to perform their best. Also it is likely that the optimal level of arousal will be different for the same person, depending on the activity they are doing. For example, if you were going out to play hockey, your optimal arousal level is likely to be different from if you were going out to play golf. It is likely to be different again, if you were going to play snooker.

••• *Focus Activity* —

AROUSAL-PERFORMANCE RELATIONSHIP

Purpose

To learn what factors can affect your level of arousal.

Procedure

1. Make three copies of the X and Y axes from figure 2.2.
2. On the graph, plot a curve that matches your arousal-performance relationship for three different activities.
3. Discuss the differences with members of your group. What would you do to control your arousal to an optimum level for each activity?

Written Task

Other than the activity itself, make a list of factors that might influence arousal levels.

Recently, researchers have suggested that the inverted-U hypothesis is too simplistic and more complex models have been proposed. These new models try to separate the effects of cognitive anxiety and physiological arousal. For example, in catastrophe theory (figure 2.3) it is predicted that if cognitive anxiety is low, increases in physiological anxiety will follow the inverted-U, with performance decreasing when physiological anxiety rises beyond optimal levels. However, if cognitive anxiety is high, once physiological arousal passes an optimal level, there will be a sudden decline in performance, or a catastrophe. In this theory, the effects of physiological arousal are markedly different

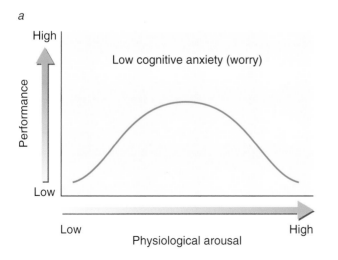
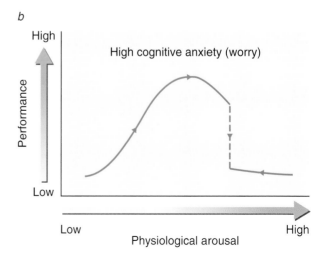

Figure 2.3   Model of catastrophe theory: *(a)* low and *(b)* high cognitive anxiety.

Reprinted, by permission, from R.S. Weinberg and D. Gould, 1999, *Foundations of sport and exercise psychology*, 3rd ed. (Champaign, IL: Human Kinetics), 90.

depending on the level of cognitive anxiety. This means that when trying to manage anxiety we need to be able to manage our thoughts and worries as well as our physical responses.

••• Focus Activity —

AROUSAL AND ANXIETY

Purpose

To explain how arousal and anxiety affect performance.

Procedure

1. Explain how the inverted-U hypothesis fits within the catastrophe model.
2. Interview members of your class on how they attempt to control their cognitive anxiety.
3. Then apply this information to a coaching situation.

Written Task

If you were coaching an individual or team in a sporting situation, how would you help your athletes control cognitive anxiety? Write down some examples.

We have seen that both arousal and anxiety can affect performance. Also, we have examined some of the relationships between arousal and anxiety. We are now in a position to answer the question, Why do arousal and anxiety affect performance?

There are at least two possible answers to this question. The first is that increases in physiological anxiety may lead to increases in muscle tension that in turn lead to decreases in coordination. It is hard to move easily and competently if you are feeling tight and stiff.

The second explanation is that changes in psychological arousal result in changes to our concentration. When you are optimally aroused, you focus on the relevant details to perform the task. When you are underaroused your mind tends to wander and you take in irrelevant details such as what you had for tea last night, or what colour shirt the opposition is wearing. In contrast, if you are overaroused and worrying about what is going to happen, you are likely to find your concentration becomes too narrow and you miss some vital cues. With a focus that is too broad or too narrow, you are unlikely to perform at your best.

••• Focus Activity —

MANAGING AROUSAL AND ANXIETY

Purpose

To learn techniques for managing your arousal and anxiety.

Procedure

1. What words would you use to describe yourself when you have (a) high cognitive anxiety, (b) low cognitive anxiety, (c) high physiological arousal

and (d) low physiological arousal. Construct your own personal scale for cognitive anxiety and physiological arousal. For example, your cognitive anxiety scale might be 1 = whatever you wrote for (a) and 5 = whatever you wrote for (b).

2. To be able to effectively manage your arousal and anxiety levels you have to know how you feel when you perform at your best. After every performance for a period of 2 to 3 months, complete a form containing the following information:

   • Date:

   • Opponent:

   • Performance rank: (1 = the worst I can play, 10 = as good as I can play)

   • Rate your cognitive anxiety and physiological arousal using the scale you constructed in step 1.

   • Make note of any factors that might have influenced how you felt (e.g., weather, opponent, who was watching, importance of the game).

3. When you have several of these ratings you should start to see a pattern between how you feel and how you perform. Use this information as a guide for managing your arousal and anxiety before performing.

4. In a group, discuss ways to manage arousal and anxiety before performance. Remember to discuss ways to both increase and decrease these levels.

Written Task

Make a list of at least three ways up and three ways down for both cognitive anxiety and physiological arousal. Your list should be personal to you and include ways that you know or feel would work for you.

CONFIDENCE

One of the most consistent findings in the research literature is the relationship between **confidence** and success. When we feel confident, we tend to perform well. When we lack confidence, we tend to perform poorly. Confidence is important because what you think or say to yourself before performing is critical. If you don't think you can achieve your goals, then you probably won't. For example, if you think your gymnastics routine is too difficult, then it will likely prove so.

confidence:
The realistic belief that you have the ability to achieve your goals.

Being confident does not guarantee you will perform well. But it certainly helps the process and enables you to ride out the rough patches more easily. For example, compared with someone who lacks confidence, a confident person is more likely to react positively to correct a mistake or poor performance. Someone with little confidence is likely to view the mistake as a further sign that they aren't very good. They may then be less likely to try to correct the mistake or improve in the future.

When we have negative **self-talk,** we start to doubt ourselves. Doubts can increase anxiety. They interfere with concentration and they can make someone indecisive or tentative. Sometimes losing confidence in one part of a game can lead to a loss of confidence in other game skills. For example, a batter in cricket going through a run of low scores might then start to make mistakes when fielding. Keeping self-talk positive and realistic is the key to confidence.

self-talk:
The things we say to ourselves.

••• *Focus Activity* —

SELF-CONFIDENCE

Purpose

To explore what it means to be self-confident.

Procedure

1. In a paragraph, define self-confidence in your own terms.
2. Then write a half-page description of a confident person you know personally.
3. In a small group, share and discuss what you have written.
4. Summarise similarities and differences in definitions and characteristics of the descriptions.

Managing Self-Talk to Keep It Positive

As with managing arousal and anxiety, the first step in managing self-talk is to be aware of the things you say to yourself in different situations. Think of a situation in which you felt really confident. Make a note of the situation and what you were saying to yourself. Now think of when you lacked confidence. Again, make a note of the situation and what you were saying to yourself. In the latter situation where you lacked confidence, there is a good chance you had some self-doubts. Maybe you were telling yourself, 'I'm so useless' or 'I can't believe I'm playing so badly'.

Having built up a list of negative things we typically say to ourselves, we can then build up another list of positive statements to counter them. We can tell ourselves such things as *Be calm and focused—remember all the good training you have done* or *Hang in there, one shot at a time.* These positive statements should be task oriented; that is, they should be encouraging statements that focus on what you have to do at present.

When you find yourself thinking negatively, try repeating one of the positive statements to yourself to switch your thinking around. When you use the positive statements, say them to yourself with conviction and emotion, as if you really believe them. Recall your performance goals, as this can also be an effective reminder of what you are trying to achieve.

••• *Focus Activity* —

MAINTAINING CONFIDENCE

Purpose

To learn how to counter negative statements with positive ones.

Procedure

1. Design an interview to investigate the negative things people typically say to themselves.

2. Use this plan to interview your partner and then assist her or him to come up with positive counter statements.

Written Task

Imagining that you are a team-mate of your partner, how could you use this information to help them maintain confidence? Write down your suggestions. Remember, it's important not just to note what your partner says, but also what the situation is.

CONCENTRATION

Concentration is a vital factor in quality performances in any setting. When someone is performing at their best, they seldom have difficulty with concentration. It seems to happen naturally and easily. However, when they are anxious or lack confidence, concentration can waver and the quality of their performance decrease.

Concentration is selective. It involves paying attention to the right things at the right time. So it involves focusing attention on certain sources of information while ignoring others. For example, a golfer attempting to sink a vital putt must focus on the task at hand and be oblivious to things that might distract him. Golfers thinking about other things cannot give their full attention to the putt.

Concentration involves the ability to shift between cues depending on the situation. For example, in football a player has to be able to make rapid shifts from a broad focus, scanning the pitch for the position of other players, to a narrow focus when shooting. Concentration involves parking your mind in the present and nowhere else. The only thing you have control over is here and now. You cannot do anything about things that have already occurred and you cannot do anything about things that might happen in 5 minutes' time. Thoughts about events that have already occurred or thoughts about the future are wasteful and distracting. If you are thinking *What if I lose?, How could I have made that mistake?,* or *What if I miss this basket?* then your mind is off task and you decrease the chance of performing well.

concentration:
The ability to focus on relevant cues at the right time and to maintain this focus for the duration of an event.

Improving Your Concentration

If you can develop a consistent mental and physical preparation routine, this will assist you to do your best more consistently. Softball players who do exactly the same thing each time they come to bat are more likely to be appropriately focused when the ball is pitched. For example, they may imagine themselves hitting the ball while waiting to bat. When they step up to the plate they always go through exactly the same routine: left foot in position, right foot in position, couple of easy swings, check balance and bat position, look at the pitcher, take a deep breath, and use cue words such as *target* to narrow in on the pitcher and the ball.

Such routines are effective because they help players learn to focus on task-relevant cues and avoid distracting ones. They also create a mental set. A mental set involves the idea that, by doing the same thing at the same pace every time, the player is ready to 'go'.

Finally, routines give you a familiar activity to return to after distraction. In free-flowing games such as hockey or rugby, routines may only be appropriate at set plays. However, you can use cue words to focus on what is happening. For example, in hockey you might use the words *ball* and *player* to focus your attention on where the ball is and where your opposition is. We have already noted how arousal and anxiety can affect concentration. So controlling your arousal and anxiety levels can help maintain concentration. Likewise, a focus on performance goals helps to maintain a focus on what has to be done here and now.

••• *Focus Activity* —

PREPARATION ROUTINES

Purpose

To learn about and test different ways to mentally and physically prepare yourself for an activity.

Procedure

1. Make a list of any mental and physical preparation routines you already use.

2. Talk with other people to find out what routines they use.

3. Then try out some of the routines in a selected activity and monitor your progress.

TEAM COHESION

The skills and techniques already discussed in this chapter apply to individuals. However, in team games how well the members of the group get on and share common goals can affect the overall team performance. It is often assumed that the best players go together to make the best team, but this relationship is not perfect. Simply summing the abilities of team members does not accurately describe team performance. Rather, it is necessary to consider team or group processes as well as the individual skills of the players.

team cohesion:
The tendency for group members to stick together and remain united in the pursuit of team goals.

An important group process is **team cohesion.** Team cohesion is the tendency for group members to stick together and remain united in the pursuit of team goals. There are two dimensions to team cohesion:

• Social cohesion refers to how much team members like each other and enjoy each other's company.

• Task cohesion refers to how team members work together to achieve a specific goal.

The relationship between cohesion and performance depends on the amount of interaction required from team members in the sport being examined. Sports requiring a high level of mutual interaction are influenced by task cohesion to a greater degree than sports requiring little interaction between team members.

For example, basketball requires passing between players and the use of offensive and defensive team patterns. In the case of basketball, task cohesion will be more important than in a sport such as rowing, where team members simply have to do the same thing at the same time. However, rowing will be influenced by task cohesion more than team events in archery or triathlon, where individual scores or times are added at the end of the event and no interaction is required during the event. Social cohesion appears to have little effect on performance although it can help an event be more enjoyable.

••• *Focus Activity* —

THE TEAM COHESION CONTINUUM

Purpose

To learn how different sports are positioned along the team cohesion continuum.

Procedure

1. With a group, make a list of 10 different sports, including at least 2 invasion games, 2 striking-fielding games and 2 net-racquet games.

2. Position these sports along the continuum illustrated in figure 2.4.

3. Discuss and make a note of differences in the positioning of each sport.

Team cohesion is important	Team cohesion is not important

Figure 2.4   Team cohesion continuum.

Adapted, by permission, from D. Kirk et al., 2002, *A-level physical education: A reflective performer* (Champaign, IL: Human Kinetics), 52.

Although a positive relationship has been found between cohesion and performance, it is not clear whether increased cohesion causes improved performance or the other way around. At the moment, researchers think that it is a circular relationship with successful performance leading to a greater sense of cohesion, which leads to further success. Success leads to greater satisfaction and cohesion and consequently further improvements in performance and so on. Because of this circularity, sport psychologists suggest that when new teams are formed, players should be given the chance to experience early success as a team in friendly matches or small-sided games.

There are many ways of developing team cohesion. Early and ongoing success has already been mentioned. Obviously, if having a commitment to a common goal defines team cohesion then involving team members in deciding what that goal is and how it will be achieved is an important step. In large teams where there are natural subgroups it can be useful to have performance goals for each subgroup that fit together to help the whole team reach their goal.

For example, in Rugby Union, the front row have a distinct job and can set goals for this job, whereas the back line have a different job with different goals. With each group setting relevant performance goals and taking pride in them, the overall team goal is more likely to be reached and cohesion increased. Remember that success is not the same as winning, so look for indicators of success and good performance, particularly after a loss. Displaying a team identity, by way of a uniform or on training T-shirts, can help a group feel more together.

DEVELOPING TEAM COHESION

Purpose

To learn how coaches develop team cohesion.

Procedure

1. Interview the coach of a local team or club.
2. Write a one-page description of what they do to develop team cohesion.

1. Define the following terms:

    Motivation

    Arousal

    Cognitive anxiety

    Somatic anxiety

    Self-confidence

    Self-talk

    Social cohesion

    Task cohesion

    Task orientation

    Ego orientation

2. Describe the mental climate associated with your best performance. Describe the strategies you might use to achieve this optimal mental climate.

3. Explain how attributions for success or failure might influence a performer's motivation for future participation.

4. Explain why task orientation is viewed as motivationally adaptive.

5. Kelsey is a talented young swimmer who is looking to make the Olympic team in 4 years' time. However, the 4 years seems like a long, long time and she is unsure whether she can make the improvements necessary to bring her times down. Explain why goal setting might help Kelsey, and describe the steps involved in effective goal setting.

6. Robert is a mid-level tennis player. He reports to you that sometimes he feels 'physically really tight' before a game, but this doesn't seem to affect his performance once the game starts. However, on other days this tightness really worries him and he starts wondering why he's so tight; on these days his performance seems to suffer. From your knowledge of the arousal-performance relationship, explain the reasons for this difference.

7. Explain the relationship between arousal, concentration and performance.

8. If an athlete experiences an overly high level of preperformance physiological anxiety, what techniques would you recommend to lower this level and why?

   If an athlete experiences an overly high level of preperformance cognitive anxiety, what techniques would you recommend to lower this level and why?

9. Explain how having a consistent mental and physical preparation routine would help a performer obtain or maintain concentration in a sport of your choice. Provide an example of a routine from this sport.

10. Self-talk is associated with an individual's confidence level. Describe a strategy for manipulating self-talk to enhance confidence.

11. Explain how the type of sport task influences the relationship between cohesion and performance.

12. Outline three strategies you would use with a junior hockey team to increase team cohesion.

Describing Motion When Learning Physical Skills

Learning Outcomes

When you have studied this chapter, you should be able to

- describe motion using linear and angular kinematic terms;
- explain the distinction between linear and angular displacement and distance, speed and velocity;
- use examples from physical activity to illustrate Newton's law of inertia; and
- predict the consequences of this law for the motion of projectiles.

The movement of the human body is complex. Biomechanics helps us to understand the moving body. By applying the laws of physics to simplified physical models, you can predict the behaviour of the moving body in various circumstances. However, before you can talk about the movement of the body in physical terms, you must understand the language of physics. You probably already use terms like distance, displacement, speed, velocity, acceleration, inertia, momentum, work, energy, power and force in daily speech, but these words have very specific meanings within the field of biomechanics.

KINEMATICS: DESCRIBING MOTION

linear motion:
Movement in a straight line.

angular motion:
Rotation about an axis.

kinematics:
A collective term for descriptors of motion including distance, displacement, speed, velocity and acceleration.

The first step in understanding the movement of the body is to describe the movement. **Linear motion** refers to movement of the body or parts of the body in a straight line. **Angular motion** refers to rotation of the body or parts of the body. Rotation always occurs around an axis, and this axis might be inside or outside of the body. You can describe any movement of the body through a combination of linear and angular distances, displacements, speeds, velocities and accelerations. These components are referred to collectively as **kinematics.**

LINEAR MOTION

Figure 3.1   Average velocity is greater for sprinters like Cathy Freeman than for marathon runners.
© Sport The Library

Movement occurs in time and space. Linear distance is the distance in metres (m) that a person or object moves during a given time, measured in seconds (s). Linear displacement is the distance and direction in which an object moves in a straight line during a given time.

Linear Speed, Velocity and Acceleration

Linear speed is the rate of change of distance during the time interval, or distance divided by time. Linear velocity is the rate and direction of change of displacement in a time period, or displacement divided by time. The units of speed and velocity are metres per second (m/s). Linear acceleration is the direction and rate of change of velocity in a time period, and the units are metres per second per second (m/s/s or m/s^2). Linear displacement, velocity and acceleration all have both magnitude and direction, whereas linear distance and speed have magnitude only.

Consider the movement of a sprinter from start to finish in a 100-metre race (see figure 3.1). The sprinter's time for the race was 12 seconds. If you define the start as 0, and the finish line is 100 metres away in a positive direction, then the displacement of the sprinter at the finish line is +100 metres. The average velocity during this time is the displacement divided by time (100 m ÷ 12 s) or +8.33 m/s.

Linear Displacement

Unfortunately, knowing the sprinter's average velocity over the duration of the race does not tell us anything very useful. It does not tell us what the velocity of the sprinter was at any particular time, what the sprinter's maximum velocity was or how she ran the race. How quickly did she leave the blocks? Was she slowing down at the end of the race? To answer these questions, you need to know the **displacement** of the sprinter at many more times throughout the race.

If you measure the displacement of the sprinter every half second throughout the race, you can tabulate the information in a fashion similar to table 3.1. You can then calculate the difference in displacement between each half second, and divide by 0.5 seconds to calculate the average velocity of the sprinter for each half second of the race.

displacement:
The distance and direction that an object has moved in a given time period.

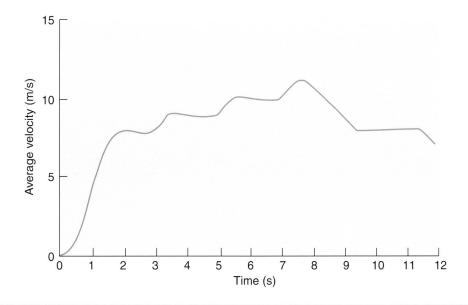

Figure 3.2   Velocity versus time for 100-m sprint.

If you plot these numbers on a graph like figure 3.2, you then know something about the way the sprinter ran the race. You can see, for example, that she increased her velocity rapidly at the start, continued to increase velocity gradually until about 7 seconds, maintained this higher velocity for 2 seconds but then slowed down until the end of the race. Although more useful than knowing the average velocity for the race, these velocities are still only averages for each half second, and they do not tell us exactly what the velocity of the sprinter was at any point in time—that is, her **instantaneous velocity** at any point.

instantaneous velocity: The velocity of an object at a particular instant in time, such as the moment of impact with another object.

If you wanted to know something about how the sprinter's velocity changed during the race (her acceleration), you could estimate her approximate **average acceleration** (m/s^2) during each half second by calculating the differences between average velocities and dividing by a half second. Suppose that a difference between average velocities is 2 m/s as seen in table 3.1. Divide this average by 0.5 seconds, and the sprinter's average acceleration is 4 m/s/s or 4 m/s^2. To be accurate, we would need to know what the sprinter's actual velocity was at each point in time, not just her average velocity.

average acceleration: The rate of change of velocity during a given time interval.

TABLE 3.1   Displacement, Velocity and Acceleration Versus Time for 100-m Sprint

Time (s)	Displacement (m)	Velocity (m/s)	Acceleration (m/s/s)
0.5	0.5	1	2
1.0	2.5	4	6
1.5	6.0	7	6
2.0	10.0	8	2
2.5	14.0	8	0
3.0	18.0	8	0
3.5	22.5	9	2

(continued)

TABLE 3.1 (Continued)

Time (s)	Displacement (m)	Velocity (m/s)	Acceleration (m/s/s)
4.0	27.0	9	0
4.5	31.5	9	0
5.0	36.0	9	0
5.5	41.0	10	2
6.0	46.0	10	0
6.5	51.0	10	0
7.0	56.0	10	0
7.5	61.5	11	2
8.0	67.0	11	0
8.5	72.0	10	–2
9.0	76.5	9	–2
9.5	80.5	8	–2
10.0	84.5	8	0
10.5	88.5	8	0
11.0	92.5	8	0
11.5	96.5	8	0
12.0	100.0	7	–2

••• Focus Activity —

LINEAR VELOCITY AND ACCELERATION

Purpose

To understand the concepts of linear velocity and acceleration.

Many physical activities require speed of movement. By calculating the linear velocity of sprinters within your class and manipulating the calculations, you will gain a basic idea of acceleration. Without sophisticated timing devices, however, your extrapolations will be rough estimates at best. By comparing and contrasting the results, you will develop a better understanding of linear velocity and acceleration.

Equipment

Access to a 100-metre running track, a starting gun or whistle, five dome markers, a 100-metre measuring tape and five stopwatches.

Procedure

1. Use the measuring tape and dome markers to divide the 100-metre track into five 20-metre segments.

2. A student holding a stopwatch stands at each marker, while the remaining students get ready to sprint the 100 metres, one at a time.

3. The students at the markers start their stopwatches when the starting signal (a gun or whistle) is given, and stop their stopwatches at the precise moment that the sprinter passes their marker. Some previous stopwatch practice would be useful, to make the results as accurate as possible.

4. One student at a time sprints in the lane adjacent to the markers.

5. The student at each marker writes down the stopwatch time next to the sprinter's name on a list.

6. Rotate the stopwatch responsibility until each student has sprinted the 100 metres so that all the students can have their results recorded.

Calculation Tasks

• Obtain your own results by sharing information.

• Calculate your average linear velocity for each of the distances: 20, 40, 60, 80 and 100 metres. Each of these distances represents your displacement at each marker. Remember, linear velocity measures both the rate and direction of change of displacement. For example, if you were timed at 3.66 seconds for the first 20 metres, then your average velocity (at that point) would have been 5.46 m/s (distance divided by time).

• When you have calculated your average velocity for each of the distances, record the information on a simple graph that plots distance against velocity. Such a graph might look like the one in figure 3.3.

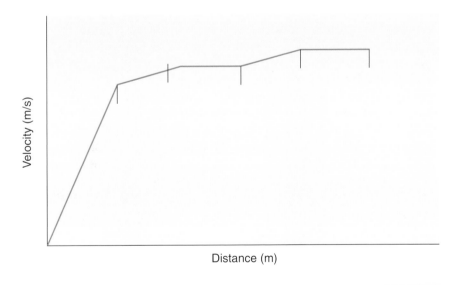

Figure 3.3 Example of a graph that plots distance against velocity.

(continued)

To accurately measure acceleration, sophisticated data and calculation are required. As a general indication, however, your graph will show your average velocity at five different stages. The shape and direction of your graph determines whether the change in your velocity, from one point to the next, was positive (accelerating) or negative (decelerating). Compare and contrast your graph and results with those of the other students.

Written Task

- Compare and contrast your results with those of other students.
- Evaluate your 100-metre performance in terms of your acceleration and average velocity at various stages of the sprint.
- Write down any factors that might affect the accuracy of your calculations.

ANGULAR MOTION

Not everything moves in a straight line. You might also be interested in the rotation of an object, the body or limbs about a joint. In this case, you need to describe the movement in terms of angular kinematics, using angular displacement, angular velocity, angular speed and angular acceleration.

Remember that movement occurs in time. Angular displacement is the angular change that occurs during a specified time and is measured in degrees ($°$). One complete rotation equals $360°$. If an object rotates all the way around to its initial orientation, then the angular displacement is zero. The angular distance is the distance the object rotated through during the time interval—in this case, $360°$. Angular velocity refers to the rate and direction of change in angular displacement of a body in a given time, whereas angular speed is the angular distance divided by time. Angular speed and angular velocity are measured in degrees per second ($°/s$). Angular acceleration refers to the rate and direction of change in angular velocity during a specified time ($°/s^2$).

Imagine you are playing a chip shot in golf. You can use angular kinematics to describe the movement of your club during the downswing. If you define the position of the club at the moment of impact as zero and the direction of the downswing (anticlockwise) as positive, then in the illustrated swing, the angular displacement of the club during the downswing is $90°$. If the duration of your downswing is 0.5 seconds, then the average angular velocity for the downswing is $90°$ divided by 0.5 s, or $180°/s$.

Average angular velocity is not the angular velocity of your golf club at the moment of impact. If you measure the actual angular velocity of your club at the moment of impact, you will find that it is greater than the average velocity across the duration of the downswing.

••• Focus Activity —

ANGULAR KINEMATICS

Purpose

To develop an understanding of angular kinematics by considering how variations of a golf swing can affect the outcome of a shot.

Procedure

1. Examine the text regarding angular displacement, angular velocity and angular acceleration. How can this information help golfers understand how to improve their chip shots?

2. Imagine that you are a golfer and that your chip shot has landed in a bunker in front of the putting green, instead of landing on the green as you had planned. Aside from changing clubs, what could you have done differently to improve the shot?

3. Discuss these questions with another student and write down at least two or three solutions. After you have completed the written task, check your answers against the explanations below.

Explanation

One factor determining the outcome of any golf shot is the linear velocity, or direction and speed, of the head of the golf club at the moment of impact with the ball. The greater the linear velocity of the club head at impact, the greater the velocity of the ball after impact. All else being equal, a ball struck with a higher velocity club head travels further. Therefore, one way to land the ball on the green instead of in the bunker is to increase the linear velocity of the club head at the moment of impact with the ball.

The linear velocity of the head of the club at impact is equal to the angular velocity of the club at impact, multiplied by the distance of the head of the club from the axis of rotation of the club. One way to increase the linear velocity of the club head is to keep the angular velocity the same but increase the length of the axis of rotation by choosing a longer club. That is, keep your swing the same but use a seven iron instead of a nine iron.

Another way to increase the distance the shot carries is to increase the angular velocity of the club at impact. The angular velocity of the club at impact is determined by the angular acceleration of the golf club throughout the swing. If you increase the distance through which the golf club rotates during the downswing, you increase the duration of the downswing (assuming that you can continue to accelerate the club through the whole swing). Consequently, the angular velocity of the club at impact increases. If your chip shot lands short of the hole, therefore, increase the height of your backswing while you maintain the same angular acceleration to increase the linear velocity of the club head at impact, and consequently the distance the ball travels.

Written Tasks

- Write down ways in which angular displacement occurs in your chosen physical activity.
- Investigate the physical activity through video or observation and identify aspects of the activity in which angular velocity and angular acceleration are relevant to improved performance. Write down your observations.

EXTENSION ACTIVITY

ANGULAR KINEMATICS

Consider the physical activity that you are currently studying. If it contains the use of an implement for striking a ball, then it is highly likely that the activity will be affected by variations in angular kinematics. Even physical activities that do not use implements involve angular kinematics. Every time there is movement at one of the body's major hinges, or at one of the ball-and-socket joints, there is angular displacement.

PROJECTILE MOTION

What would happen if you threw a ball into space, where there is no gravity or air resistance? **Newton's law of inertia** states that the velocity of a body remains constant unless a force acts on it. In the absence of any forces, therefore, the ball would maintain a constant velocity—that is, it would continue to travel in a straight line with the same speed.

What happens when you throw a ball on Earth? It does not maintain constant velocity. The velocity of the ball begins to change from the instant of release, and it continues to change until the ball stops moving. Changing velocity applies to any object in flight, such as a discus, javelin or ball. The human body is such an object, during the flight phase of activities like jumping, diving, vaulting and running. The continual changes in velocity are caused by the resistance of air against the object passing through it and by the gravitational attraction between the Earth and the object. The gravitational attraction between the Earth and an object always causes vertical (downward) acceleration. Consider the magnitude of the acceleration to be constant at about 10 m/s^2.

The accelerations caused by air resistance are not as easy to predict. In many cases, such as the shot-put or the high jump, the effects are slight and may be ignored. In other cases, such as the discus or badminton, the effects of air resistance are substantial and complex. The next chapter will discuss the effects of air resistance.

SAMPLE LEARNING EXPERIENCE

Projectile Motion and Physical Activity in Archery

Kelly was studying projectile motion as part of her archery course in physical education. Because the arrows travelled so fast when they left her compound bow, it was difficult to observe the shape of the path that the arrows followed on their way to the target. The following task illustrated clearly to Kelly that regardless of the force with which an object moves, it follows a curved path because of the pull of gravity.

Kelly had made some big improvements in her archery technique and could now fire the arrows quite consistently. She had learned how to use the sight on her bow and appreciated how it could help her find out more about her technique. In this task, the teacher used the sight to help illustrate the curved trajectories of arrows propelled by bows.

Kelly's task was to fire a total of nine arrows. She had to shoot the first three arrows from the 10-metre mark, with the sight set for 10 metres, aiming them at the gold centre of the target. She grouped the three arrows within 15 centimetres of each other in and about the gold centre.

Next Kelly had to shoot another three arrows, but this time from the 15-metre mark. Her teacher told her to leave the sight set for 10 metres and to continue to aim at the gold centre of the target. Kelly again produced a grouping of about 15 to 20 centimetres, but this time the grouping hit the target below the gold centre.

She repeated the task with the final three arrows from the 20-metre mark, again using the 10-metre sight and aiming for the gold centre. This time the grouping struck the target about 25 centimetres below the last grouping of arrows.

Explanation

Kelly explained the findings of the experiment in the following way. When the compound bow imparted a force to the arrows, they had an initial velocity. The force of gravity then affected the trajectory or path of each arrow.

During the journey of each arrow from the bow to the target, the greatest rate of acceleration of the arrow occurred at the last point at which the bow string contacted it. After this point, the arrow was under the influence of other factors governing projectile motion, including air resistance, the angle of release and the height of release. The arrow began decelerating from the point immediately after the bowstring applied force to it.

Because each consecutive arrow was fired with reasonable consistency, the propelling force remained reasonably constant, as did the height of release (dictated by Kelly's height) and the angle of release (the result of the consistent use of the 10-metre sight for each of the three distances). Each of the arrows was identical, so the air resistance characteristics were much the same. The only relevant variable was the distance from the target.

Kelly understood that the trajectory of the arrow would be a product of all of these factors, especially the size of the propelling force, according to Newton's law of acceleration and because of the constant force of gravity. She was able to predict that the greatest rate of curvature of the path would come later in its flight, when the decelerating arrow had its lowest velocity. Conversely, the straightest path of the arrow was in its early flight when the initial velocity was significantly greater than the force of gravity. She predicted that as the velocity of the arrow decreased and gravity began to exert a greater pull on the arrow in flight, the curvature of the path gradually increased.

The task showed that the arrows did follow a curved path, because each consecutive group of arrows hit the target lower than the last. The reason was that the constant force of gravity pulled the arrows closer to the centre of mass of the earth. If both forces had been constant, then the direction and path of the arrow would have been a vector resulting from a product of the two forces. This outcome did not occur, because the only constant force in the task was gravity. The arrow lost its acceleration because of frictional air resistance. Thus the force of gravity affected it more and more, producing the curved path.

EXTENSION ACTIVITY

PROJECTILE MOTION

Consider This

Consider the physical activity that you are currently studying. Whenever an implement (for example, a ball) or body is moving through the air in this activity, it is a projectile and is affected by the principles of projectile motion.

Think and Write

- Write about a typical movement scenario in this activity. In doing so, examine the various forces that work to determine the path of the body or projected object.
- What factors under your personal control could alter the path of your body or projected object?
- What particular techniques do experts in this field utilise to improve the effectiveness of projectile motion?
- If you are studying a sport that involves a projected implement, what equipment design features are used to maximise projectile motion outcomes?

mass:
The amount of matter in an object, measured in kilograms.

centre of mass, or centre of gravity:
The point of an object on which the force due to gravitational attractions appears to act.

parabola:
The curved path that the centre of mass of an object follows during flight.

CENTRE OF MASS

All objects are composed of matter. **Mass,** measured in kilograms (kg), is the amount of matter in an object. The **centre of mass,** or **centre of gravity,** of an object is the point on which the force due to gravity appears to act. The location of the centre of mass of an object depends on the arrangement of mass within the body. If an object is a regular shape and its mass is evenly distributed, then the centre of mass is at the centre of the object. Objects with irregular shapes or irregular arrangements of mass can have a centre of mass quite distant from the centre of the object, and sometimes even outside the object, as shown in figure 3.4.

If a body rotates during flight, it rotates around the centre of mass. Forget about air resistance for the moment and assume that the only force acting on an object is that due to gravity. In this case, the centre of mass of the object in flight travels in a curve called a **parabola** and continues on this curve until acted on by another force. The initial velocity of the object, as well as its initial position and the gravitational acceleration, determines the precise details of the curve.

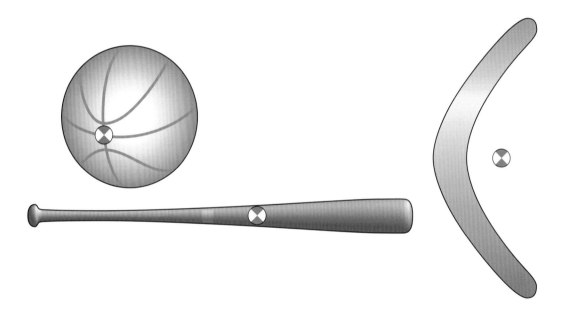

Figure 3.4   Different objects have different centres of mass.

The example shown in figure 3.5 illustrates how you can use this knowledge in a throwing activity such as the shot-put. The velocity of the shot at release and the height of release determine the horizontal displacement of the shot when it hits the ground. Increases in the height of release will increase the horizontal displacement at landing, as will increases in the speed of release. For any given height and velocity of release, there is an optimal angle of release that maximizes the horizontal displacement at landing.

When the human body is in flight, its centre of mass also travels in a curve that cannot be altered during flight. However, unlike rigid objects, you can alter the location of the centre of mass of the human body during flight by altering the arrangement of the body's mass. Raising your arms, for example, raises the

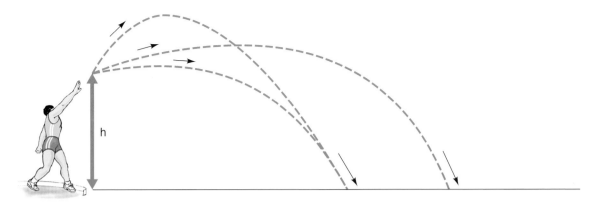

Figure 3.5 For any height at release (h), there is an optimal release angle to achieve maximum horizontal distance. The optimal angle is always less than 45°. Shown here is the relationship between release angle and horizontal displacement (distance) for a shot-putter.

location of the centre of mass of the body relative to the trunk (see figure 3.6a). Adopting a piked position or arching the spine backward can cause the centre of gravity of the body to move outside of the body, like that of a boomerang, as you can see in figure 3.6b.

Volleyball blockers sometimes seem to hang in the air forever, but they have not discovered the secret of flight. What they have learned to do is raise their legs by bending their knees after take-off and then lower their legs by straightening them as they reach the peak of the jump. Lowering the legs has the consequence of lowering the centre of mass of the body relative to the upper body and arms. This causes a player's trunk to remain higher for longer than it would have if the legs had not been lowered.

Figure 3.6 *(a)* The centre of mass in different postures. *(b)* Centre of mass passes under the body when performing the Fosbury flop.

Two other sport activities in which the location of the centre of mass within the body changes during flight are the high jump and pole vault events. In these events, the body arches over a bar. At the moment of passing over the bar, the centre of mass of the body may actually be outside of the body, and perhaps even under the bar. Even though you can manipulate the location of the centre of mass relative to your body, after take-off you cannot change the flight of the centre of mass itself.

• • • Test Yourself —

1. How might biomechanics contribute to our understanding of human movement?

2. Compare and contrast linear and angular motion. Select from your current physical activity two skills, one utilising linear motion and the other angular motion. Justify your selection.

3. When an object is rotating, the axis may be inside or outside of the body. Where would the axis be for a person completing a 360° swing around a high bar? What about a pike somersault off a vault box in gymnastics?

4. Complete the following statement: The combined value of linear and angular distances, displacements, speed, velocity and acceleration is known as _____.

5. Match Column A with the correct statement from Column B.

Column A	Column B
___Linear speed	a. The distance and direction an object moves in a straight line during some time period.
___Linear acceleration	b. The rate of change of distance during the time interval.
___Linear distance	c. The direction and rate of change of velocity in some time period.
___Linear velocity	d. The rate and direction of change of displacement in a short period of time.
___Linear displacement	e. The direction of change of displacement in some time period.

6. What units are used to measure (a) linear distance, (b) time, (c) linear speed, (d) linear velocity and (e) linear acceleration?

7. Brainstorm a range of physical activities or skills that would improve through analysis by linear kinematics. Underline those that come from your current physical activity.

8. Complete the following sentences by inserting the missing words: Angular displacement is the _____ change that occurs during a _____ _____ and is measured in _____. One complete rotation equals _____°, but if an object has rotated back to its initial orientation, then the _____ _____ is zero, whereas the _____ _____ is the distance the object has rotated through during the time interval, in this case, _____°. _____ _____ refers to the rate and direction of change in angular displacement of a body in a time period, whereas angular speed is the _____ _____ divided by _____.

(continued)

9. Define Newton's law of inertia. Give examples of how it affects your current physical activity.

10. Applying the law of inertia, describe the changing velocity of a basketball in flight during a free throw shot at the basket.

11. What effect does the varying shape of an object have on the centre of mass? Draw three objects from your current physical activity, marking the centre of gravity for each and explaining why you have placed it in that position.

12. What influences the parabola (curve of flight) of an object?

13. How can you manipulate the body's centre of gravity in a volleyball block or a jump shot in basketball? Provide examples of some other sports in which manipulation of the centre of gravity could benefit performance in the activity.

Understanding Forces and Torques in Learning Physical Skills

Chapter Overview

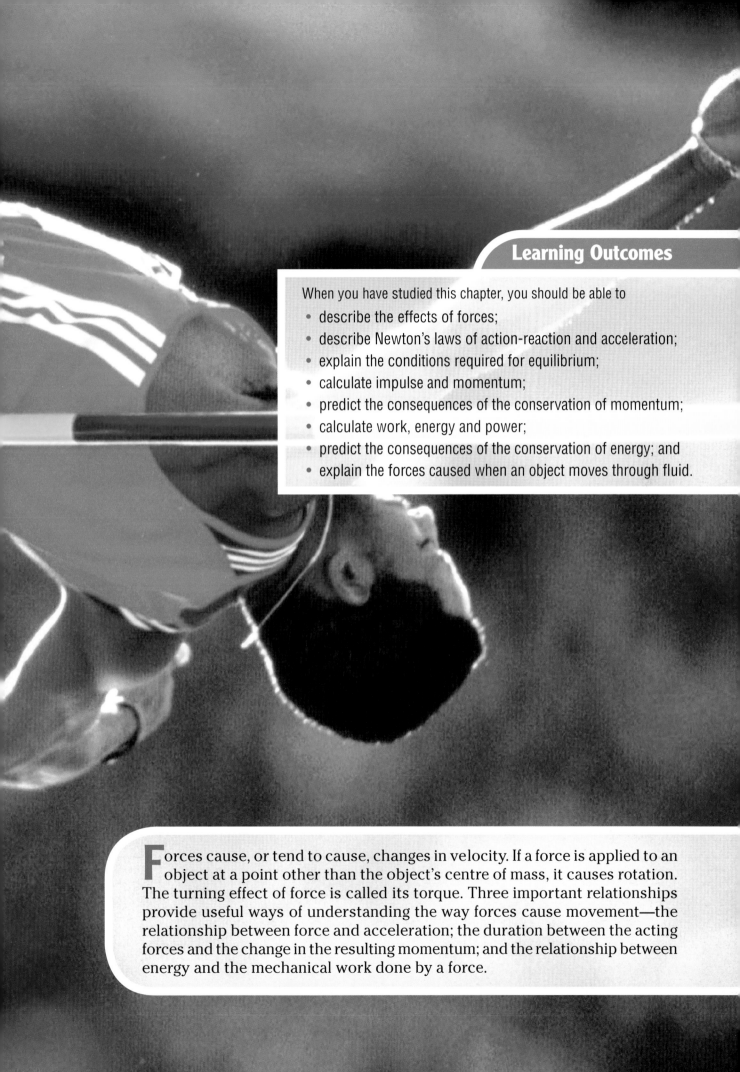

When you have studied this chapter, you should be able to

- describe the effects of forces;
- describe Newton's laws of action-reaction and acceleration;
- explain the conditions required for equilibrium;
- calculate impulse and momentum;
- predict the consequences of the conservation of momentum;
- calculate work, energy and power;
- predict the consequences of the conservation of energy; and
- explain the forces caused when an object moves through fluid.

Forces cause, or tend to cause, changes in velocity. If a force is applied to an object at a point other than the object's centre of mass, it causes rotation. The turning effect of force is called its torque. Three important relationships provide useful ways of understanding the way forces cause movement—the relationship between force and acceleration; the duration between the acting forces and the change in the resulting momentum; and the relationship between energy and the mechanical work done by a force.

FORCE HAS MAGNITUDE AND DIRECTION

Forces cause, or try to cause, a change in the velocity of an object. Force has both magnitude and direction, and it is measured in Newtons (N). Two examples of forces are gravity and air resistance. Examples of forces that physical activities can involve are the forces exerted by muscles on bones by means of tendons, and the forces that occur during contact between objects, such as friction, impact forces and reaction forces.

Applying a force always entails an interaction between objects. Every action by a force is accompanied by an equal action in an opposite direction. This principle is Newton's law of action-reaction. An object resting on the ground exerts a vertically downward force on the ground that is equal to the object's mass multiplied by the acceleration due to gravity. The ground also exerts a force on the object that is equal in magnitude and opposite in direction, vertically upward in this case. This force is called a reaction force.

If all the forces that act on an object act through the object's centre of mass, then you can think of the object as a point. Consider the force you apply to a softball when you strike it through its centre with a bat. Assume that the centre of the ball is a point. In this case, the only change in velocity that the impact of the force causes is a change in linear velocity. In the moment before impact, the ball has a substantial linear velocity in one direction—toward the bat. An instant later, the ball has quite a different velocity as it speeds over the fence. The change in the ball's velocity is a result of the force that the bat applies to the ball during the time they are in contact. The ball applies an equal force to the bat, but in the opposite direction.

TORQUE: THE TURNING EFFECT OF FORCE

It is not always helpful to use the point model for the object you are considering, so imagine another impact situation. Suppose you are taking a free kick in soccer and you want to curve the ball around a defensive wall, as shown in figure 4.1. How can you do it? By kicking the ball slightly off-centre you can spin it, causing it to curve in flight. Before you kick the ball, when it is stationary, its

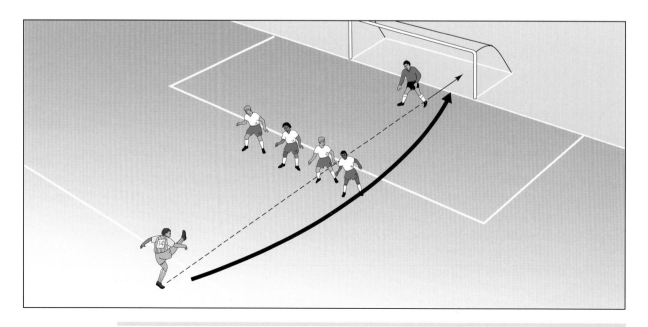

Figure 4.1   Kicking a ball off-centre creates spin, leading to a curved trajectory.

linear and angular velocities are zero. When your foot applies force to the ball at contact, the ball's linear velocity changes, as does its angular velocity.

The change in angular velocity occurs because the force's line of action does not pass exactly through the ball's centre of mass. The change in angular velocity depends on the turning effect, or **torque,** of the force. The amount of torque a force causes depends on the size of the force and the perpendicular distance from the line of action of the force to the axis of rotation (in this case, the centre of the ball). The distance of the line of action of the force from the axis of rotation is called the moment arm. The torque of a force is equal to the magnitude of the force multiplied by the moment arm, expressed as torque = force × moment arm.

torque:
Turning effect.

Another situation in which the torque of forces plays an important role is the movement of your arms and legs. The human body moves because muscles generate forces that cause the limbs to rotate. The torque caused by the contraction of a muscle depends on both the size of the force the muscle produces and the distance the muscle acts from the axis of rotation (its moment arm). Consider, for example, the muscle shown in figure 4.2. The biceps brachii lies on the front of the upper arm. When contracted, this muscle applies a force by means of its tendon to the forearm. This force tends to rotate the forearm toward the upper arm. The size of the turning effect, or torque, is equal to the force multiplied by the moment arm.

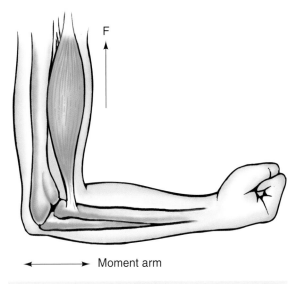

Figure 4.2   Moment arm of biceps brachii causing elbow flexion.

RESULTANT FORCES AND TORQUES

If multiple forces act on an object at any moment in time, the effect of the combined forces is the same as if one equivalent force and torque, which is the sum of all the applied forces and torques, acts on the object. This equivalent force and torque is called the resultant force and torque.

Suppose you are a football player. When you jump to catch a high ball, two opponents tackle you simultaneously, one from the back in a tackle around your waist, and the other from the front in a tackle around your shoulders (as shown in figure 4.3). The back tackle applies a force of 400 N to 0.1 metre below your centre of mass. The front tackle applies a force of 600 N to 0.2 metres above your centre of mass. The effect of these two forces is the same as if a single force of 200 N to the back and a torque about the centre of mass of 80 N/m anticlockwise were applied.

Effects of Forces and Torques

The magnitude of the linear acceleration that occurs when a resultant force acts on the centre of mass of an object depends on the mass of the object. If the mass of the object is small, then the linear acceleration caused by a given force is greater than if the mass is large. This principle is Newton's law of acceleration. The relationship is expressed as force = mass × acceleration, or acceleration = force ÷ mass.

In the previous example, if you were a fullback with a mass of 50 kilograms (50 kg), the linear acceleration resulting from the tackle would be 200 N divided by 50 kg = 4 m/s^2. If you were a forward whose mass was 100 kilograms, the linear acceleration would have been half as much (2 m/s^2).

Moment of inertia:
The resistance of an object to turning about an axis of rotation

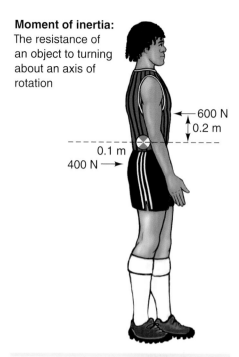

Figure 4.3   If the resultant force between front and back = 600 N – 400 N, then the net force = 200 N. Since acceleration is calculated as force ÷ mass, for a person whose mass is 50 kilograms, acceleration = 4 m/s². The resultant movement is 600 × 0.2 m anticlockwise – 400 × 0.1 m clockwise = 80 N/m.

The angular acceleration caused by a given torque depends on how resistant an object is to turning about its axis of rotation. This property of an object is called the moment of inertia, and it depends on the mass of the object and the way in which the mass is arranged relative to its axis of rotation. The moment of inertia increases when the mass is located further from the axis of rotation.

If an object's resistance to turning is less (that is, its moment of inertia is less), then a given torque causes a greater angular acceleration. In the same way that force = mass × acceleration, torque = moment of inertia × angular acceleration. In the previous example, the 100-kilogram player has a larger moment of inertia than the 50-kilogram player does. Consequently, the angular acceleration that the heavier player experiences from the resultant torque is less.

The relationship between moment of inertia and angular acceleration explains how mass, as well as the distribution of mass within an object, affects the speed with which a person can rotate an object. Imagine swinging a wooden tennis racquet, then changing the racquet to one made of aluminium. If both racquets are the same length and shape, but the aluminium one is lighter, the resistance of swinging the aluminium racquet is less. With the lighter racquet, you can cause a greater change in angular velocity by exerting the same torque with your arms and body. If the duration of the swing is constant, the outcome is a higher velocity of the racquet at the moment of impact.

Changing the mass of the object is not the only way to change the moment of inertia. If you shift your grip up the handle of the racquet, you change the arrangement of the mass of the racquet relative to the axis of rotation. The result is that the moment of inertia of the racquet is reduced, and the same torque produces both a greater angular acceleration and, as long as the swing duration is constant, a higher angular velocity of the racquet at impact.

This same principle explains why field hockey players sometimes drop their hands lower down the stick to hit the ball, as shown in figure 4.4. If they have

Figure 4.4   Reducing the moment of inertia of the hockey stick by lowering their hands lets hockey players execute a hard hit quickly, before a tackle can be made.
© Sport The Library

lots of time, then the best way for them to hit the ball hardest is to grip the end of the stick and use a large backswing. This creates a large moment of inertia, so the angular acceleration for the given torque is small. If the small angular acceleration is applied for a long time, however, the result is a large angular velocity. When multiplied by the length of the stick, a large angular velocity gives a high linear velocity of the head of the stick at impact.

However, if opposition players are close, they can easily make a tackle if the hit takes a long time to execute. Instead, when the hit time available is short, players can reduce the moment of inertia of the stick about the axis of rotation by lowering their hands on the stick. This technique lets them produce a greater angular acceleration by the same torque, and produces a hard hit in a short time interval.

• • • Focus Activity —

MOMENT OF INERTIA

Purpose

To study how technique evolution and equipment design have taken advantage of manipulating the moment of inertia in many physical activities.

Procedure

1. Select an appropriate piece of equipment and consider its evolution over time.

2. Write down your understanding of what technology has done for the equipment. Make particular reference to how technology and design have manipulated the moment of inertia when striking an object such as a ball.

3. What effect has the design improvement had on the implement's velocity at impact?

4. If the physical activity you are studying does not use an implement, there might have been technique improvements over the years that have been able to manipulate the moment of inertia of body parts. You can find excellent examples in dance, gymnastics, aerobics and other aesthetic events, as well as in several track and field events.

EXTENSION ACTIVITY

MOMENT OF INERTIA

• Try a series of hits of a stationary ball with your stick, bat or racquet. Start by holding the implement at the very end of the handle. Move your grip progressively down the handle, effectively making the handle shorter for each consecutive hit. Write down your observations and attempt to explain them in terms of manipulating the moment of inertia. What applications could this phenomenon have in physical activities?

• Find an office chair that swivels. Sit on the office chair, curl your knees up to your chest and wrap your arms around your knees. Have another student spin you around on the chair—notice how well you spin. Repeat the experiment, but this time stick out your arms and legs as far as you can. Have the same student spin you, and note how well you spin compared to the first spin. Write down your observations and attempt to explain what you have experienced in terms of manipulating the moment of inertia. What applications could your findings have in physical activity?

Equilibrium: When Velocity Is Constant

Sometimes forces do not cause changes in velocity—they only tend to do so. Changes in velocity do not occur if other forces of equal size but opposite direction resist. In this case, the object is said to be in equilibrium.

Imagine you are standing still. No change in velocity is occurring, but are any other forces acting on you? Figure 4.5 shows that gravitational attraction is acting on you, which tends to cause a change in velocity of approximately 10 m/s² vertically downward. What is stopping you from sinking into the ground? The ground is exerting an equal and opposite force through your feet, often called a ground reaction force. The resultant force is zero, and no change in velocity occurs.

A more complex example of equilibrium is that of a toddler and his mother playing on a seesaw, as shown in figure 4.6. The seesaw is stationary; that is, there is no change in its velocity. However, the mother has much greater mass than the toddler does. How can the seesaw possibly remain stationary?

Recall how to calculate the turning effect of a force. The gravitational attraction between the mother and the ground causes the mother to exert a force that is equal to her weight (mass × gravity) vertically downward on the seesaw, at a small distance from the fulcrum (the axis of rotation) of the seesaw. The torque caused by the mother is equal to the product of her weight and her distance from the fulcrum. Similarly, the toddler causes a torque in the opposite direction, equal to the product of his weight and his distance from the fulcrum. If the difference in distances from the fulcrum is just right, the resultant torque is zero, and the change in velocity is zero.

In general, if the linear and angular velocities of a rigid object are constant, then you know that the forces and torques that are acting on the object cancel out and the resultant force and torque are zero. Note that the velocity of an object does not need to be zero for the object to be in equilibrium, just not changing.

If a rigid body experiences a change in linear or angular velocity, then the resultant force and torque is proportional to the linear and angular acceleration. This principle is only true for a rigid object. If the object's mass, or more likely its moment of inertia, is changing, then changes in velocity can occur in the absence of resultant forces or torques.

Weight/2   Weight/2

Figure 4.5   Equilibrium equals weight balanced by ground reaction force, so weight = mass × gravity.

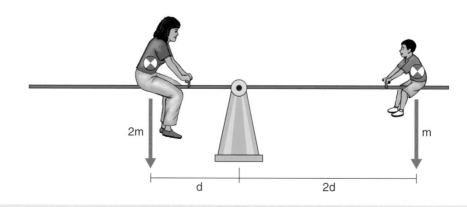

2m   m

d   2d

Figure 4.6   This seesaw is in equilibrium. The mass (m) and distance (d) are equal: 2m × d = 2d × m.

IMPULSE AND MOMENTUM

Another way to think about the effects of force is in terms of the impulse applied to an object and the consequent change in momentum. If a force is constant, then the impulse is equal to the force multiplied by the length of time it is applied to an object: impulse = force × time. The momentum of an object is equal to the object's mass multiplied by its velocity, expressed as momentum = mass × velocity.

Impulse and momentum are related quantities. When you apply a force to an object for a specified time, the impulse is equal to the change in momentum that results. The relationship between impulse and momentum provides one way of understanding, for instance, the generation of high velocities. There are two ways you can propel a ball at high velocity. You can either apply a powerful force for a very short time, such as when you hit a ball with a bat, or you can apply relatively small forces for a longer period, such as when you pitch a softball or baseball.

The relationship between impulse and momentum also provides a way to understand how a gymnast can avoid injuries when landing from a dismount or vault. When the gymnast first touches the ground, he has a large linear momentum, equal to the product of his mass and the velocity with which he approaches the ground. A moment later he is standing still, and his velocity (and consequently his momentum) is zero. What caused the change in momentum? From the time his feet first touched the ground to the time he was stationary, a ground reaction force was exerted on the gymnast. This force can be substantial and can cause injuries. What can the gymnast do to reduce the magnitude of these ground reaction forces?

As noted earlier, impulse equals change in momentum. Assuming that the gymnast's mass and his initial and final velocities remain constant, the impulse required to produce the change in momentum is constant. Impulse is force multiplied by the time interval over which that force acts. Therefore, increasing the time interval allows a smaller force to produce the same impulse. The gymnast can increase the time over which the force is applied during landing by bending his knees as he lands. This bend reduces the size of the ground reaction forces and the potential for injury. Landing mats in the high jump and pole vault prevent injury in the same way.

Angular Impulse and Angular Momentum

A similar relationship holds true for angular impulse and angular momentum. Angular impulse is equal to torque multiplied by the time during which it is applied, so angular impulse = torque × time. Angular momentum is equal to angular velocity multiplied by the moment of inertia of the object about the axis of rotation, and is expressed as angular momentum = angular velocity × moment of inertia. The impulse of a torque is equal to the change in angular momentum.

When discus or hammer throwers rotate around and around before releasing the implement, they increase the time during which they can generate torque, and consequently increase the angular impulse. A larger angular impulse means a larger change in angular momentum and a higher velocity of the implement at the time of release. A common goal of many sporting techniques is to increase the impulse applied by the body either to an object or to the ground.

Conservation of Momentum

Another important insight arises from the relationships between linear and angular impulse and momentum. What happens if the resultant force or torque is zero? If there is no resultant force acting on an object, then the impulse is zero and there is no change in momentum. Similarly, if there is no resultant torque acting on an object, then the angular impulse is zero and there is no change in angular momentum. In other words, momentum remains constant when no resultant forces or torques are acting. This principle is called conservation of momentum, another way of stating Newton's law of inertia.

If momentum is constant and the mass of the object is constant, then the velocity is also constant. Likewise, if angular momentum is constant and the moment of inertia of an object is constant, then angular velocity is also constant. However, whereas the mass of an object usually remains constant, there are many instances when the moment of inertia of an object (particularly the human body) does not remain constant.

Remember that the moment of inertia refers to the resistance of a body to rotating around a particular axis; it is dependent on the mass of the object and the distribution of the mass relative to the axis of rotation. You can decrease the moment of inertia by locating the mass close to the axis of rotation, and you can increase it by locating the mass further from the axis of rotation. If you change the arrangement of the mass of an object, then the angular velocity of the object can change in the absence of any resultant torque.

You encounter this principle commonly in physical activity. As you can see from figure 4.7, the angular velocity of a springboard diver when she leaves the board is relatively small. During her flight to the water, the only external force acting is the force due to gravitational acceleration. This force acts through her centre of gravity and causes no resultant torque. Consequently, the angular momentum of the diver during flight remains constant.

If the diver stretches out her body when she leaves the board, her mass is distributed a long way from her axis of rotation. She consequently has a relatively large moment of inertia about her centre of gravity. For her to rotate fast enough to complete, for example, a double somersault before hitting the water, she goes into a tuck. This position brings the mass of her limbs closer to the axis of rotation, to reduce her moment of inertia. Her angular velocity increases to maintain constant angular momentum, and she is able to complete the required number of revolutions in the time available. Because she does not want to be rotating quickly when she enters the water, she straightens her body before entry. This increases the moment of inertia again, which results in a reduction of her angular velocity.

Another activity that involves conservation of angular momentum in determining which techniques to use is the long jump, as shown in figure 4.8, a and b. When a long jumper leaves the board, she is leaning forward. The line of action of the reaction force that propels her into the air passes some distance behind her centre of mass, and consequently has a rotational effect as well. Because of this torque, the jumper has some angular momen-

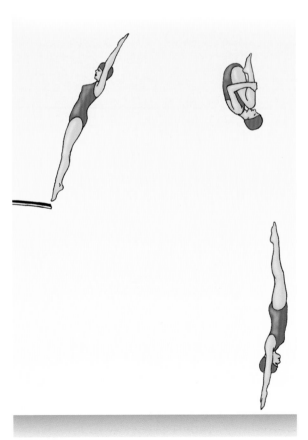

Figure 4.7   Divers change their angular velocity by changing their moment of inertia.

Figure 4.8   *(a)* The hitch-kick long jump technique. *(b)* The somersault long jump technique.

tum in a clockwise direction during the flight. This situation presents her with a problem. She would like to land in the sand with her feet ahead of her centre of gravity, which follows a parabola—a fact she cannot alter. If she continues to rotate forward at the same rate, her feet will be a long way behind her centre of gravity at landing.

The various techniques of long jumping are each devised to cope with this problem in a different way. If the jumper uses a hang technique, she tries to minimise the forward rotation during flight by maximising her moment of inertia and hence reducing her angular velocity clockwise. In the last moments before impact, she draws her legs and upper body forward to land.

Another technique is the hitch kick, shown by the jumper in figure 4.8a. Here the jumper rotates his legs as if he were pedalling a bicycle. The pedalling goes in the same direction as the angular momentum that the jumper had at take-off. However, the total angular momentum of the jumper must remain constant. Consequently, the angular velocity of the whole body is reduced as the jumper tries to minimise the forward rotation during flight by maximising his moment of inertia.

A third way of dealing with angular momentum during the long jump is illustrated by the jumper in figure 4.8b. This technique involves not reducing the angular velocity, but increasing it by adopting a tucked position, much the same as a diver. The aim is to perform a complete rotation in the form of a somersault during the time of the flight, then extend the legs at landing. This technique was briefly popular before it was banned for safety reasons.

SAMPLE LEARNING EXPERIENCE

Newton's Laws and Volleyball

Mitchell's class was studying volleyball. They had just been learning about Sir Isaac Newton and the three fundamental laws of physics that he described. Mitchell wondered what Newton's principles had to do with volleyball. How was his knowledge of these laws going to help him to become a better volleyball player?

Mitchell's teacher seemed to guess what he was thinking, because the next thing they did was a set of volleyball drills. The teacher asked the class to practice an underarm serve and to try to hit the ball so that it travelled over the net and landed close to the back line. Most of the class could perform this serve successfully.

After they had been practicing for a while, the teacher brought them together in a circle to discuss how Newton's laws related to volleyball. The teacher gave them a handout that summarised the three laws described by Newton, and asked them to suggest examples of each in volleyball.

Then the class did another drill. One player set volleyballs to the other students, who attempted to spike the balls over the net. Every student participated in the drill. The teacher encouraged them to closely observe and discuss both players' actions and the actions of the ball in relation to Newton's laws of motion. Many students had trouble with this drill, especially with jumping high enough to spike the ball effectively. After they had performed the drill for a while, the teacher asked the students to write about how Newton's laws applied to spiking.

Explanation

Here is what the handout said:

- Newton's law of inertia—The velocity of a body remains constant unless a force acts on it.
- Newton's law of acceleration—The change in velocity caused by a force acting on a body is proportional to the force, and inversely proportional to the mass of the body.
- Newton's law of action-reaction—Every action by a force is accompanied by an equal action in an opposite direction.

Amanda said, 'Well, before I serve a ball, it's not moving. It's just sitting in my hand. To get it to go up and over the net, I have to hit it with my hand. That is an example of the law of inertia. The ball doesn't change velocity until I apply a force to it with my hand.'

'Yeah,' said Beth. 'And if you hit it hard, the change in velocity is greater, and the ball travels further. That's the law of acceleration.'

'That's the first part of the law of acceleration,' said their teacher. 'What about the second bit; how does the mass of the object fit in?'

'Um, if the volleyball were heavier, it wouldn't go as far?' suggested Beth.

'Right. Imagine trying to serve a basketball. A basketball is heavier than a volleyball, and if you hit it with the same force that you hit a volleyball with, it doesn't change velocity as much,' explained their teacher. 'What about the action-reaction law?'

The class thought. This question had them a bit stumped. Colin was looking down at his hands and forearms. He really did not enjoy volleyball very much. He found that his arms got red and sore from hitting the ball. Then he wondered where the force that made his arms red came from, and he realised that this force was an example of action-reaction. 'Whenever I hit the ball, I apply a force to the ball. The law of action-reaction says that the ball also exerts an equal force on me, on the skin that contacts the ball. That's why my arms get red.'

Mitchell wondered what to write. He started with the law of inertia. 'The velocity of a body remains constant unless a force acts on it.' The problem was that the velocity of the ball during the spiking drill was always changing. First he threw the ball to the setter, then the setter set the ball so that it travelled a long way up into the air before coming down again to where he could intercept it and hit it over the net. Therefore, many forces must have been involved. He listed the various forces. The initial throw applied a force to the ball, the set applied a force to the ball and the spike itself produced a force that changed the ball's velocity. Was that all? Then he remembered the effect of gravity. Gravity was also a force that acted on the volleyball. That was why the ball did not keep going up after the setter had hit it.

Then Mitchell thought about how some of the changes in velocity were greater than others. The throw was a small change in velocity, the set was a bigger change and the spike was the biggest of all. What was the law of acceleration? It said something about changes in velocity depending on the force and the mass of the object. Mitchell knew that the mass of the volleyball did not change, so differences in the force applied to the ball must cause any differences in its change of velocity. He wrote down that the force applied to the ball during the spike must be greater than that applied during the set.

The biggest trouble Mitchell had with performing the spike was his jump. If he could only jump higher, he was sure he could hit a better spike. Mitchell thought about the forces involved in jumping. When he jumped he exerted a force on the ground, but the ground did not seem to go anywhere. Instead, his body changed velocity. That change must have occurred because of the law of action-reaction. Mitchell wrote that when he jumped, he exerted a force on the ground, and the ground exerted an equal force on his body in the opposite direction. It was this force that caused the change in velocity of his body.

EXTENSION ACTIVITY

NEWTON'S LAWS OF MOTION

Consider This

Consider the physical activity that you are currently studying. Newton's laws of motion apply to everything that you do in life, including this physical activity.

Try This

Work together with some other students in the following task, which is designed to identify examples of Newton's laws in practice:

- Make a three-columned table in your notebook, and head each column with one of the three laws of motion.

(continued)

- Arrange for members of your group to perform various skills that are involved in the physical activity you are studying.
- While each person performs different skills, have the rest of the group analyse parts of the skills to identify examples of Newton's laws of motion occurring in practice.
- Make sure everyone has a go at demonstrating and analysing skills.

Compare and Contrast

Share your findings with the other groups in the class. You can have a representative of each group explain the group's observations and ideas, while others demonstrate the skills. How did your group's findings compare with those of other groups? Discuss points of disagreement in an attempt to find the best explanation.

Think and Write

Now that you have investigated Newton's laws thoroughly, write down a detailed example of how to demonstrate each of the laws in physical activity.

WORK, POWER AND ENERGY

work:
The force applied to an object multiplied by the displacement through which the object is moved by the force; force × displacement.

The term *work* is very common in our ordinary language. In mechanics, the term has a very specific meaning that is somewhat different from its normal use. Here, mechanical **work** is defined as the force applied to an object multiplied by the displacement through which the object is moved by the force: work = force × displacement.

This definition leads to some confusion for people used to the common meanings. For example, a person holding a heavy box in his arms for a long time may get extremely tired doing so, but in mechanical terms he has done zero work, because he is not moving the object. Even more confusing is a situation in which the person lifts the box from the ground and then puts it down again in the same place. During the lifting phase, he did positive work on the box. During the lowering phase, the work done was negative. The total mechanical work done was still zero.

If you consider the lifting phase only, the force necessary to lift the load against gravity is equal to the mass of the load multiplied by the acceleration due to gravity. If you know the distance that he lifted the load, then you can calculate the work he did on the load as the force multiplied by the height he lifted it. Thus if a person lifts a 30-kilogram load from the floor to a shelf at 1.5 metres above the floor, and if you approximate gravity as 10 m/s^2, the work done on the load by the lifter = mass (30 kg) × gravity (10 m/s^2) × displacement (1.5 m), or 450 N/m.

Power Is a Rate of Change

In the same way that velocity is the rate of change of displacement, power is the rate of change of work. You can calculate the average power the lifter can achieve in the previous example if you know how long the person took to lift the load. If he lifted the load very quickly, in half a second, then the average rate of change of work was 450 N/m divided by 0.5 s, or 900 N/m/s. If he did the lift slowly, over a 2-second period, then the average power was 450 N/m divided by 2 s, or 225 N/m/s.

You can use a similar calculation in simple measurements of power like the stair-climbing test. In this test, a person must climb a set of stairs as fast as possible. The total height of the stairs is known, and you measure the time that the person takes to climb the stairs as accurately as possible. You then calculate the average power as the work done (mass of the person × gravity × height of the stairs), divided by the time taken to climb the stairs.

Energy Is Conserved

To understand the usefulness of the concept of mechanical work, you must know the definition of energy. A fundamental law of physics is that energy is conserved. It is never created or destroyed. Energy can only be changed into different forms.

Energy comes in many forms. For the body to move, the contractile elements within muscles convert the chemical energy stored in the body to mechanical energy and thermal energy. Where this energy comes from is the subject of chapter 5. The muscles in turn transfer this energy into movements of the body and objects with which the body interacts. When transformed into movement, the energy is called kinetic energy. The kinetic energy of a moving object depends on its mass, its linear velocity, its moment of inertia and its angular velocity. Other forms that energy can take include gravitational potential energy, which an object possesses because of its height above the ground, and elastic energy, which is stored in tendons (or springs) when they stretch.

Exploring the different forms of energy, and especially how energy is transferred between forms, provides another way to understand the movement of the body. A good example is a trampolinist. The trampolinist in figure 4.9 is flexing his knees and then jumping straight up with no rotation. The movement starts as his muscles turn chemical energy into kinetic energy and cause

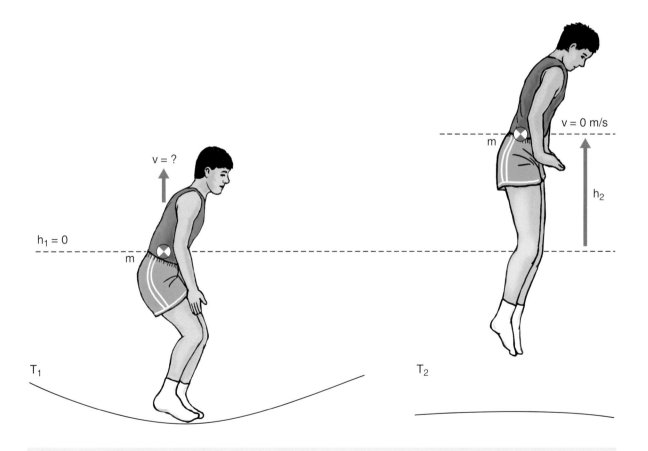

Figure 4.9 Energy $= 1/2\ mv_1^2 = mgh_2$. Therefore $v_1^2 = 2gh_2$, and $v_1 = \sqrt{2gh_2}$. If $g = 10$ m/s^2 and $h^2 = 1$ m, then $v_1 = 4.5$ m/s.

angular rotations of the lower limbs. These angular rotations in turn give the body's centre of mass linear velocity upward as the trampolinist leaves the trampoline (time = T_1). If you define the height of the centre of mass of the trampolinist at this instant (h_1) as zero displacement, then all his energy at this instant is kinetic. The kinetic energy is equal to 1/2 the mass of the trampolinist multiplied by the square of the velocity at the moment he leaves the trampoline; that is, $1/2 \times m \times v_1^2$.

As the trampolinist gains height, he slows. His kinetic energy decreases, but his potential energy due to gravity increases. When he reaches his maximum height (at time = T_2), his velocity is zero, all his energy is potential energy due to gravity, and (if we ignore the effects of air resistance) it is equal to mass (m) × acceleration due to gravity (g) × maximum height (h_2), or $m \times g \times h_2$. All the kinetic energy possessed by the trampolinist at T_1 has now become potential energy due to gravity.

If you can measure the maximum height reached by the trampolinist's centre of mass, then you can work out what his initial velocity must have been. If $1/2 \times m \times v_1^2 = m \times g \times h_2$, then $v_1 = \sqrt{(2 \times g \times h_2)}$. That is, regardless of the trampolinist's mass, the initial velocity is equal to the square root of two times gravitational acceleration times the maximum height of the trampolinist. Assuming an approximate value for g of 10 m/s², if the trampolinist reaches a maximum height of 1 metre, then the initial velocity must have been the square root of 20, or approximately 4.5 m/s. With what velocity would he have to leave the trampoline to reach a height of 2 metres?

You can use the same logic to discover that when the trampolinist again reaches zero height and gravitational potential energy is again zero, the velocity must be equal in magnitude but opposite in direction to the initial velocity. What happens then? The trampolinist again slows as the springs holding the trampoline mat stretch and his height becomes negative. At the moment of lowest height, when the trampolinist is again stationary for an instant, all the energy that he possessed is now stored as elastic potential energy within the springs of the trampoline, before being returned to the trampolinist as he jumps again.

Work and Energy Are Related

Did you notice the similarity between the calculation of the work done by a person lifting a box and the change in gravitational potential energy of the trampolinist? Both were equal to mass times gravitational acceleration times the height through which the object moved. This is just one example of the equality between work done and the change in energy. In the same way that the impulse of a force equals the change in momentum of an object, the mechanical work done by a force is equal to the change in energy. The work-energy relationship provides another way of understanding the movement of the body and its interaction within an environment. Imagine struggling up a steep hill on a bicycle. The mechanical work you do to reach the top of the hill is equal to your mass times the acceleration due to gravity times the height of the hill. Because you know that work equals the change in energy, you also know that the mechanical work done to reach the top of the hill is equal to the additional gravitational potential energy gained in climbing the hill.

Where did this energy come from? Your muscles converted the chemical energy stored in your body into the necessary kinetic energy. However, your body also provides energy to overcome friction within the bicycle, and your body produces a lot of heat. If you could measure (or estimate from heart rate) the oxygen you consumed at the same time, you could also estimate the total amount of chemical energy required to cycle up the hill. The ratio of mechanical work done to the total amount of energy is a measure of the efficiency of the system.

IMPACT MECHANICS

Many sports involve situations in which moving objects (such as balls) make contact with other moving or stationary objects (such as bats or racquets), or with surfaces (such as floors). The results of these contacts, or impacts, depend in part on the properties of the objects.

Elasticity and Coefficient of Restitution

When a ball contacts another object or surface, the ball is temporarily deformed by the impact before returning to its normal shape. The tendency of the ball to return to its original shape after deformation is referred to as its *elasticity*. This property varies—some balls return quickly to their original shape, whereas others do so more slowly. Elasticity determines how much of the kinetic energy of the ball before impact is returned to the ball after impact—that is, how fast the ball rebounds.

If a collision between a ball and a surface was perfectly elastic, then all the kinetic energy would be returned. The ball would rebound at the same speed that it approached at (although in the opposite direction). This does not occur in the real world because some kinetic energy is always transformed into heat and sound during the impact, resulting in decreased speed after the impact. The ratio of the speed of the ball after impact to the speed of the ball before impact is a measure of the elasticity of the collision, called the *coefficient of restitution*.

The speed of the ball after impact with a stationary surface is always less than the speed with which it hit the surface. This fact means that a ball dropped on a stationary surface will always rebound to a height lower than that from which it is dropped. You can use these values to calculate the coefficient of restitution for a collision between a ball and surface, using this formula: coefficient of restitution = $\sqrt{(hb/hd)}$, where hd is the height from which the ball is dropped and hb is the height to which the ball bounces after impact.

The coefficient of restitution varies from 0 for a perfectly inelastic collision (in which the ball does not bounce at all) to 1 for a theoretical perfectly elastic collision. The magnitude of the coefficient varies with the nature of the ball and the surface, as well as with other factors such as the temperature of the ball.

Centre of Percussion

Another example of impact in physical activity occurs when a ball is struck by an implement such as a bat. As mentioned at the beginning of this chapter, when a batter exerts a force on a ball by hitting it, the ball exerts an equal and opposite force on the bat. This force causes an acceleration of the bat, which the batter's hands must resist. Sometimes the batter notices this acceleration as a jarring effect. If the ball is contacted in just the right place on the bat, however, no jarring occurs and the ball is said to have been hit in the *sweet spot*. This location on the bat is called the *centre of percussion*.

Consider the bat illustrated in figure 4.10. When the ball contacts the bat, the bat applies a force to the ball, and the ball applies an equal and opposite force to the bat at the point of contact. This force on the bat imparts a linear and angular acceleration to the bat, and this acceleration is resisted by the hands located at point H. The linear acceleration caused by the ball moves in the same direction as the force applied by the ball. The angular acceleration around the bat's centre of gravity, caused by the force of the ball, in turn causes a linear tangential acceleration of point H on the bat, in the direction opposite from that of the force applied by the ball. If the contact with the ball occurs at the sweet spot or centre of percussion, these accelerations cancel each

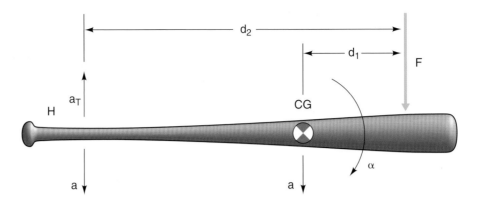

Figure 4.10   Calculation of centre of percussion. $F = ma$; $a = F/m$; $T = I_{CG} \times \alpha = F \times d_1$; $\alpha = F \times d_1/I_{CG}$; $a_T = \alpha \times d_2 = (F \times d_1/I_{CG}) \times d_2$. When F occurs at the centre of percussion, the linear acceleration at point H (a) is equal and opposite to the tangential acceleration at point H (a_T). That is, $a = a_T$; $F/m = (F \times d_1/I_{CG}) \times d_2$; $I_{CG}/(d_1 \times m) = d_2$; where F is the force applied to the bat by the ball, m is the mass of the bat, a is the linear acceleration of the bat caused by F, T is the torque about the bat's centre of gravity caused by F, I_{CG} is the moment of inertia of the bat about its centre of gravity, α is the angular acceleration of the bat caused by T, and a_T is the tangential acceleration of point H on the bat caused by T.

other exactly, and the batter's hands do not need to apply any force to resist the acceleration. The exact location of the sweet spot depends on where the hands grip the bat, the moment of inertia of the bat about its centre of gravity, the location of the centre of gravity and the mass of the bat.

FLUID MECHANICS

As the human body, or an object propelled by the human body, moves through air or water, the air or water exerts forces on the object. In some cases, such as shot-putting or gymnastics, these forces are insignificant and can be ignored. In other cases, such as the discus, the javelin, cricket fast bowling and golf, the forces are too large to ignore, and you usually must include them in analysis. Swimming, rowing and canoeing are examples of sports in which these forces exercise the greatest influence.

The forces that air and water apply to an object passing through them can be divided into two general groups: those forces that act in opposition to the object's direction of motion, known as drag; and those that act at right angles, known as lift. An example of drag in water is the frictional force created by contact between a moving object and particles in the fluid. A drag force always acts to slow the movement of the object. For activities in which drag forces are significant, such as cycling, speed skating, swimming and rowing, a person may expend considerable effort to try to reduce the magnitude of the drag. Attempts to reduce drag in these sports include experimenting with helmet design, frame shape, full-body costume, swimming costume material and boat hull design, respectively.

If the shape of an object passing through a fluid is asymmetrical in cross-section perpendicular to the direction of movement, or if it is spinning, then lift forces act perpendicular to the direction of movement. For an asymmetrical object, particles of fluid on one side of the object travel further around the object than particles on the other side do, in the same length of time; therefore, they have a higher velocity than the particles on the other side. The increased velocity on the first side causes a decrease in pressure on that side. The result is a lift force that tends to cause a change in velocity toward the side of lower pressure.

As shown in figure 4.11, a discus is thrown so that the body of the discuss travels at an angle, relative to the direction of movement. Drag forces act to slow the discus, but lift forces occur because of the asymmetrical cross-section. The lift forces prolong the duration of the flight by reducing the acceleration due to gravity.

A similar effect occurs with a spinning ball. On one side of the ball, the spin opposes the direction of motion, increasing the fluid pressure on that side. The consequence is a lift force acting toward the side of lower pressure, shown in figure 4.12. The consequence of spin is to alter the trajectory of the ball.

A golf ball normally leaves the club with a large amount of backspin. The ball spins so that the bottom of the ball travels in the direction of flight. This spin causes higher air pressure on the bottom of the ball. It also causes a lift force to act in a direction that reduces the gravitational acceleration and prolongs the duration of the flight. As novice golfers quickly notice, it is common for the spin to be more than just backspin. If the club's face is not exactly perpendicular to the direction of travel of the club at impact, then the spin is not perfectly vertical. The result is that the lift force acts to one side, causing the ball to curve sideways in flight. This occurrence is known as a hook or slice in the language of golf.

Lift forces are even more essential in swimming. Until quite recently, experts believed that drag forces created as the hands moved backward through the water produced propulsion in swimming. However, it now seems likely that lift forces created by the hands moving sideways through the water are just as important, and might even be more critical than drag forces.

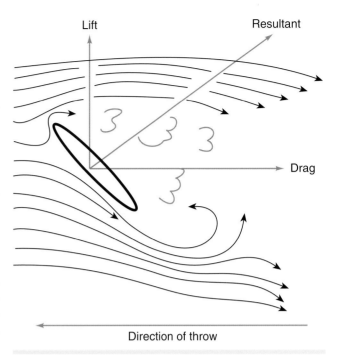

Figure 4.11   Drag and lift forces on a discus in flight.

Reprinted, by permission, from G. Carr, 1997, Mechanics of sport (Champaign, IL: Human Kinetics), 118.

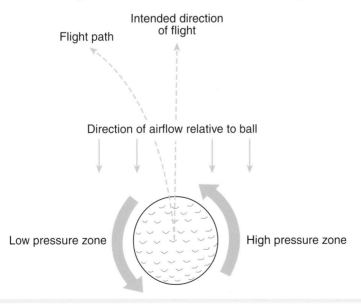

Figure 4.12   Effects of spin on a ball in flight.

From J.G. Hay, 1978, Biomechanics of sports techniques, 4th ed. (Needham Heights, MA: Allyn & Bacon), 181. Reprinted by permission of Pearson Education, Inc.

SPINNING

Purpose

To understand how to control and manipulate the effects of spin on a ball in various physical activities.

Procedure

1. If the activity you are studying involves throwing a ball or implement, experiment with spin around every conceivable axis of rotation.
2. If the activity you are studying involves hitting a ball, experiment with spin around every conceivable axis of rotation.
3. If the activity you are studying involves kicking a ball, experiment with spin around every conceivable axis of rotation.

Written Tasks

- Consider the effects of spin on this ball. Is there any design feature on the surface of the ball that affects the movement of the ball when it is propelled with a spinning motion? Do players in the sport employ any techniques that are designed to manipulate spin and to take advantage of it?
- Determine the advantages of being able to control the flight of the ball through spin in the physical activity you are currently studying, and write them down.

••• *Test Yourself* —

1. Force is measured by _____.
2. Supply four examples of force that may influence the performance of a physical activity.
3. By using Newton's law of action-reaction, supply the action and the reaction in the following physical activities: (a) jumping off the middle of a canoe, (b) kicking a moving soccer ball and (c) hitting a cricket ball with a cricket bat.
4. Consider the following action-reaction situations and describe the variation that would cause the specified result for (a) a hook shot in golf, (b) a fly ball in softball and (c) a spike in volleyball.
5. Define the term torque. Apply the formula to an action within the skill or activity you are currently studying.
6. Using the example of topspin in a tennis forehand shot, what has determined the torque of the ball?
7. What is the formula that explains Newton's law of acceleration?
8. Complete the following sentence: The moment of inertia is when _____ _____ caused by a given _____ is dependent on the _____ of the object to turning around the axis of rotation.

9. Using the above biomechanical principles, explain why it is better to have a greater body mass in a scrum in Rugby Union and a smaller body mass when performing a somersault in gymnastics.

10. Supply the formula for calculating (a) impulse and (b) momentum.

11. What is the relationship between impulse and momentum?

12. List some skills that can utilise an understanding of impulse and momentum to improve performance, preferably from your current physical activity.

13. Supply the formula for calculating (a) angular impulse and (b) angular momentum.

14. Define Newton's law of inertia.

15. How does the principle of conservation of momentum apply to a gymnast completing a double-tucked somersault during a tumbling sequence of a floor routine?

16. Supply the formula for calculating (a) work and (b) power.

17. List the different forms in which energy is found in the body.

18. List some skills that gravitational potential energy influences.

19. What influences the rebound of a ball? Can you think of examples that result in various rebound heights?

20. Why is the sweet spot important when using striking implements in sport?

21. What is meant by *drag* or *lift* when used to describe the influence on objects by air or water?

22. Sports such as athletics and downhill skiing have made adaptations to minimise the effects of drag. List three sports and supply the adaptations each has made in these same efforts. Include any adaptations from your current physical activity.

23. Lift forces are used in many ball sports and athletics to maximise performance. List some physical activities that use lift, justifying your choices by supplying the benefits that result.

Physiological Dimensions of Physical Activity

The physiology of sport and exercise performance has traditionally occupied an important place in the study of physical education. The three chapters in part II provide key information about the relevant physiology and develop important concepts across the spectrum of knowledge in this field.

Chapter 5 discusses the molecular level of physiological knowledge. It focuses on the ways in which the body produces energy and uses it to make physical activity possible, from short-duration, high-intensity activities to longer, lower-intensity activities (endurance activities). Chapter 6 explores the physiological processes that take place at the interface between the molecular level and the systems level of the body. This chapter focuses on metabolic and cardiorespiratory capacity and on oxygen transport and use. It also explains core concepts such as $\dot{V}O_2$max. Chapter 7 explains a number of the principles of training, including specificity and progressive overload. It applies the information from chapters 5 and 6 to the design of training programs for both sport performance and general health.

Energy for Physical Activity

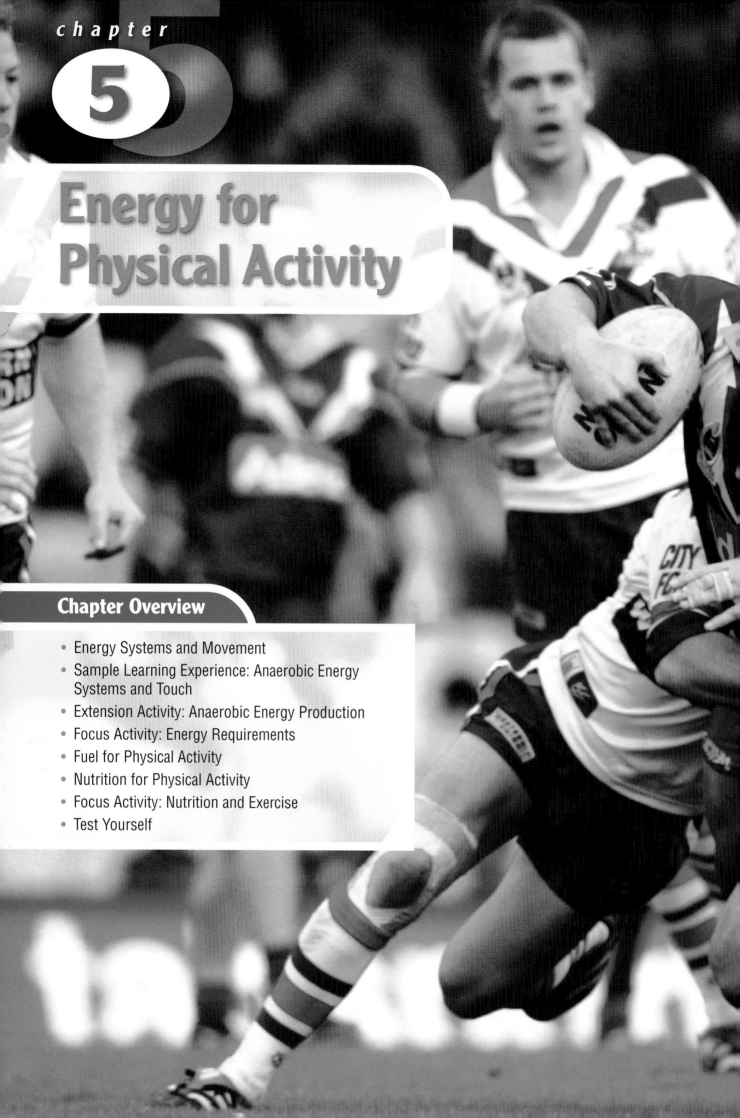

Chapter Overview

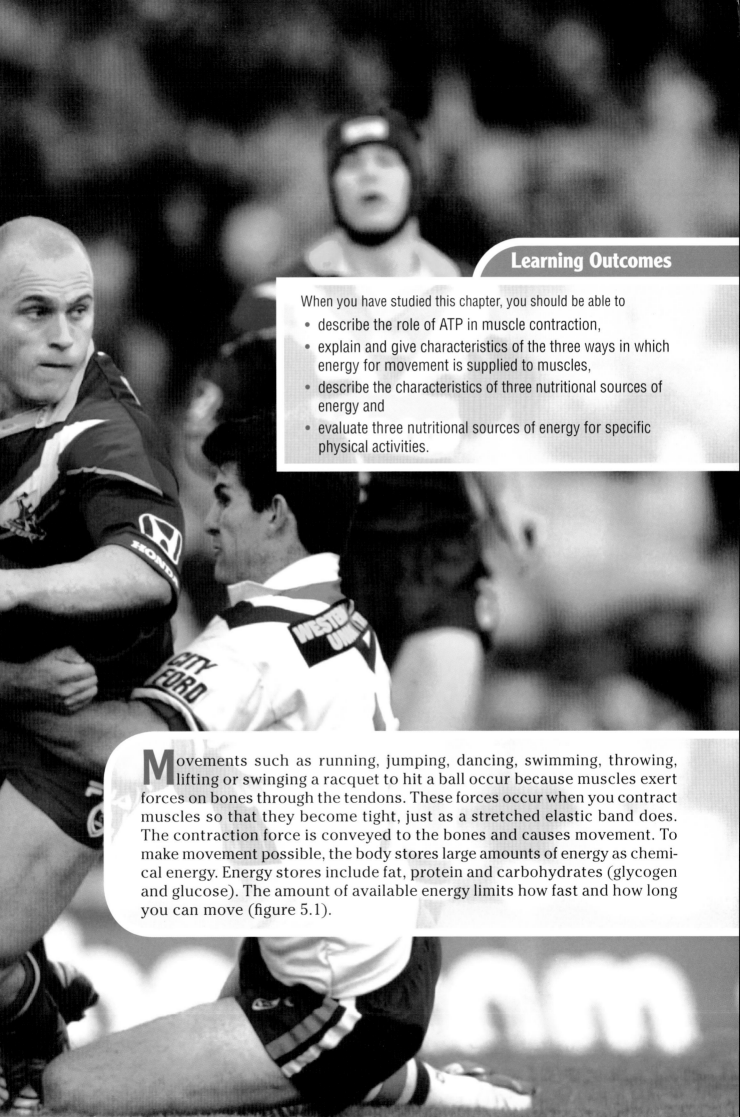

Movements such as running, jumping, dancing, swimming, throwing, lifting or swinging a racquet to hit a ball occur because muscles exert forces on bones through the tendons. These forces occur when you contract muscles so that they become tight, just as a stretched elastic band does. The contraction force is conveyed to the bones and causes movement. To make movement possible, the body stores large amounts of energy as chemical energy. Energy stores include fat, protein and carbohydrates (glycogen and glucose). The amount of available energy limits how fast and how long you can move (figure 5.1).

ENERGY SYSTEMS AND MOVEMENT

The energy that muscle fibres use comes from turning a molecule called adenosine triphosphate (ATP) into adenosine diphosphate (ADP). An enzyme (ATPase) splits one of the three phosphate molecules (P) from ATP. This action releases chemical energy that the muscle fibres turn into mechanical energy. Figure 5.2 is a schematic description of this process.

Only a very small amount of ATP is stored within the muscle cells—about enough for a single weight lift, volleyball spike or golf swing. For movement to continue, other parts of the muscle cell use energy obtained from other sources to turn the ADP back into ATP. The cycle is then ready to start again, and can continue for as long as energy is available to turn the ADP back into ATP.

Three sources of energy exist for turning ADP back into ATP. Although all three systems work at the same time, they differ in terms of the speed with which they can make energy available and the amount of energy that they can provide. The relative importance of each source of energy for any particular physical activity depends on the intensity and the duration of the activity.

Figure 5.1 Endurance athlete near exhaustion.
© Sport The Library

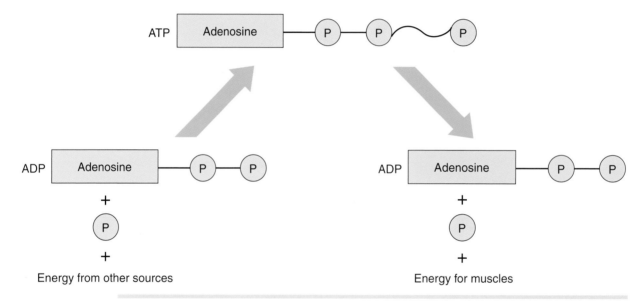

Figure 5.2   ATP = ADP + P + energy.

Creatine Phosphate

creatine phosphate:
A molecule stored within muscle cells that,when broken down, releases energy that is used to rapidly rebuild ATP molecules.

The fastest way of turning ADP back into ATP involves another molecule, called **creatine phosphate** (CP), in a process illustrated in figure 5.3. Muscle cells store small amounts of CP, which an enzyme called creatine kinase can break down very quickly to provide energy to turn ADP back into ATP. Although this system acts very quickly, it does not last long. It provides only enough energy for about 10 to 15 seconds of maximum effort before the muscle's store of CP runs out.

Athletes competing in events of short duration rely predominantly on the energy released from CP. Examples of short duration events are

- the 100-metre sprint,
- throwing and jumping events in track and field,
- weight-lifting and
- vaulting in gymnastics.

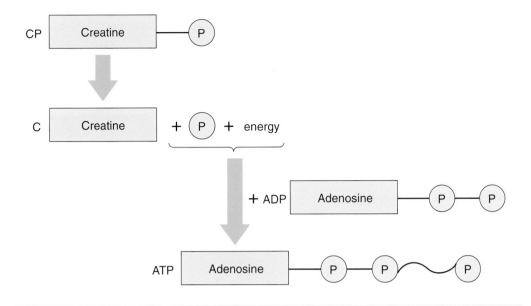

Figure 5.3 The creatine phosphate (CP) energy system.

Replenishing the stores of creatine phosphate takes 5 to 6 minutes of recovery after the end of the exercise. Performance is impaired if athletes attempt another maximal effort before their bodies have had time to replenish CP stores.

Anaerobic Glycolysis

The second fastest way to obtain the energy to keep muscles contracting is called **anaerobic glycolysis,** because it involves breaking down **glycogen** or glucose (glycolysis) without using oxygen (anaerobic). Anaerobic glycolysis is illustrated in figure 5.4. The body breaks down glycogen (stored in the muscles and liver) and glucose (stored in the blood) in a complex process involving 12 enzymatic reactions. A by-product of this process is **pyruvic acid.** If sufficient oxygen is not available, the cells convert the pyruvic acid into **lactic acid.** If lactic acid accumulates in muscles, the anaerobic glycolysis process slows, resulting in fatigue.

Getting energy from anaerobic glycolysis takes a bit longer than getting it from creatine phosphate, but it also lasts longer. Anaerobic glycolysis provides energy for up to 3 minutes of maximal effort before the build-up of lactic acid prevents further energy production by this system. Athletes competing in longer sprint events usually run out of creatine phosphate before they finish the event and end up getting most of the energy they need from anaerobic glycolysis. Examples of longer duration events are

- the 200- to 800-metre events in track,
- the 50- to 200-metre events in swimming and
- a competitive aerobics routine.

It takes about 20 to 60 minutes to remove the accumulated lactic acid after maximal exercise.

anaerobic glycolysis:
The breaking down of glycogen or glucose without using oxygen.

glycogen:
A product of the breakdown of carbohydrates. It is stored in the liver and in muscles and is a key source of energy.

pyruvic acid:
A by-product of anaerobic glycolysis.

lactic acid:
A product that accumulates in muscles as a result of anaerobic glycolysis.

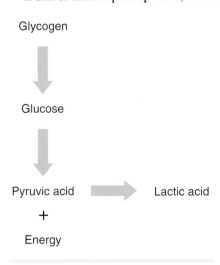

Figure 5.4 Glycogen utilisation (anaerobic glycolysis) energy system.

Anaerobic Energy Systems and Touch

Jody's class was learning all about energy systems. The students were having trouble understanding the difference between anaerobic exercise that uses creatine phosphate for energy production and anaerobic exercise that uses anaerobic glycolysis for energy production. Because the class was studying a unit on the game of touch, the teacher used a two-part exercise to help students understand the concepts.

The class performed two versions of a touch drill. For the drill, the students repeatedly sprinted 5 metres from one line to the next, simulating a defensive line in touch. They touched the ground and then ran backward to the starting line before performing the next sprint.

Their instructions were simple. In the first version of the task, the students had to perform the drill for 8 seconds. Most of the students were able to cover the distance around two or three times. At the end of the task, they received a 1-minute break before they had to perform the task again. Jody and the rest of the students performed this procedure six times. During each rest period, they wrote down observations regarding the distance they covered, heart rates, breathing rates, muscle soreness and anything else of note.

Jody's observations indicated that after each 60-second rest interval she had fully recovered from the 8-second burst of exercise; therefore, the distances she covered on each shuttle run were very consistent. She also found that although her heart and breathing rates were up after each shuttle run, they dropped rather quickly during the rest period and were slightly above normal before the start of the next shuttle run. Jody and the class produced 48 seconds of exercise in total (six repetitions of the 8-second task). She felt that she could go on for quite some time if required.

After a group discussion about their observations, the class lined up for a similar task. The teacher gave them the same exercise drill, but this time the students had to complete a single 48-second shuttle at top speed. At the end of the shuttle, the teacher again instructed them to record their observations.

Jody was trying to catch her breath and write at the same time. Although she had tried her hardest, the total number of times that she covered the 5-metre distance was significantly less than the total covered in the first drill. Her heart rate was up considerably, as was her breathing rate. She felt quite hot and sweaty, and her leg muscles were burning intensely toward the end of the task. She felt as if it could not end soon enough. Most of the class felt the same, although some of the fitter athletes fared better.

Explanation

The energy for the first drill was supplied almost entirely by creatine phosphate. The duration was less than 10 seconds, and the 60-second recovery period was sufficient to rebuild the CP stores that were used to resynthesise ATP during the exercise phase. Jody was therefore able to exercise maximally on each occasion, without becoming fatigued.

During the second drill the intensity remained at maximum effort, but the duration was significantly longer. The result was that after approximately 10 seconds, Jody had depleted her CP supplies. Although her heart and lungs worked hard trying to deliver oxygen to create energy aerobically, they could not keep up. Thus, the dominant source of energy for ATP resynthesis was anaerobic glycolysis. The exercise intensity was so high that when her body metabolised glycogen anaerobically, the pyruvic acid produced was converted to lactic acid, causing Jody's muscles to fatigue. Her heart rate and breathing remained elevated for a while after she stopped the exercise to deliver enough oxygen to metabolise the lactic acid and remove the carbon dioxide (CO_2). The fitter students had cardiorespiratory systems that worked more effectively and were able to do more of the work aerobically, turning the pyruvic acid into energy instead of lactic acid.

EXTENSION ACTIVITY

ANAEROBIC ENERGY PRODUCTION

Consider This

Consider the characteristics of exercise in the physical activity that you are currently studying. Does your sport involve short bursts of energy dispersed among longer periods of lower-intensity energy? If so, you can create an experiment that simulates exercise and energy production for this sport.

Try This

The sample learning experience simulated part of a touch game defensive strategy—the 5-metre shuttle runs. Think of an activity that you and other class members can perform that examines anaerobic energy production in the same way. You should confine your activity to short distances and utilise high-intensity exercises. An example for basketball might be to practice sprints from one end of the court to the other, with rapid turnarounds that simulate fast breaks in game play. What can you devise for your sport?

Arrange for someone to be a timekeeper. This person is to signal the start and stop of exercise intervals. On the *go* command, you and the other students must perform the activity at maximal effort for 8 seconds and then recover for 1 minute before repeating the exercise in the same manner. As in the previous case study, perform the activity six times. During recovery intervals, make notes in a journal that reflect how your body is feeling in response to the exercise.

After completing the first task, put the second task to the test. Have the timekeeper signal the start of a 48-second period of maximal effort exercise. After the 48 seconds, sit down with the rest of the students and again make notes on your body's response to this rigorous task.

Think and Write

- After you have all had a drink and a rest (and perhaps have returned to the class-room or sat under a nice shady tree), evaluate what has happened.

- Using the explanation from the sample learning experience as a guide, explain in writing how your body used and replenished energy for each of the two tasks.

- In terms of energy systems and their functions, what were the limitations to exercise in both cases?

- What ramifications does this knowledge have for the way you train for your particular physical activity?

Aerobic System

A third way of obtaining energy does require oxygen. It is called the **aerobic energy system,** or oxidative system. Figure 5.5 shows that this system converts the pyruvic acid produced by glycolysis into more energy, instead of turning it into lactic acid. The aerobic energy system also produces by-products that the body

aerobic energy system: A system that uses oxygen in the process of creating energy in the form of ATP from carbohydrates, fats and proteins.

$$O_2 \quad + \quad \begin{pmatrix} \text{Pyruvic acid} \\ \text{or} \\ \text{Fatty acid} \\ \text{or} \\ \text{Amino acids} \end{pmatrix}$$

$$CO_2 \quad + \quad H^+ \quad + \quad e^- \quad + \quad \text{Energy}$$

Figure 5.5   Aerobic energy system.

Figure 5.6   Creatine phosphate (CP) supplies energy for high-intensity activities, such as jumping to defend a netball shot.

© Sport The Library

eliminates in two different ways. Electrons and hydrogen ions are eventually turned into water and excreted through sweat. The blood transports carbon dioxide to the lungs, where it is exhaled.

In addition to using glucose or glycogen derived from carbohydrates, the aerobic system fuels itself with fatty acids that come from fat stores in the body, or with amino acids that come from protein stores.

The aerobic system is the slowest way of providing the energy needed to produce movement, but it can provide much more energy than the creatine phosphate or anaerobic glycolysis energy systems can. If the heart and lungs can deliver enough oxygen, then the body can continue to supply energy for as long as its supplies of glucose and glycogen (derived from carbohydrates, fat and protein) last. Compared with the two anaerobic systems, it maintains energy production for a long time. The aerobic system supplies most of the energy required in activities that last longer than about 3 minutes.

For most exercises, sports and games, the body utilises all three ways of obtaining energy. Netball players provide an example. Although their aerobic systems supply the majority of the energy required to move around the court, creatine phosphate and anaerobic glycolysis provide energy for short periods of high-intensity activity (such as jumping for a ball or sprinting for a pass) when the body requires it. When the players are not sprinting or jumping, their aerobic systems work overtime to remove the lactic acid created by the last surge. They turn it back into pyruvic acid, then into more energy. The aerobic system also replaces creatine phosphate, to help the players get ready for the next energy surge (see figure 5.6).

••• Focus Activity —

ENERGY REQUIREMENTS

Purpose

To understand that, in most cases, the three energy systems work together to provide the energy required for exercise.

Consider This

Consider the physical activity that you are currently studying. Using the previous netball example as a guide, analyse the segments of exercise that occur in your physical activity and attempt to account for how the body provides energy for these phases. Consider the intensity and duration of each phase to help you determine which energy system is providing the energy for that phase.

Written Task

After you have worked out the energy requirements for the phases of activity, write an exposition that explains how the body provides energy for an elite performer in the physical activity you are studying. Assume that the reader knows nothing at all about energy systems. Your exposition must first explain the three basic energy systems and then demonstrate how they apply to various phases of activity in your chosen sport.

FUEL FOR PHYSICAL ACTIVITY

The food that we eat supplies the energy our bodies need for movement. The energy contained in food comes in three basic forms: carbohydrate, fat and protein. The body uses a mixture of fuels at any one time, although it uses some more than others. The relative contribution made by each fuel depends on what is available in the body and on the intensity of the physical activity it is performing.

Once it has digested them, your body stores most carbohydrates (such as grains, fruit, vegetables and sugar) in your muscles and liver in the form of glycogen. To be used by the muscles, glycogen must first be turned into glucose. The anaerobic glycolysis system uses glucose to provide energy that the body uses to synthesise ATP and produce pyruvic acid. The aerobic system can then use the pyruvic acid to provide more energy. As long as sufficient stores of glycogen are available, carbohydrates provide most of the energy required during exercise of moderate to high intensity.

The fat that you eat in meat, dairy products and vegetable oils is stored as triglycerides in adipose tissues under your skin and around your body organs. Your body turns the triglycerides into fatty acids, which the aerobic system can use as fuel. Fat provides most of the energy you require at rest and during low-intensity exercise.

Joules (J):
The SI unit of energy.
For example, the energy
content of food can be
expressed in kilojoules
per gram (kJ/g).

The body stores protein from meat, eggs, dairy products and vegetables in muscles and in the liver. Your body can turn it into amino acids that the aerobic system can use as fuel. Protein is not normally a major source of energy, but your body might use it when it runs out of supplies of glycogen.

Imagine that you are sitting around, relaxing. Your energy needs are relatively small—about 360 kJ/hr—and your aerobic system supplies the energy. Most of the energy, about 70%, comes from fat. Fats are a high-energy food, providing 37 kJ/g (carbohydrate contains about 16 kJ/g). Sitting around watching television uses about 7 g/hr of fat, and about the same amount of carbohydrates.

Suppose you tire of sitting around and decide to go for a jog. For the first few minutes, stores of creatine phosphate and anaerobic glycolysis supply the energy you need. Soon, however, your rate and depth of breathing increase, as do the rate and volume of blood that your heart pumps.

If you continue jogging at a relatively slow speed, your rate of oxygen consumption levels out. The levelled-out rate of oxygen consumption is sufficient to allow the aerobic system to use all the pyruvic acid produced by the anaerobic glycolytic system as fuel. Therefore, no lactic acid accumulates in your muscles. When you jog slowly, the energy you need normally comes from both glycogen and fat. However, should you use up all the glycogen, fat and protein can still supply enough energy for you to continue jogging. If there were no other limitations, you could continue jogging at this pace for as long as your stores of fat lasted. Ultra-marathon runners and long-distance swimmers rely on this process.

Imagine, however, that instead of continuing to jog slowly, you gradually pick up the pace. Running faster involves taking longer strides and completing more strides per minute. Such acceleration requires both greater muscle forces and more frequent muscle contractions. Your body needs more energy to keep turning ADP back into ATP that your muscles can use. Since your muscles now require energy more quickly than before, the anaerobic system accelerates its production of energy, using glycogen as fuel. This process creates pyruvic acid, which the aerobic system then uses in preference to fat. Aerobic use of pyruvic acid is advantageous, because otherwise the pyruvic acid would be turned into lactic acid, leading to fatigue. The result is that as you increase the intensity of exercise by running faster or running uphill, glycogen supplies an increasingly higher proportion of your energy needs (see figure 5.7).

Your supply of glycogen, however, is limited. In a 65-kilogram person, the liver stores about 110 grams of glycogen, and the muscles store about 250 grams. Glycogen supplies about 16 kJ/g, so these stores contain about 5,760 kJ [(110 g + 250 g) × 16 kJ/g = 5,760 kJ]. Running at 16 km/hr requires about 1.3 kJ/kg/min, which is 85 kJ/min for this 65-kg person. Assuming the person can consume enough oxygen to maintain this pace, the glycogen stores will last about 70 minutes (5,760 kJ ÷ 85 kJ/min = 67.8 min).

Glycogen provides energy faster than fat does and results in more energy per litre of oxygen consumed—about 21.2 kJ per litre, versus 19.7 kJ per litre. When glycogen stores are depleted, athletes must either reduce their intensity of exercise or increase their oxygen consumption by increasing both the volume of air they breathe and the volume of blood that the body pumps. Endurance athletes refer to this state as hitting the wall.

Figure 5.7   As you run faster, glycogen supplies a higher proportion of your energy.
© Sport The Library

NUTRITION FOR PHYSICAL ACTIVITY

The amount of glycogen stored in the muscles and liver partially determines how long you can continue to exercise at moderate to high intensities. This length of time shrinks if your diet contains insufficient carbohydrates, or if you do not allow sufficient time between exercise sessions for glycogen stores to replenish. The body requires between 24 and 48 hours to replace completely depleted glycogen stores.

You can increase the amount of glycogen stored in your muscles and liver by eating more carbohydrates. Athletes who train intensely for several hours each day should consume a high carbohydrate diet. That is, 60% or more of their energy intake should be carbohydrates, as you can see in figure 5.8. The body can store only a limited amount, however, and it stores excess carbohydrate intake as fat.

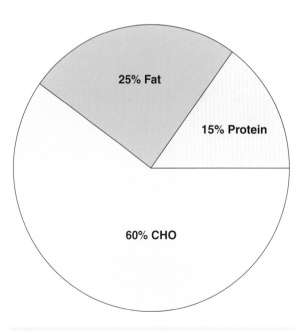

Figure 5.8   The recommended daily intake for fat, carbohydrates (CHO) and protein.

Although an athlete's protein needs may be slightly higher than a non-athlete's, a normal diet typically supplies sufficient protein. Protein should supply about 15% of the energy used by the body. High protein diets or supplements are unnecessary and may lead to kidney problems.

Adequate supplies of vitamins and minerals are essential for the body to function, and a balanced diet normally provides them. Taking vitamin and mineral supplements to provide levels above normal body requirements does not lead to improvements in performance.

We have been examining how the body uses energy to create movement. The body is not a very efficient machine, however, and the majority of energy liberated from the body's chemical stores actually ends up as heat. The body can only tolerate a narrow range of temperatures. Therefore, another factor that limits athletic performance is the body's ability to get rid of this heat.

The major way that the body removes heat is by sweating and then evaporating sweat at the skin. Although water is not a fuel, it is essential that you consume sufficient water before, during and after exercise. A typical recommendation is that you consume 500 ml of water in the 20 minutes before exercise and 250 ml during every 15 minutes of exercise. Feelings of thirst actually lag behind the body's need for water, so drink more water than your thirst dictates, especially when you are exercising.

• • • Focus Activity —

NUTRITION AND EXERCISE

Purpose

To analyse nutritional intake and determine the suitability of personal diet for a specific exercise.

Procedure

1. Make a plan for keeping a diary of your food intake for a full week. A commitment that lasts a full week will give you a more accurate analysis of your diet. Honesty and accuracy are essential factors in this commitment.

2. Use the dietary information provided on most processed food labels, together with dietary information accessible through your library, and work out your total energy intake for the week.

3. Determine the proportion of your diet that belongs to each of the three food sources: carbohydrates, fats and proteins.

Written Tasks

- Based on the general discussion during class time about the energy requirements of the physical activity you are currently studying, appraise your current diet in terms of its suitability for providing energy for the sport you are studying. Write down your findings.

- What improvements could you make to your diet so that it is more specifically suited to this physical activity?

1. Complete the following sentences by inserting the missing terms: The energy source that muscle fibres use comes from the change of a molecule called _____, or _____ for short, into _____, or _____. ATP is stored within the _____ _____ in sufficient quantities for one explosive action such as a _____ _____ or _____ _____. Once this action has occurred, the muscle cell must resynthesise _____ _____ back into _____ _____ by using other sources within the cell or bodily systems. The cycle will continue as long as _____ is available to turn ADP back into ATP.

2. Fill in the diagram showing the energy sources required for the resynthesis of ADP into ATP:

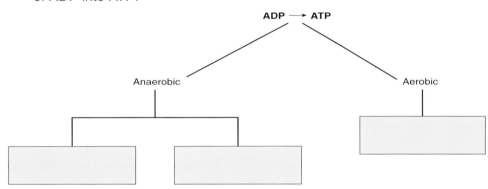

3. Complete the table:

Energy source for ADP → ATP resynthesis	Creatine phosphate	Anaerobic glycolysis	Aerobic (oxidative)
Is oxygen used?		No	
Source			Glycogen (carbohydrates), fats, protein
Storage of source	Cell		
Length of source		3 min	
Resynthesis length			
By-products			Water, CO_2
Is fatigue developed?	No		
Intensity of physical activities	Maximum effort	Maximum effort	Sub-maximum effort

(continued)

4. Take a partner and a stopwatch to the track. After a warm-up, one of you runs a total of 800 metres at maximum speed, while the other measures the time for each 100-metre segment. What energy sources predominated in each 100 metres, and why did the segments vary in speed?

5. Which energy sources are utilised in (a) a competitive aerobics routine, (b) a competitive triathlon, (c) a competitive hockey game for the midfield player and (d) a competitive hockey game for the hockey goalie? Give examples of energy sources for each activity with your answers.

6. Reflect on your current sport. Does it utilise a range of energy systems? Give examples of the energy sources.

7. Complete the following table, providing the missing information for each of the fuel sources for physical activity:

Food source	Carbohydrates	Fats	Proteins
Fuel source	Glycogen	Fatty acids	Amino acids
Utilised aerobically or anaerobically	→ ATP	→ ATP	→ ATP
Storage of fuel source			
Level of exercise intensity			

8. Complete the following graph to show that energy sources do not work in isolation but in a continuum to provide ATP resynthesis:

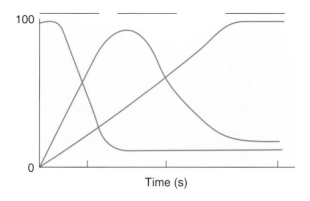

100

0

Time (s)

9. What does the term *hitting the wall* mean?

10. Supply a dietary guideline for training athletes to maximise their performance potential (a) 3 to 7 days before the event, (b) 1 to 2 days before the event, (c) 20 minutes before the event and (d) during the event. For each suggested guideline, justify the choice in terms of the physical performance outcomes.

Physiological Factors Affecting Physical Activity

Chapter Overview

When you have studied this chapter, you should be able to

- describe the physiological factors affecting performance,
- explain the short-term physiological changes that occur during physical activity and
- predict the long-term physiological adaptations that occur in response to increased physical activity.

Human bodies constantly change, and the pace and nature of the change vary throughout the life cycle. When you exercise, your body adapts to physical demands in ways that are very specific to the type of exercise that you perform. The body parts and energy systems that you exercise grow stronger. Muscles respond quickly to changes, because large blood supplies provide energy and nutrients to well-used muscles. Ligaments, tendons and bones change more slowly, because they receive smaller blood supplies. Your nervous system also adapts to exercise in specific ways.

METABOLIC CAPACITY

As explained in chapter 5, three different systems supply energy to the body: creatine phosphate (CP), anaerobic glycolysis and the aerobic system. The capacity of each energy system to supply energy determines the limits of your performance. That capacity improves when specific forms of exercise place regular demands on a particular energy system.

High-intensity, short-duration exercise like strength training or short sprinting requires the body to rapidly obtain energy from ATP and CP stored in muscles (see figure 6.1). This type of exercise leads to an increase in the amount of ATP and CP that the muscles can store. The result of training for short, high-intensity exercise is an enhanced ability to quickly generate large amounts of energy for producing force.

Exercises of moderate to high intensity, such as sprint training, require the body to obtain energy through anaerobic glycolysis. This requirement leads to an increased storage of muscle glycogen and increased activity of the enzymes involved in anaerobic glycolysis. As a result, muscles are more capable of tolerating lactic acid accumulation. All of these changes enhance the body's capacity to produce energy rapidly in the absence of oxygen.

Exercises of moderate to low intensity and long duration, such as endurance training, also cause increased storage of muscle glycogen. The enzyme activity that liberates the energy from pyruvic acid, fatty acids and amino acids increases, as do the number and size of the cell mitochondria, where chemical reactions take place inside the cell. These changes enhance the body's ability to utilise energy from the aerobic system and therefore decrease the body's reliance on the anaerobic system at any exercise intensity (see figure 6.2). Endurance-trained muscles are also more capable of removing lactic acid from the blood, delaying the onset of fatigue due to lactic acid accumulation.

The aerobic energy system requires oxygen. The body's capacity to utilise energy from the aerobic system is closely linked to the muscles' capacity to obtain oxygen from the blood. The capacity of muscles to extract oxygen from the blood and transport it within the muscle cells grows with endurance training. These capacities in turn rely on the ability of the heart and lungs to deliver oxygenated blood to the muscles.

Figure 6.1 High-intensity, short-duration activities like putting a shot require the body to rapidly obtain energy from stored ATP and CP.
© Sport The Library

Figure 6.2 Long-distance swimmers get most of their energy from their aerobic systems.
© Sport The Library

CARDIORESPIRATORY CAPACITY

Imagine you are at home relaxing with a friend and watching television. Your energy needs are small, and your body usually provides sufficient oxygen by normal breathing and a resting heart rate. Suppose you decide to go for a jog. The rate and depth of your breathing increases and the rate and volume of blood pumped by your heart also increases. If you continue to jog at a relatively slow speed, your rate of oxygen consumption levels out; it maintains a rate sufficient to metabolise all the lactic acid produced by your anaerobic energy system, as well as fatty acids. In this situation, the amount of oxygen you consume is a good measure of the amount of energy you require to perform the activity.

If you pick up the pace, the rate at which you consume oxygen increases to keep pace with your mounting energy needs (see figure 6.3). Eventually your heart and lungs cannot deliver oxygen to your muscles any faster. The rate at which your muscles consume oxygen at this point is your maximum rate of oxygen consumption, expressed as $\dot{V}O_2$max. The relationship of oxygen consumption over time is shown in figure 6.4.

$\dot{V}O_2$max refers to the rate of oxygen consumption; that is, the volume of oxygen the body consumes over a period of time (for example, 3 litres per minute). Energy needs are related to body mass, so $\dot{V}O_2$max is usually reported relative to a person's mass and is expressed as millilitres of oxygen per kilogram of body mass per minute (ml/kg/min). If your maximum rate of consuming oxygen is 3 L/min and your mass is 60 kg, your $\dot{V}O_2$max is 50 ml/kg/min. Typical $\dot{V}O_2$max values for untrained young adults are about 45 ml/kg/min, whereas elite distance runners may have a $\dot{V}O_2$max of up to 70 to 80 ml/kg/min.

Return to the jogging example mentioned earlier. As you increase your running speed and rate of oxygen consumption, your anaerobic energy system increases the rate at which it produces pyruvic acid. We learnt earlier in the chapter that at low speeds, your aerobic system can metabolise pyruvic acid. As the exercise intensity increases, however, the aerobic system cannot keep up with the amount of pyruvic acid the anaerobic system produces and instead turns the pyruvic acid into lactic acid.

Figure 6.3   The more intense the physical activity, the more oxygen the body requires.
© Sport The Library

Fatigue results rapidly if you increase the intensity of exercise above this level. The exercise intensity above which lactic acid accumulates is the lactic acid threshold. In untrained people, the intensity of exercise is equivalent to an oxygen consumption that is about 60% of their $\dot{V}O_2$max. Endurance-trained athletes might not reach this point until 80% of their $\dot{V}O_2$max. The relationship of blood lactic acid concentration and exercise intensity is illustrated in figure 6.5.

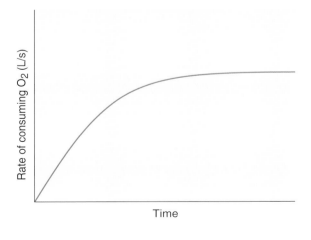

Figure 6.4   Oxygen (O_2) consumption versus time during submaximal running.

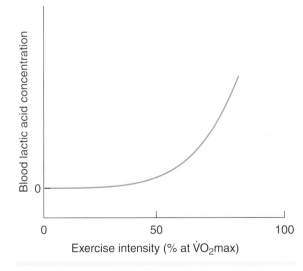

Figure 6.5   Lactic acid accumulation as a function of exercise intensity.

When you stop running and go back to watching television, your energy requirements return to what they were originally, but your rate of oxygen consumption remains elevated above resting level for some time. Your body uses this oxygen in part to create the energy it needs to replace the stores of creatine phosphate and glycogen you used up when you were exercising. It also uses extra oxygen so that your heart can pump extra blood to return your body temperature to normal and to clear the build-up of carbon dioxide from the blood. This process is called elevated post-exercise oxygen consumption. It may last for several hours after high-intensity exercise of long duration.

SAMPLE LEARNING EXPERIENCE

Anaerobic Threshold, $\dot{V}O_2$max and Netball

Mark and his class were studying energy systems as part of a netball unit. His teacher had been using terms like anaerobic threshold and $\dot{V}O_2$max. Mark and the other students were having trouble understanding what these concepts meant and how they could apply them to netball. To help the students grasp the concepts, the teacher attached a heart rate monitor to Mark, who had volunteered to be a subject for this learning experience. The teacher gave him the job of playing centre, which would allow him to be actively involved in game play in all areas of the court. Mark's main sporting pastime was golf.

The teacher formed three teams from the class of students. The players on the first team had average netball skills and ability. The second team was better than average, and the third team was made up of the top seven students in the class. Mark was a member of team 2.

The teacher then set up a 15-minute game between teams 1 and 2, and two of the expert players from team 3 umpired. Mark's resting heart rate was measured at 78 beats per minute before the start of play. Team 2 quickly asserted itself as the superior team and easily raced to a significant lead. Mark effortlessly evaded his opposite centre player and barely raised a sweat while moving around the court at a moderate pace. He seldom had to exert himself by bursting into speed to jump or get into position. He finished the 15-minute game feeling good. His heart rate fluctuated between 105 and 115 beats per minute during the game. His breathing rate was elevated, but he was not puffed by any means. He felt that he could play at this pace all day.

In the next game the teacher put Mark's team up against team 3, which contained the more highly skilled regular netballers. Now the tables were turned, and team 3 gave Mark's team a lesson in how to play netball. Mark's opposite centre was very fast around the court. She had excellent evasive strategies that left Mark rapidly and repeatedly changing directions in an attempt to keep up with her. She was also tall, and Mark had to jump extra high to contest the high ball. These challenges continued for the entire duration of the 15-minute game. By the end, Mark could no longer provide credible opposition for his skilled and fit counterpart. His heart rate was racing at higher than 150 beats per minute for most of the game, and he was breathing very heavily. Mark was sweating profusely, his body felt fatigued and his legs felt very heavy.

Explanation

Mark coped well with challenges in the first game. Because he was playing a team with less skill and fitness than his own, the pace of the game was quite slow. He easily evaded the opposition with low-intensity exercise that his aerobic system could easily provide the energy for. During Mark's low-intensity exercise, his body metabolised the pyruvic acid that was a by-product of aerobic glycolysis. His aerobic system created more energy, plus water and CO_2 that were easily disposed of by his body. When Mark exerted himself to sprint or jump, his anaerobic energy systems kicked in to provide the burst of energy. Even if anaerobic glycolysis did at this stage produce excess pyruvic acid, Mark's aerobic system provided plenty of oxygen to turn it into energy instead of lactic acid, thereby avoiding muscle fatigue and soreness. These modest demands on his energy systems explain Mark's moderate heart rate, comfortable breathing rate and general lack of fatigue.

The second game was a different story. The tougher opponent meant Mark had to exercise more intensely in order to remain competitive. Mark's heart rate initially rose to about 120 beats per minute, since his aerobic system required more oxygen to fuel his extra efforts. It climbed steadily to 150 beats per minute as the intensity of the game increased. He was again intermittently jumping and sprinting to get into better position. As in the first game, his anaerobic energy systems provided the power for these short bursts of extra effort. However, this time Mark's aerobic system was not providing sufficient oxygen to meet his energy needs and metabolise the pyruvic acid produced by anaerobic glycolysis. At a heart rate of 150 beats per minute, Mark's body could no longer fill his basic energy requirements by aerobic glycolysis alone. It depended increasingly on his anaerobic energy systems to bridge the energy gap. His muscles converted pyruvic acid to lactic acid because of the lack of oxygen, causing Mark to tire quickly as muscle fatigue set in. This elevated lactic acid production explains why Mark had to struggle so hard to remain competitive.

The point at which Mark's body can no longer fuel his energy demands aerobically and has to call on his anaerobic energy systems to bridge the gap is referred to as the anaerobic threshold. After this point, lactic acid begins to accumulate and adversely affects performance. Mark's $\dot{V}O_2$max is the maximum rate at which his body can consume oxygen. It is measured in ml/kg/min and is an excellent indicator of aerobic fitness. Mark's oxygen requirements in the second game began to exceed his $\dot{V}O_2$max. At this point, he had reached his anaerobic threshold.

Mark's opponent, being fitter and more accustomed to the game of netball, had a higher $\dot{V}O_2$max and a higher anaerobic threshold. Her body was able to meet more of her energy demands aerobically. When she did draw on anaerobic glycolysis for bursts of speed, her aerobic system delivered sufficient oxygen to metabolise any pyruvic acid produced by anaerobic glycolysis. Therefore, she did not suffer the lactic acid build-up or subsequent fatigue that Mark did.

EXTENSION ACTIVITY

$\dot{V}O_2$MAX AND PHYSICAL PERFORMANCE

Consider This

Consider the physical activity that you are currently studying. How does an athlete's $\dot{V}O_2$max influence the level at which she can perform? Does your physical activity involve intermittent bursts of effort interspersed with longer periods of lower-intensity play? If so, it is highly likely that $\dot{V}O_2$max is a significant determinant of appropriate fitness for performance.

(continued)

Try This

Arrange with your teacher for the class to participate in your physical activity at a level that the class agrees is low intensity. Do the activity for 5 minutes and observe the effect that the performance has on you and your classmates.

For the next 5 minutes, participate in the activity at medium intensity. What effect does this increase in intensity have on various class members? Are some starting to struggle? Are others still coping effortlessly and without signs of fatigue?

For the final 5 minutes, perform with maximum effort and intensity in your chosen physical activity. What do your observations reveal now? Have some students been able to last longer than others have, before becoming fatigued? Are there some students who still do not appear to be fatigued? How did you cope with the exercise?

Think and Write

- You probably saw marked variations in the observable signs of fatigue at the end of each of the three periods of exercise. Using the explanation from the netball sample learning experience as a guide, write down an explanation of how your energy systems provided energy for you during the three phases of exercise. Make particular reference to the role of your $\dot{V}O_2$max during exercise and its relationship to your body's ability to provide ATP through aerobic metabolism.

- At what point during the three stages do you think you reached your anaerobic threshold? Write about why you think it occurred at that particular time.

- What ramifications does this information have for you in your pursuit of appropriate fitness for your physical activity?

Measurement of Oxygen Consumption

The scenario above is very similar to the way you measure $\dot{V}O_2$max in a laboratory. In a typical test, a person exercises while the intensity of the pace, gradient or resistance gradually increases. As shown in figure 6.6, the person breathes through a mouthpiece and hose connected to a gas analyser. You measure the average concentration of oxygen in the air breathed out each minute and compare it to the concentration of oxygen in the air breathed in, then work out the difference. Multiply the difference by the volume of air inhaled during that time to determine the volume of oxygen the person consumed.

As the intensity of exercise increases, the rate of oxygen consumption also goes up. The test continues until the person can no longer increase the intensity of exercise, at which time you determine the maximum rate of oxygen consumption in millilitres per minute (ml/min). As noted earlier, oxygen consumption is related to body mass. Thus, $\dot{V}O_2$max is usually expressed relative to the person's body mass, in terms of millilitres per kilogram per minute (ml/kg/min).

Measuring $\dot{V}O_2$max is useful for determining a person's appropriate intensity of exercise. Athletes can train at a high percentage of their $\dot{V}O_2$max (80% or above), whereas appropriate intensity for an untrained person is in the range of 50% to 80% of their $\dot{V}O_2$max.

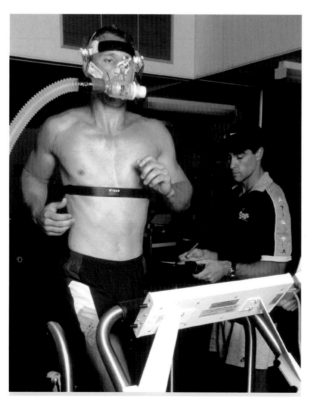

Figure 6.6 $\dot{V}O_2$max test on a treadmill.
© Sport The Library

Delivery of Oxygen to Muscles

For the aerobic energy system to provide energy, the body must deliver oxygen to the muscles. Oxygen begins its journey to your muscles when you draw air into your lungs, as shown in figure 6.7. The volume of air brought into the lungs each minute is known as *minute ventilation*. Minute ventilation is the rate of breathing in terms of breaths per minute (breaths/minute) multiplied by the volume of air inspired in each breath. It is expressed in terms of litres per breath (litres/breath). During exercise, both the rate and volume per breath increase, and the minute ventilation can increase from about 10 L/min at rest to a maximum of about 160 L/min. Maximum minute ventilation increases with endurance training and leads to an enhanced capacity to excrete carbon dioxide.

Oxygen enters the blood in the alveoli within the lungs. This process is quite efficient, and even in maximal exercise the blood leaving the lungs is almost saturated with oxygen. This saturation means that the respiratory system is not the limiting factor for the rate at which the blood can deliver oxygen to the muscles.

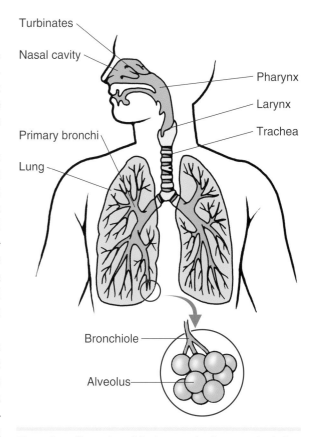

Figure 6.7   Illustration of the lungs and pulmonary circulation.

The rate at which the body can deliver blood to the muscles is the factor that limits the rate of oxygen consumption. Oxygenated blood returns from the lungs to the heart by means of the pulmonary veins, as shown in figure 6.8, and is then pumped to the muscles. The rate at which the heart pumps (beats per min) increases during exercise from a resting value of about 70 beats/min for an untrained person to a maximum value that varies with age. The maximum heart rate is normally quoted as 220 beats/min minus your age. Thus a 17-year-old might be expected to have a maximum heart rate at or just above 200 beats/min (although the rate varies significantly among different people). The volume of blood that the heart pumps for each beat is called the *stroke volume*. Stroke volume also increases during exercise, from about 60 ml at rest to about 120 ml during maximal exercise.

The total volume of blood pumped to the muscles per minute is the *cardiac output*. Cardiac output is the product of heart rate and stroke volume. For a resting value of 70 beats/min and stroke volume of 60 ml (0.06 L), cardiac output is 4.2 L/min (70 beats/min × 0.06 L/beat). It would increase to 24 L/min at maximum exercise intensity (200 beats/min × 0.12 L/beat).

Since the heart is a muscle, its size and strength increase with endurance training, leading to an increase in the stroke volume. Consequently, the resting heart rate of trained athletes may be much lower than it is for people who do not exercise, whereas resting cardiac output remains the same. Maximum heart rate does not change with training, but because of the increase in stroke volume, the cardiac output of endurance-trained athletes at maximal heart rates is much larger, perhaps up to double that of untrained people.

The increase in cardiac output during exercise is not distributed evenly throughout the body. Figure 6.9 shows that at rest, about 20% of blood ends up

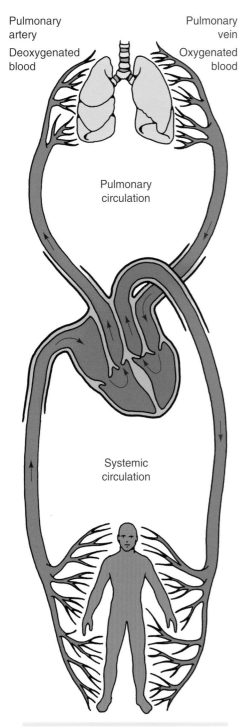

Pulmonary artery

Deoxygenated blood

Pulmonary vein

Oxygenated blood

Pulmonary circulation

Systemic circulation

Figure 6.8 Schematic diagram of cardiac circulation.

at muscles, and the other 80% goes to the brain and internal organs such as the stomach. When a person begins to exercise, the body redirects the blood flow to the muscles that are doing the work and to the skin. The body achieves the redirection by narrowing the arteries that take blood to the internal organs and widening the arteries that take blood to the muscles involved. Besides carrying oxygen to the muscles, blood also delivers the fatty acids and glucose that fuel the muscles and removes carbon dioxide, lactic acid and heat from the muscles.

Not only do muscles receive more blood during exercise, they also extract a greater proportion of oxygen from the blood than they do when at rest. Muscles extract about 25% of the oxygen at rest and up to 85% during exercise. The changes that occur with exercise help to increase the rate at which oxygen is made available to the muscle cells, up to a person's $\dot{V}O_2$max. The increased rate means that the aerobic energy system can produce additional energy and the muscles can turn the pyruvic acid produced by anaerobic glycolysis into carbon dioxide, hydrogen and electrons, rather than accumulating it as lactic acid. However, fatigue develops if the exercise intensifies to the point that the rate of pyruvic acid production exceeds the rate at which the muscles can metabolise it. This point of exercise intensity is called the lactic acid threshold.

The maximum rate at which oxygen can be delivered to and consumed by the muscles ($\dot{V}O_2$max) and the lactic acid threshold (percent of $\dot{V}O_2$max) determine the intensity of exercise that a person can maintain for prolonged periods without fatigue. Because of the many adaptations that occur with endurance training, $\dot{V}O_2$max may increase by 20% to 40%. Endurance training also increases the lactic acid threshold.

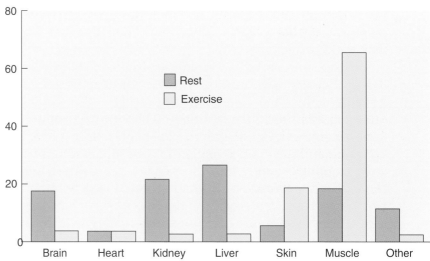

Figure 6.9 Percentages of blood distribution to various organs during exercise and rest.

Adapted, by permission, from J.H. Wilmore and D.L. Costill, 1994, *Physiology of sport and exercise* (Champaign, IL: Human Kinetics), 172.

• • • Focus Activity —

CARDIAC OUTPUT

Purpose

To calculate personal cardiac output and cardiac output for family members. The calculations will give you a greater understanding of the relationship between cardiac output and elite endurance performance.

Procedure

1. First, here is some fictitious personal and family information that you can use to make your calculations. Assume that your personal resting stroke volume was scientifically measured at 0.05 L/min and that your maximum stroke volume was measured under maximum effort at 0.1 L/min. To calculate your personal resting cardiac output, you must measure your pulse rate for 1 minute and then multiply it by your resting stroke volume. To calculate your personal maximum stroke volume, you must first calculate your maximum heart rate by subtracting your age from 220 (as in the formula mentioned earlier) and then multiplying this new heart rate by your maximum stroke volume.

2. Next, assume you have a family member who has a resting stroke volume of 0.067 L/min, a maximum stroke volume of 0.134 L/min, and a resting heart rate of 88 beats/min. Calculate his cardiac output. Subtract his age from 220 as you did above and use this new heart rate to calculate his maximum stroke volume.

3. Finally, assume you have a family member who has a resting stroke volume of 0.09 L/min, a maximum stroke volume of 0.18 L/min and a resting heart rate of 88 beats/min. Calculate her cardiac output. Subtract her age from 220 and use this new heart rate to calculate her maximum stroke volume.

Written Tasks

- Write down an explanation of the relationship between age and cardiac output for the general population.
- What factors might cause an individual to be an exception to the rule?
- What role does cardiac output have in the physical activity that you are currently studying?

NEUROMUSCULOSKELETAL CAPACITY

Muscle fibres supply the force that makes movement possible, but movement involves more than just muscles. Nerves deliver the stimulus for muscles to contract, and the contracting muscles transmit forces to the bones by means of tendons. Ligaments limit movement to particular directions. All of these structures together form the neuromusculoskeletal system. The capacity of these structures contributes to our ability to perform physical activity, and all neuromusculoskeletal structures respond to use and disuse.

Types of Muscle Fibre

Different types of muscle fibres make up skeletal muscle. The major distinction is between slow-twitch fibres (type I) and fast-twitch fibres (type II). Fast-twitch fibres are in turn divided into two types—IIA and IIB.

slow-twitch (type I) muscle fibres:
Muscle fibres that contract slowly and use energy from the aerobic process.

fast-twitch (type II) muscle fibres:
Muscle fibres that contract faster than slow-twitch fibres and use both anaerobic and aerobic energy systems.

Slow-twitch (type I) muscle fibres have a high capacity for using energy from the aerobic energy system and do not fatigue rapidly. They are not, however, as large as fast-twitch fibres. As their name suggests, they do contract more slowly than fast-twitch fibres. Consequently, they are useful for physical activities requiring low forces over long periods. **Fast-twitch (type II) muscle fibres** are larger and contract faster than slow-twitch fibres, but they fatigue rapidly. The two kinds of fast-twitch fibres differ in the metabolic sources of energy they use. Type IIB fibres have a high capacity for glycolytic release of energy, whereas type IIA fibres use both aerobic and glycolytic energy sources. The large type II fibres that contract quickly are useful for physical activities requiring large forces. Because they obtain energy from anaerobic glycolysis, however, they produce lactic acid.

Type I fibres are smaller than type II, and the body uses them to produce force before it uses the larger type II fibres. Only when it needs to produce more force does the body use the larger type II fibres as well.

A typical muscle has about 50% type I fibres, 25% type IIA and 25% type IIB, although the proportions differ between muscles and among people. Muscles primarily used for posture have a higher proportion of type I fibres, whereas muscles that produce large forces rapidly typically have more type II fibres than average.

If you are standing around waiting on the sideline to play a game of basketball, one of the muscles that must continually produce low levels of force to keep you upright is the soleus, which lies deep on the back of the calf. In normal standing, the soleus acts to stop you from falling flat on your face. The soleus is primarily composed of type I fibres, which means that you can stand around for long periods without getting tired.

If you are on the basketball court getting ready to perform a jump shot, your soleus does not help much. It cannot generate forces very quickly, which is what a muscle needs to do in order for you to jump. Fortunately, you have another muscle in your calf called the gastrocnemius that is composed of a high proportion of type II fibres. This is exactly the kind of muscle you need to help you perform the jump shot.

These two calf muscles are extreme examples of different muscle functions. Most muscles are general purpose and are able to both contract at low levels for long periods and generate relatively high forces for short periods. Most people do many different things, so it is an advantage to have different fibre types.

It seems that some elite athletes have different distributions of fibre types than the average person. Elite endurance runners, for example, have large proportions of type I fibres, whereas bodybuilders and elite sprinters, like the one shown in figure 6.10, have larger proportions of type II fibres. It is not clear whether fibre type changes in response to extreme exposure to either endurance or strength activities. Another possibility is that these fibre distributions are to some extent genetically determined, and the performance of elite athletes is a consequence of the abnormal distribution of fibre types. Both possibilities may be true to an extent.

Figure 6.10   Elite sprinters' muscles have larger proportions of type II fibres.
© Sport The Library

Neuromusculoskeletal Responses to Training

Some parts of the neuromuscular system definitely do respond to training. The number of capillaries within muscles increases with endurance training. This increase allows the body to deliver more oxygen to the muscle cells. It also accounts in part for the enhanced ability of muscles to extract oxygen from blood delivered to them by the cardiorespiratory system.

Changes that are even more remarkable occur in the neuromusculoskeletal system in response to strength and speed training. The initial gains in strength that occur in response to training are a result of refinements in the functioning of the nervous system. Enhanced skill and coordination of muscle contractions account for this change in nervous system functioning in part, but the ability to activate muscle fibres also improves.

After the initial gains in strength due to neural changes, any further gains are a consequence of growth in the size or number of muscle fibres. Increase in the size of muscle fibres is called **hypertrophy.** Hypertrophy is the body's primary response to training.

The strength of a muscle is roughly proportional to its cross-sectional area. Which fibres increase in size depends on the specific nature of the training performed. Type I fibres increase in size as a result of endurance training, whereas the size of type II fibres increases in response to strength and sprint training. Type IIB fibres in particular, although having the greatest potential for hypertrophy, grow in size only if near maximal forces are involved in training.

An increase in the number of fibres is called **hyperplasia.** Hyperplasia is less common than hypertrophy, but can occur in response to high-load and high-volume training.

hypertrophy:
An increase in the size of muscle fibres.

hyperplasia:
An increase in the number of muscle fibres.

PHYSIOLOGICAL CAPACITY AND AGE

A person's capacity for physical activity increases through childhood and early adulthood and then decreases after about age 30. Our bodies, however, never stop responding to the demands placed on them, and you can reduce the inevitable decline in physiological capacity associated with aging by training (figure 6.11).

Maximum oxygen consumption declines after about age 30. This decline occurs in large part because of a decrease in the maximum heart rate and a consequent reduction in maximum cardiac output, even though stroke volume may remain the same. The number of capillaries decreases, as does the ability of the vascular system to redirect blood to working muscles. Both of these changes diminish the amount of oxygen the body can deliver to muscles. Training can reduce the rate and amount of this decline in maximum oxygen consumption.

Training can also slow the rate of muscle loss. Strength appears to decrease by about 2% to 4% per year in non-athletes, primarily because of shrinkage of muscle mass. This decrease in muscle mass is predominantly caused by atrophy of the larger type II fibres—fibres that the body only recruits for high-force contractions.

Figure 6.11   The capacity for physical performance may decrease with age, but the health benefits or enjoyment will not.

© Sport The Library

PHYSIOLOGICAL CAPACITY AND SEX

People differ in their physiological capacity for physical activity. Differences exist between the typical male and female. On average, $\dot{V}O_2$max is higher in males than in females, although the magnitude of the difference is small until after puberty. When trained female and male endurance athletes are compared, the differences in aerobic capacity are not that great (less than 10%). Many females have a higher $\dot{V}O_2$max than many males.

In general, the differences in physiological capacity between male and female children are minor. They are probably caused by differences in activity levels due to social rather than biological factors. After puberty, greater average differences exist between females and males, especially in terms of muscle mass and consequently of strength and power. Females and males respond similarly to training, and discrepancies in strength diminish when you compare similarly trained females and males. It is unknown how much of the average strength difference is a consequence of social factors affecting activity levels and how much is a consequence of physiological differences.

Several performance factors are specific to female athletes. The effects of the menstrual cycle on performance are highly individual, and no generalisations are possible. Some female athletes, up to 40% in some sports, experience disruptions of their normal menstrual cycles as a consequence of their participation. The likelihood of menstrual disruption grows with increased quantity and intensity of training, especially when such training is combined with insufficient energy intake (inadequate diet) or psychological stress. Female athletes should note that absence of menstruation does not necessarily mean absence of ovulation—pregnancy may still be possible.

osteoporosis:
Decreased density and increased porosity of bones.

Osteoporosis occurs when bone density decreases and bone porosity increases. It predominantly affects post-menopausal women. The loss of bone density leads to a heightened risk of fractures, and fractures of the neck and femur are especially common. Osteoporosis is a major public health concern.

The most effective way to prevent osteoporosis later in life is to engage in regular weight-bearing exercise throughout childhood and adulthood, while also maintaining an adequate calcium intake and normal hormonal balance. Some women who engage in substantial amounts of intense physical activity find that they suffer hormonal disruption, associated with disruption of the normal menstrual cycle. Hormonal disruption is also more likely if women restrict their energy intake or experience psychological stress. The consequences of hormonal disruption are reduced bone density and a greater likelihood of developing osteoporosis in later life.

• • • *Focus Activity* —

PHYSICAL DIFFERENCES AND THE EFFECT ON PERFORMANCE

Purpose

To examine the differences between males and females in your class concerning characteristics related to physical performance. This analysis will help you to understand performance differences between the sexes.

Procedure

This exercise works best in a class made up of both sexes. In a single-sex class you can still make the same measurements on class members to illustrate differences. Then you can make extrapolations from assumptions in the text, concerning the average differences between males and females in society.

1. Consider the physical activity you are currently studying. As a group, brainstorm the physical abilities that make one player more competent than others in this sport. For example, you might choose the capacity to jump higher, throw farther, run faster, be more agile or be stronger.

2. Brainstorm some ideas for creating simple tests to measure and profile physical characteristics of everyone in the class. For example, as a test of a person's ability to jump high, you might have the person hold a piece of chalk, jump up against a wall, make a mark and measure the height with a tape measure. It would also make sense to measure the height of the person jumping as well.

3. After you have all decided and agreed on the tests, make a table in your journals for recording the results beside the names of students you are going to test.

4. Perform, measure and record the tests. It may take several lessons to complete these tasks.

5. After measuring all students and entering their results into your personal table, calculate the average performance for each of the tests. Add together all of the scores for each of the tests and divide each total by the number of students who performed the test. Then use the same formula to calculate the average performance of males in the group and of females in the group.

Written Tasks

- Are there any significant differences in the average measurements of males and females compared to the averages for the whole group? How do you account for these differences? Can you attribute them to physical capacity differences, or are they manifestations of social circumstances?

- Explain your thoughts in writing and justify your ideas with arguments that are based on scientific facts rather than on stereotypes.

- What implications do physical differences between the sexes have for competition rules in the physical activity that you are studying? Are facilities, equipment or playing conditions altered to allow for differences between the sexes? Do you think that these alterations are entirely justified? Write down your thoughts.

• • • Test Yourself —

1. The body's adaptation to exercise is based on the intensity level of the person exercising. Complete the following table outlining the changes that happen as a result of training:

Energy stored	Creatine phosphates	Anaerobic glycolysis	Aerobic
Training: intensity level			
Training: duration			
The body's physical adaptation			

(continued)

2. Define $\dot{V}O_2$max. If able to complete the 20-metre shuttle run test, what level of $\dot{V}O_2$max did you obtain? Why is a high $\dot{V}O_2$max a good indication of strong cardiovascular fitness?

3. Define the lactic acid threshold. Why is the lactic acid threshold lower in untrained people than in trained people? What impact did your lactic acid threshold have on your $\dot{V}O_2$max test?

4. After exercise stops, why do heart and breathing rates remain elevated? Why do some athletes return to their pre-exercise heart rate faster than others do?

5. How is knowing your $\dot{V}O_2$max reading useful when designing your individual fitness program?

6. What is minute ventilation? Why is it important for exercise?

7. Define (a) stroke volume, (b) cardiac output and (c) maximum heart rate.

8. What is the difference between cardiac output at rest and cardiac output during exercise?

9. What is your maximum heart rate? What influence will it have on your threshold of training, compared to that of a 60-year-old?

10. How do changes in age affect a person's exercise potential?

11. What impact will long-term, high-endurance training have on (a) maximum heart rate, (b) heart size, (c) stroke volume, (d) cardiac output at rest, (e) resting heart rate and (f) cardiac output during exercise?

12. What changes occur in the circulatory, respiratory and muscular systems when the body goes from rest to exercise?

13. What is the relationship between $\dot{V}O_2$max and the lactic acid threshold? How will it affect your performance in your current physical activity?

14. Complete the following table differentiating between the types of muscle fibres:

Muscle fibres	Types	Main energy source	Fatigue rate	Rate of contraction	Type of movement
Slow twitch	I				
Fast twitch	IIA				
	IIB				

15. Complete the following sentences by inserting the missing words: Different muscles within the body and between _____ have different combinations of _____ and _____-twitch fibres. Explosive physical activity requires _____ fibres, whereas _____ activities require slow-twitch fibres. Elite athletes such as endurance runners have a high predominance of _____ fibres, whereas _____ and _____ have larger portions of type II fibres.

16. State three physiological changes that occur within the muscular system as a response to training.

17. What is the influence of age on physical capacity?

18. List the physiological changes that occur after approximately 30 years of age.

19. How does physical training affect the changes caused by aging?

20. When you compare similarly trained adult athletes of different sexes, what variations would you expect to find in their (a) $\dot{V}O_2$max and (b) strength?

21. People can prevent loss of bone density, known as osteoporosis, through regular exercise. Explain how exercise inhibits the onset of this degeneration.

chapter 7

Improving Physiological Capacity for Physical Activity

Chapter Overview

- Principles of Training
- Focus Activity: Training Specificity
- Sample Learning Experience: Training Specificity and Athletics–400 m
- Focus Activity: Energy System Specifics
- Training Program Design
- Training for Health
- Extension Activity: Training Principles
- Test Yourself

When you have studied this chapter, you should be able to

- describe four principles of training,
- apply the principles to designing a training program to achieve a specific goal,
- apply the notion of periodisation with a training program and
- explain some health benefits associated with exercise.

If you carry out exercise in a haphazard or random fashion, then the changes that occur in the body are also haphazard. If you carry out exercise according to a planned program, however, you can develop your capacity for physical performance systematically. By applying the principles of specificity, progressive overload, reversibility and individuality to designing a sound training program, and then carefully following the program, you can improve your physical performance. Other factors you must consider when you exercise are the effects of various types of training on physiological functioning and a strategy for periodising training to allow peak performance at the right time in a competitive sport season.

PRINCIPLES OF TRAINING

When you plan your exercise program, keep in mind the factors that will affect your progress. By attending to the principles of training that follow, you can develop your most effective training program.

Specificity

specificity:
A principle of training that emphasises that movements should be identical to those involved in the actual athletic activity.

The most important principle of training is **specificity.** As you learnt in chapter 6, changes that occur in the body are very specific to the types of physical activity we engage in. For example, gains in strength you achieve by lifting weights only affect the muscles you use to lift the weights. The strength gains are even specific to the speed of movement. If you are training for the shot-put and your goal is to improve your ability to exert large forces very quickly, then there is little to gain not only from lifting light weights but also from lifting heavy weights slowly.

To gain maximum benefit and improved physiological capacity, your training should utilise movements that are as similar as possible to the movements involved in the actual activity. You should involve the same joints and muscles, and the movements should ideally involve movements of the same force, speed and direction.

The changes that occur in your body's ability to use energy are specific to the demands placed on the different energy systems. To enhance your body's capacity to perform a specific activity, your training should be similar in frequency, duration and intensity to that of the physical activity you perform. For instance, if your aim is to improve sprint performance, you should engage in relatively short bouts of high-intensity exercise in your training to improve the function of the creatine phosphate and anaerobic glycolytic energy systems. Sprint performance does not gain much from long-duration, low-intensity sessions that improve cardiovascular functioning and the aerobic energy system. Such sessions are more suitable for training your systems to supply the energy necessary for completing an ultra-marathon.

• • • Focus Activity —

TRAINING SPECIFICITY

Purpose

To investigate training methods for your physical activity—specifically, how your training methods reflect the real activity.

Procedure

1. Form groups of three or four students. List as many training drills as possible that you commonly use in the general training process for the physical activity you are currently studying.

2. Take turns demonstrating the various drills that the group has identified, while the other students observe.

3. Analyse the drills one by one and determine whether the skills shown are relevant or useful to your chosen sport. Examine each drill carefully. Remember that training should be as close as possible in force, speed and duration to the physical activity you are studying.

SAMPLE LEARNING EXPERIENCE

Training Specificity and Athletics—400 m

Simon's class was studying training principles in the context of an athletics unit. He had achieved considerable success in the past with long-distance running, particularly in the 3000-metre event. Simon wanted to diversify his running ability and so chose the 400-metre event to specialise in during his physical education course. He figured that since he was already very fit and was used to running longer distances, he would not have any difficulty with the shorter distance. He could enjoy the luxury of continuing with his normal training program and benefit from a little variety.

Much to Simon's dismay, he could not match the specialist 400-metre runners in his class. He finally found the explanation for his problem when his teacher introduced him to the training principle of specificity.

Explanation

The training program that Simon was using seemed to be adequate for him to achieve significant success in his favourite event, the 3000 metres. When he found that he could not compete against the specialist 400-metre runners, he was very frustrated. When Simon heard his teacher referring to the training principle called specificity, he thought that he might have found the source of his problem.

The teacher explained to Simon that training for maximum performance outcomes needed to be similar in most respects to the physical activity the athlete was training for; it must simulate the specific characteristics of that particular physical activity. The teacher also explained that specificity applied not only to the primary actions involved (in this case running) but also to the energy systems that training was developing.

Simon was confident that his training program was specific enough with respect to primary actions. He was doing plenty of running, and it was fairly regular (see table 7.1). When he analysed his training program more closely, however, he realised that it failed to address the specific energy demands of the 400-metre race. Much of what Simon had learnt about energy systems now started to make sense.

Simon worked out that success in the 3000-metre event is largely dependent on a high $\dot{V}O_2$max, which is the maximum amount of oxygen that can be delivered to the body when exercising (commonly referred to as cardiorespiratory capacity). Cardiorespiratory capacity depends on the ability of the aerobic energy system to metabolise glycogen in the presence of oxygen.

Simon's aerobic capacity had improved from the kind of endurance activities he had been doing in his training program. In this respect, his training was meeting the specific energy demands of his favourite event, the 3000 metres, which is an endurance race.

Simon used his knowledge of energy systems to deduce that because the 400-metre race was of a shorter duration and a much higher intensity than the 3000 metres, it must utilise a different energy source. He realised that the 400-metre event must draw on the anaerobic energy systems and that because the race lasts for longer than 10 seconds, the energy must be provided by anaerobic glycolysis. Simon realised that he was training specifically for endurance events, yet was expecting success in a short-distance race. He was not adequately training his anaerobic glycolysis energy system. As a result, he was suffering from fatigue due to lactic acid production during the more intense 400-metre race.

Simon's predicament became even clearer when he examined the training programs of the serious 400-metre runners in the class. They did very little endurance work in their programs. Most of their physical activity consisted of submaximal and maximal sprinting over short and middle distances. The training activities were organised in intervals, with rest intervals of varying degrees. The athletes performed several 400-metre runs in each session. Clearly these programs were designed specifically to train the lactic acid system, since most of the activities needed to draw on anaerobic glycolysis for energy production.

After thinking carefully, Simon determined this sort of training would have a two-fold effect. First, the lactic acid systems of the 400-metre runners were more efficient and effective than his, and produced less lactic acid for a given anaerobic workload. Second, their working muscles were used to exercising in the presence of lactic acid. This lactic acid tolerance had enhanced the muscular endurance that is essential for successful 400-metre running. Simon evaluated his own training program and concluded it did not address these areas, which is why he was not successful at competing in the 400-metre event.

TABLE 7.1   Simon's Current Training Program

Sunday	Rest day; recovery after competition
Monday	10-km road run
Tuesday	Track work; two sub-max 1500-m runs; one max-effort 3000-m run
Wednesday	5-km cross-country run
Thursday	Rest day; part-time job
Friday	Track work; two sub-max 1500-m runs, one max-effort 3000-m run
Saturday	Athletics club competition day; one 1500 m plus one 3000 m

Progressive Overload

Your body adapts to the demands placed on it in order to build up its ability to accommodate those demands. Once your body can meet these demands, further improvements in physiological capacity do not occur unless the demands increase. For continued improvements in physiological capacity to occur, your training program must include progressive increases in the demands you place on your body. This strategy is known as progressive overload. You can raise the demands by changing the frequency, intensity or duration of your training. Which element (or elements) you increase depends on the specific requirements of the physical activity. For example, if your goal is to increase your endurance, extend the duration of the exercise. If you want to get stronger, increase the weight you lift once weights that were previously heavy for you become easier to lift (figure 7.1).

Figure 7.1   When the weight you currently lift starts to feel lighter, increase the weight to get stronger.
© Sport The Library

• • • *Focus Activity —*

ENERGY SYSTEM SPECIFICS

Purpose

To determine the prominent energy requirements for elite performance in various physical activities, including the physical activity you are currently studying.

Procedure

1. Draw a continuum with aerobic energy production at one end and anaerobic energy production at the other end.

2. Examine the following list of physical activities, then place each activity on the continuum according to the proportion of aerobic and anaerobic energy requirements it demands from an elite athlete:

   • 400-metre sprint

   • 1500-metre swim

   • A gymnastics vault

   • 15 minutes of rock climbing

   • 1 minute of boxing

   • 2 minutes of competitive aerobics

   • A complete hockey match for a goalkeeper

   • A single dive from a platform

   • A complete soccer match for a mid-fielder

   • A 3-minute jive routine

Written Task

   • Mark down where you think the physical activity that you are currently studying fits on the continuum.

   • Compare and contrast where you placed the various activities on the continuum with where one of your classmates put them. Discuss the differences with this student and justify why you chose the positions you did for the various activities.

Reversibility

The flip side of the principle of progressive overload is **reversibility.** The changes that occur in response to increased demands remain for only as long as the demands on the body remain. If the demands on your body suddenly fall to much lower levels, then the changes in physiological capacity reverse to match the new levels of activity.

A dramatic example of reversibility is the astronaut who spends a long period in a weightless environment. During that time, the muscles that the astronaut would normally use to maintain posture are not required and consequently get very weak. The astronaut's bones get weaker in a similar way, because they are not bearing the astronaut's weight under gravity. The same sort of thing happens to anyone who remains inactive for prolonged periods.

Individuality

People's bodies differ in many obvious ways, such as size and shape; and in less obvious ways, such as the relative proportions of muscle fibre types they possess. An important realisation for anyone involved in athletic training is that people also differ in how quickly, and to what extent, they respond to a training program. Consequently, any training program must be flexible and must adapt specifically to each individual, especially regarding the timing and extent of progressions in its exercise demands. If training loads are too high or increase too quickly, then overtraining may occur.

Overtraining

It is possible to overload your body through **overtraining.** When you increase your training load by increasing its frequency, intensity or duration, you must match the training increases to your body's capabilities. You must also keep in mind the speed with which you respond to training. If you make the load too high, or increase it too quickly, your body will become fatigued and will no longer respond to the demands you place on it. Your capacity for physical activity will diminish, as will your performance levels. On top of these setbacks, your susceptibility to injury and illness will increase. An athlete who has been exhausted by overtraining may require weeks, or even months, to recover.

TRAINING PROGRAM DESIGN

Different types of training promote different types of changes in your body. The types of training may be broadly categorised as resistance, interval and continuous.

Resistance Training

Resistance training uses a relatively low number of movement repetitions operating against relatively high forces. The forces can be either static (which means you exert them without movement) or dynamic (which means you exert them with movement). Dynamic actions include the use of free weights and a variety of different mechanical devices.

In dynamic actions, you can exert forces while a muscle is shortening, as in concentric training; or while it is lengthening, as in eccentric training. For example, during the upward movement in a biceps curl, your biceps brachii shortens as it generates tension. This shortening is called a concentric muscle contraction. When you lower the load, the biceps brachii provides the tension, but it now lengthens in what is called an eccentric contraction. Muscles are stronger when they are lengthening, so eccentric training can involve higher loads and, theoretically, lead to greater strength gains.

A typical resistance-training program for developing maximal strength consists of 3 to 6 sets of 1 to 8 repetitions of various movements. Each movement resists a load that is from 80% to 100% of the maximum load you are able to lift. Use lower loads and higher repetitions to develop health-related rather than performance-related improvements in strength.

If you use free weights during training, then the load stays constant. However, your ability to generate force changes throughout the movement due primarily to the changes in muscle lengths that occur as your posture changes, and consequently free weights do not lead to the same strength gains throughout the range of movement. Another way to train is to use mechanical devices to match the resistance to the strength of your body throughout the whole range of movement. Other devices, known as isokinetic devices, maintain a constant speed of movement while the force you exert varies through the range of movement.

Another resistance-training technique is to prestretch the relevant muscles just before exerting force in a rapid explosive movement, which involves both eccentric and concentric muscle contractions. This type of resistance training is known as **plyometrics.** An example of plyometrics is depth jumping, in which you jump down to the floor from a height before jumping upwards with maximum effort. Plyometrics is ideal for developing take-off movements for blocking and spiking in volleyball and in a range of other sports that involve jumping. As the volleyball player's knees bend to absorb the body's weight on landing, the quadriceps lengthen in an eccentric contraction. After the big muscles of the quadriceps absorb the landing force, they shorten rapidly in a concentric contraction when the volleyball player jumps as high as possible.

plyometrics:
A particular type of resistance training that uses both eccentric (lengthening) and concentric (shortening) muscle contractions.

Interval Training

Interval training intersperses periods of relatively high-intensity exercise with periods of rest. The changes that occur in your body depend on the intensity and duration of exercise bouts as well as the duration of rest periods. To achieve maximum sprint performance, your training bout should be of very high intensity (95% to 100% of maximum speed) and short duration, up to about 30 seconds. Rest breaks of about 5 to 20 minutes allow the muscles to replace creatine phosphate stores. If you reduce the intensity to 60% to 80% of maximum speed and increase the duration of the exercise bouts to between 30 seconds and 2 minutes, such training improves your body's ability to utilise the energy produced from anaerobic glycolysis, rather than that from creatine phosphate. Longer bouts of exercise at even lower levels of intensity primarily lead to changes in the aerobic energy system.

interval training:
Training that combines periods of exercise with periods of rest.

Continuous Training

Continuous training involves performing relatively low-intensity exercise at about 50% to 80% of $\dot{V}O_2$max for relatively long durations. This type of training improves the body's ability to utilise energy derived from the aerobic energy system. The appropriate intensity of exercise for continuous training depends on the individual and on the aim of the training program. Elite runners train at a high percentage of their $\dot{V}O_2$max, possibly up to 80%, whereas a lower intensity of 50% of $\dot{V}O_2$max is appropriate for recreational runners who exercise for health benefits.

continuous training:
Training that involves a steady level of relatively low-level exercise.

If you wish to improve your strength, resistance training is the best choice. If you are after speed, short interval training is the answer. If your aim is endurance, continuous training is appropriate. Many physical activities require a combination of the three types of training. The emphasis that each form of training should receive depends on the relative importance of each element in the sport you are training for.

Periodisation

Training is frequently planned in blocks in which the frequency, intensity and duration of training activities vary along with the types of activity. Dividing the training cycle into blocks or periods of training is known as **periodisation.** The most common example of periodisation is the training cycle for athletes who play team sports—they undergo off-season, preseason and competitive season training. These athletes usually undertake different types of training during each period.

periodisation:
Organising training into blocks that vary in frequency, intensity and duration of training.

Varying training in this way has a number of potential advantages. Coaches and athletes frequently plan reductions in training load to coincide with important competitions, when they desire maximal performance. This process is called tapering. Variations in training also help to develop different physiological capacities, prevent boredom, maintain motivation and reduce the risk of overtraining.

Many team sports, such as field hockey, netball and the various football codes, require a combination of general aerobic capacity, capacity for frequent anaerobic efforts such as sprinting, and strength to perform specific skills like hitting, throwing or kicking a ball. In these sports, training can address different aspects of the physical capacities and skills each sport requires at different stages of the season and off-season.

Warm-Up, Flexibility and Stretching

Warming up before you exercise elevates your heart rate and breathing and reduces the risk of injury. For most activities that involve running, 5 to 20 minutes of stretching combined with low-intensity aerobic activity such as walking, jogging or striding is an appropriate general warm-up. Finishing exercise with a cooling-down period of low-intensity aerobic exercise is also beneficial. It reduces muscle soreness by speeding up the process of removing accumulated lactic acid.

For some specific movements, such as many gymnastics skills, a broad range of joint flexibility is necessary to perform the movements successfully. In many other activities, an abnormally small range of motion can impair the performance of movements and increase the risk of injury.

The bony structure of a joint, the ligaments, and the length of the tendons and muscles surrounding the joint determine the range of motion through which the joint is able to move. You can increase the range of movement or flexibility of a joint by stretching the muscles and tendons that surround it. Stretching before and after exercise sessions is a useful way to reduce the risk of injury. Regardless of the reason for stretching, you should always perform stretching movements slowly, never with rapid bouncing movements (figure 7.2).

Figure 7.2 By slowly stretching the muscles and tendons surrounding a joint, you can improve the joint's range of motion.
© Sport The Library

TRAINING FOR HEALTH

Improving your physiological capacity for physical activity benefits your health in numerous ways, including preventing or reducing the risks of obesity, osteoporosis, heart disease and diabetes. A training program appropriate for maintaining the health of normal adults should call for them to participate in a regular form of whole-body exercise that they can maintain for a prolonged period. Walking, running, cycling and swimming are examples of whole-body exercises. People should engage in the activity 3 to 5 times per week for 15 to 60 minutes per session, at an intensity of 50% to 70% of $\dot{V}O_2$max.

Resistance training should also form part of an exercise program for general health. Sets consisting of 15 to 25 repetitions, lifting loads of around 50% of maximum, are appropriate for building the muscular strength of normal adults.

EXTENSION ACTIVITY

TRAINING PRINCIPLES

Consider This

Consider the physical activity that you are currently studying. What characteristics of this physical activity make it unique (different from similar activities)? What is the major difference between training for your physical activity and training for similar activities?

Think and Write

- Write down a list of the characteristics that make the activity you are studying unique, compared with similar activities.

- With reference to the principle of specificity, write an exposition that critically evaluates the training program you are pursuing for improvement in your physical activity.

- What elements in your training make your sessions specific to your physical activity and not specific to similar activities? What sections of your training program might have relevance for training in other sports? Explain your thoughts.

- In your estimation, how appropriate is your current training program? Justify your thoughts with reasons founded in the training principles. Make suggestions about how you could improve the program to make it even more specific to your chosen physical activity.

• • • Test Yourself —

1. Match the term in Column A with the correct statement in Column B:

Column A	Column B
___ Specificity	a. Adaptations made by the body due to exercise demands require that you gradually increase subsequent workloads to continue the adaptations.
___ Progressive overload	b. Overloading the training program too rapidly can cause injury, illness, fatigue or exhaustion.
___ Reversibility	c. The principle that you get what you train for, as it relates to the type of energy source needed for muscular actions and the physical abilities needed for particular activities.
___ Individuality	d. Every person has different requirements, so training programs, timings and demands must be flexible to meet individual needs.
___ Overtraining	e. If work demands on the body decrease, physiological changes are reversed.

(continued)

2. Define (a) static force, (b) dynamic force, (c) repetitions, (d) sets, (e) maximum load, (f) eccentric training and (g) concentric training.

3. Complete the following table:

Purpose	Maximum strength	Health-related strength
Weights		
Reps		
Sets		
Speed		

4. Define plyometrics. How could you apply this training method to the sport you are currently studying?

5. What is interval training?

6. Complete the table below by providing information for developing the energy pathways named:

Purpose	Creatine phosphate	Anaerobic glycolysis	Aerobic system
Intensity			
Duration			
Recovery time			
Recovery type			

7. What does continuous training involve, and what is its purpose?

8. The training cycle can be broken up into three phases. Draw a pie chart that illustrates the time periods of the phases in this training cycle. Include tapering as a fourth phase. Place yourself in the pie chart at your current phase of training for your physical activity. Explain the reasons for your placement.

9. Outline the components of a typical training session. Does this outline reflect one of your typical training programs? Explain.

10. List the benefits of completing a warm-up and stretching session before exercise and then a cool-down period afterward. Design a warm-up and cool-down for your current physical activity to present to your class at the next session.

11. Outline the health benefits of regular exercise.

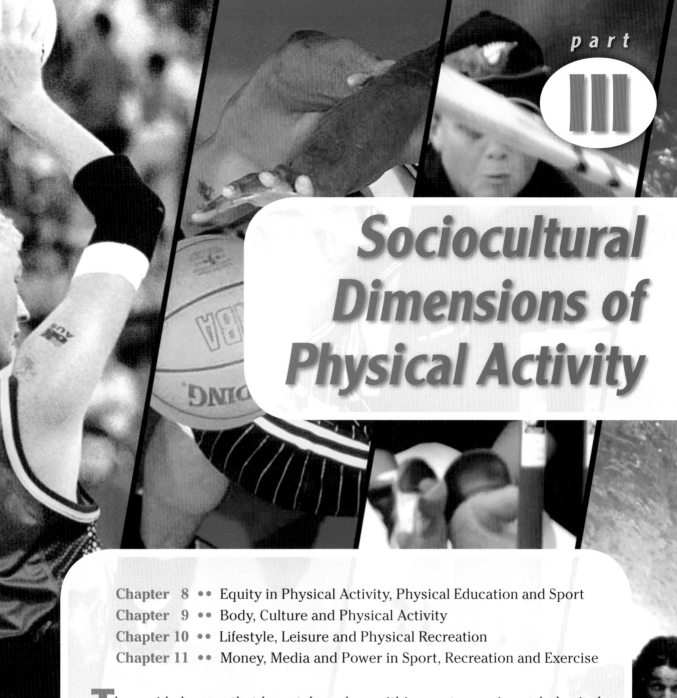

part

III

Sociocultural Dimensions of Physical Activity

The rapid changes that have taken place within sport, exercise and physical recreation over the last two decades have been matched by an increase in sociocultural research. The four chapters in part III examine how sport, exercise and physical recreation have responded and contributed to social change in Australia. These chapters draw on the fields of sociology, history, cultural studies and politics.

Chapter 8 provides an extended discussion of equality, equity and inclusion, which are key components of the principle of social justice that influences the development of new physical education and junior sport programs. Chapters 9, 10 and 11 also contribute to a better understanding of social justice and equity in physical activity. Chapter 9 examines the ways in which the body is socially constructed, including the influence of the media and advertising, body image, and the social and scientific regulation of the body. Chapter 10 analyses the notions of lifestyle, leisure and physical recreation. It assesses the effect of commodification on patterns of participation and social barriers to participation in physical activity. Chapter 11 explores the issues of money, media and power in sport, physical recreation and exercise. It includes an analysis of the commodification of sport and exercise, the social construction of gender through sport, and the relationship of sport to politics and power.

Equity in Physical Activity, Physical Education and Sport

Chapter Overview

When you have studied this chapter, you should be able to

- explain the differences between equality of access, equality of opportunity and equity in physical education and sport;
- describe some of the ways inequity can be seen in sport policies, provision and participation in Australia;
- explain, using Figueroa's framework, the various ways, times and places in which inequity is reinforced and can be challenged; and
- identify how you can personally play a part in promoting equity in and through physical education and sport.

Although you may not always realise it, whenever you participate in physical activity, you either contribute to or challenge inequities—in schools, in sport and in societies. You may be able to recall a situation in which you chose not to pass to another player who you feared would be clumsy or slow, or who might let your team down. Perhaps other players have marginalised or excluded you from play in such ways. This scenario is just one example of inequity in sport. It shows that we all have a role to play in making physical education and sport more equitable and enjoyable for more people. This chapter explores the complexities of equity and the various ways in which we may challenge inequities in physical education and sport.

DEFINING EQUITY

equity:
An idea concerned with social justice, fairness, opportunity and the valuing of differences.

Uncertainty about the meaning of the term **equity** is understandable. It is widely used in relation to policies and practices in physical education and sport. However, there is not one shared understanding of equity. Often *equity* is interchanged with *equality, equal opportunity* and (more recently) *inclusion*. Taking a closer look at these various terms is a useful starting point for discussion.

Providing Access

Historically, many of the developments that have claimed to promote equality or equal opportunities in physical education and sport have focused on the issue of access to activities and facilities. For example, schools and clubs are often concerned to extend provision in order to enable a group of people currently not participating to have access to the particular activity or facility. In England, many schools have arranged for both boys and girls to play soccer, rather than it being a sport that is only available for boys.

Exploring Opportunities

Your own school may claim that offering all students the opportunity to participate in the same physical education activities, rather than having girls and boys do different activities, provides all students with equal opportunity. However, offering the same activity does not ensure that all students have the same chance to develop their interests and abilities in the activity. Each person's experience of an activity is not the same. Some players tend to dominate a game, whereas others are hardly involved. Teachers and coaches cannot give everyone their attention all of the time. In addition, people come to the activity with different experiences and abilities that influence their participation in the activity and their levels of performance. You can see these differences when you go to a sports club for the first time, try a new activity in physical education or attend trials for a school team. You may notice people who have obviously played the sport before or people who are less experienced and skilful than you are.

Developing Inclusive Practices

Unless teachers and coaches recognise and address these kinds of differences among people, they will not succeed in providing everyone with an equal opportunity to participate. If we consider opportunity rather than merely access, we need to explore questions like these: Does everyone have an equal chance to play an active role in a lesson or club practice? Do some players dominate the lesson or practice? Does everyone have an equal opportunity to improve skills, or do the drills and expectations suit only some of the players? Differences in skills and abilities are therefore an important consideration if teachers and coaches are interested in offering everyone an equal opportunity to improve personal performance. Acknowledging these variations and developing personalised practices are essential planning steps if physical education and sport are to be meaningful for all the children involved.

TARGETING GROUPS AND PROVIDING FOR INDIVIDUALS

In Australia and elsewhere, specific groups of people have not had adequate opportunities to participate in physical activity and sport. Many initiatives have attempted to broaden participation by removing barriers to physical activity and sport. Women, young people, disabled people, people over 50 and members of ethnic groups have all, at various times, been defined as **target groups** by policy makers for a variety of sports. Initiatives have attempted to overcome barriers such as the location of facilities or clubs, the cost of participation and the timing of sessions. Activity planners have also had to consider whether particular groups of people are happy or willing to participate in mixed-sex settings. The stated aim has been to offer more people the opportunity to participate in physical activity and sport.

One of the Australian Sports Commission's initiatives is the Willing and Able Program. This program has sought to improve and extend opportunities in physical activity and sport for people with disabilities. Other programs address issues such as

- the time of day that activities are provided, so that mothers can participate when their children are at school; and
- the need for exercise classes for women only, in order to encourage the participation of women who may feel self-conscious exercising and wearing sports clothing in the company of men.

A later focus activity will highlight the way in which many equity initiatives relating to physical activity tend to focus on people who are grouped by an association with a particular personal characteristic. This approach has significant and often unintended consequences. The tendency is to view the various categories as separate from one another. For example, some programs target women as a group, separate from people with disabilities or people of a different race. Gender, ethnicity, age, socioeconomic status and disability are characteristics that equal opportunity or equity programs frequently use to identify target groups. However, is this sort of classification a sound basis from which to try to meet individual needs? In identifying groups by single characteristics, policy makers and program providers tend to ignore many individual differences within the identified social groups. Members of a group may share a common trait (such as their age), but this is only one characteristic. Individuals within the group vary, for example, in their abilities, religious beliefs, disposable income and family responsibilities. All of these differences influence a person's ability to access the opportunities provided for the target group they are placed in. Thus the target group approach overlooks critical differences found within any group.

Obviously all women do not all have the same needs when it comes to participating in physical activity and sport. Some women are confined to wheelchairs. Some women, because of their particular religious beliefs, must wear certain clothing to cover parts of their bodies that other women are happy to expose. Their clothing can make it difficult to participate in physical activity. Some women are able to pay to have a personal exercise trainer, whereas others might not be able to afford to go to a gym. Equity policies or initiatives rarely acknowledge these realities and therefore they typically create opportunities for only some members of the group that they target.

Another group that equity initiatives typically target is that of people with disabilities. Few planners appreciate the extent or importance of differences among this group. For example, you can distinguish people with intellectual impairments from those with physical impairments. Of the people with physical impairments, not all use wheelchairs; even those who do have different capacities or needs. People in wheelchairs vary greatly in terms of the extent to which their movement and physical strength are impaired. Some people can still use their abdominal muscles, whereas others cannot—a distinction that has a crucial impact on the degree of mobility they have. Those individuals without abdominal control and strength struggle to push themselves up some of the

target group:
A group of people identified as a focus of a policy or development initiative for physical activity or sport.

ramps that are supposed to provide access to people with disabilities. If they participate in wheelchair marathon racing, they need to stick to flat courses. People with disabilities also come from various cultures and have different financial resources. They can be of any age and can be male or female. Some people in wheelchairs can afford racing chairs with the latest wheel and frame technology (similar to those seen in cycling), whereas others cannot. Sport for people with disabilities generates as much of an industry as sport for those without disabilities, but not everyone with disabilities is equally able to benefit from products that the industry has to offer.

The examples of diversity among disabled people illustrate how important differences exist within as well as between groups who are categorised as disadvantaged. This diversity gives rise to inequalities in the opportunities that people have to participate in activities and improve their performances. It is the combination and interaction of many factors, rather than any single factor by itself, that give people an advantage or disadvantage in relation to the extent and quality of their participation in physical activities. Equity initiatives for physical activity and sport need to recognise the important overlaps and interactions between categories of people and the many factors that affect their participation. The danger is that initiatives do not adequately account for these complexities, a failing that limits the success of sports policies and programs.

• • • Focus Activity —

LOCAL PARTICIPATION CAMPAIGNS

Purpose

To understand the extent to which local participation campaigns can cater for all relevant groups in the community.

Materials

Brochures, posters, television advertisements and newspaper articles.

Procedure

1. Identify current local participation initiatives or campaigns by contacting and interviewing an officer of a local or state level organisation such as
   - the local town or city council,
   - the state government office of sport and recreation,
   - the state government office of health or
   - the national heart foundation.
2. Collect any brochures, posters or other materials that have been developed as part of the campaign. Scan the newspapers for relevant articles, and watch the television for advertisements and news items. Contact and interview a few people who currently participate, or previously participated, in the campaign.

Written Task

Describe the campaign, its goals, its personnel, its facilities and its procedures. Make particular note of which groups the campaign targets, which problems in existing provision the campaign attempts to address and which problems or issues you think it fails to address.

INDIVIDUAL DIFFERENCES: A PROBLEM OR AN ASSET?

Another critical shortcoming of many target group initiatives is that they start by viewing things from what we term a deficit perspective. They identify groups as not meeting expected or hoped for levels of involvement in physical activity and sport. Then they develop strategies to raise those levels and thereby reduce perceived imbalances in participation and performance statistics across social groups.

EXTENSION ACTIVITY

LOCAL PARTICIPATION CAMPAIGNS

When you have completed reading the focus activity on page 122, conduct further data collection (interviews) on the initiative or campaign that you identified. Determine whether it provided for the needs of all people within the group it targeted. Identify the people within the group whose needs the campaign met and those whose needs it failed to meet. Develop some strategies to overcome any problems you identify.

The assumptions and value judgements that are inherent in these strategies are rarely discussed. Few people stop to consider that initiatives that revolve around trying to equalise participation reflect a seriously limited approach to inclusion in physical activity and sport. The assumption is that established, dominant forms of physical activity are desirable for, and desired by, non-participants. Interests in alternative activities and personal reasons for participating are often overlooked. Programs define lack of participation in particular sports as the problem and present their solutions accordingly.

Questionable assumptions are evident when we consider attempts to increase the number of young people who participate actively in sport. Many policies have focused on recruiting more young people to become members of sports clubs. Policy makers assume that this is the type of opportunity young people want. Obviously, some young people welcome the opportunity to pursue their abilities in a particular sport and have ambitions to become involved in high-level competition in that sport (you may be one of those people). However, you may have friends who have no such desires or ambitions. They may want to be involved in physical activity and sport, but for very different reasons—perhaps for fun, friendship and general health. Can junior sports clubs provide for their needs and interests?

In addition to having varied reasons for participating, many young people may not want to commit themselves to a particular sport. They may want to have a go at several different activities instead. Some people may not want sessions to be dominated by coaching directed towards improvements in performance. Rather, they may want to enjoy taking part without pressure to reach higher levels of performance. Should we view these different interests as problematic? Should we compare people's participation to a chosen norm that we think everyone should want to achieve?

Defining a norm is not a neutral process. In making a judgement about what is normal, we are privileging some people's values and interests over others. The idea that a normal section of Australian society exists, which identified target groups should conform to, is misleading and inaccurate. The fact that fewer women participate in sports activities compared with men does not imply that women are somehow deficient. Asian-Australians may be less likely than some other Australians to participate in swimming, but this disparity does not mean that people within that ethnic group are somehow at fault or lacking. In looking at policies that target specific groups, we must once again ask some searching questions:

- What specific opportunities are provided for individuals within the various groups?
- What assumptions are made about the needs and interests of those individuals?
- Whose values and interests are reflected in and furthered by the initiatives?

SAMPLE LEARNING EXPERIENCE

Social Barriers and Cricket

Stephen's class was studying cricket. Stephen was not a good cricketer and found the unit on cricket tough going. Although he tried hard, it was obvious that his ability and experience were well behind those of some other students in his class.

While Stephen's class studied the cricket unit, his teacher set some reading about social factors affecting participation in physical activity and sport. It turned out that there were more sedentary people in Australia than was commonly thought. As the class worked through the material, Stephen began to understand that the reasons for people being physically inactive were not, in most cases, factors such as laziness or ignorance. In addition to poor health or disability, a range of social factors influenced people's level of activity—where they lived, their families' and friends' interest in sport, the amount of money available to them and how much free time they had. To illustrate the idea that there are social barriers to participation in sport, Stephen's teacher set the class an exercise for the next cricket lesson.

Stephen's class assembled on the oval for their cricket lesson. At the beginning of the lesson, the teacher gave the class a few items to make notes about. They had to

- list every item of cricket apparel that should be worn by a cricketer at different stages of the game and then attach an estimated value to each item,
- identify any family members who played cricket in the past or present,
- identify any cricket equipment that they or their families owned,
- indicate whether they were members of a cricket team for a club or school and
- estimate the distance between their homes and the nearest cricket club and training facilities.

The task was specifically designed to help students reflect on their own circumstances. Stephen found out some interesting things about his experiences of cricket and his access to the sport. This task helped him to identify possible reasons that his skill development and tactical awareness in cricket lagged so far behind those of many of his classmates.

Explanation

When Stephen began to list all of the protective equipment used by cricketers, he began to realise just how expensive the sport could be. The cost of a bat, leg pads, gloves and various other pieces of protective equipment could easily amount to hundreds of dollars (although some costs could be offset by using club or school equipment and by sharing). The class had discussed the influence of socioeconomic status on participation in sport; clearly, the cost of cricket was an example of how a person's social background could affect access to a sport. Stephen's parents had a reasonable income, but with five children in the family, they had no money to spare for the added expense of cricket. He doubted that his family could support the cost of him playing cricket, even if he did want to take it up seriously.

Stephen could not identify any family members who were particularly interested in cricket. His older brothers played basketball, and his father spent so much time working on the family farm in his youth that he hardly had time for sport of any kind. Stephen did not own any personal cricket gear, nor was he a member of a club or school cricket team. In fact, the cricket facility closest to Stephen's family farm was the school cricket ground, 35 kilometres away.

Because Stephen's parents had a farm, they tended to work long hours, and weekends were no exception. They enjoyed watching sport but generally did so only when they caught the highlights on the news at night. Stephen helped on the farm on weekends and after school. He concluded that he did not have a lot of time to spare for a sport like cricket, after helping on the farm.

Stephen recognised through the class activity that his social circumstances were not conducive to playing a great deal of cricket. His older brothers had mounted a basketball backboard on the garage, and he spent what recreational time he had playing basketball with his brothers and sisters. When he thought about it, he realised that basketball suited the family well. It was not costly in terms of equipment; a ball, a hoop and a pair of shoes were all it required. His older brothers played competition in town one night a week, and Stephen thought that he might take that up as well. Playing at night meant that his parents could drive him to play. The games lasted just on an hour, which was much more convenient for his parents than waiting around for a whole day of cricket.

The fact that Stephen's older brothers played basketball was also a factor that steered him into basketball. The same thing was likely to happen with his two younger sisters. Something of a basketball culture was present in the house. Stephen recognised that the same influences existed in cricketing families or families that valued other sports.

Stephen's conclusions became even clearer when he shared views with classmates and discovered that the best cricketers were in a different situation than he was. They had grown up with circumstances that made cricket an attractive and viable sporting option. They lived in reasonable proximity to facilities, and most had enough spare time on weekends and after school to devote time to the game. Many had a family history of cricket, and they were all from families who were able to absorb the expenses of the sport in their family budgets.

COMMITMENT TO EQUITY

Being committed to equity in physical education and sport means more than just acknowledging differences. It means celebrating and valuing differences. It means not regarding any one set of values or behaviours as superior to others—the norm to judge others against. Rather, we recognise that we must always view behaviours and values in their temporal and cultural contexts. At different times and in different places and cultures, people may regard a variety of behaviours and values as normal and desirable.

prejudice:
The practice of making judgements or holding beliefs about people on the basis of assumptions about characteristics of the groups to which they belong, rather than on the basis of personal knowledge about an individual.

stereotyping:
The belief that every individual who belongs to a particular group displays characteristics that are associated with that group. It classifies all individuals within a group as the same in particular respects.

Equity in physical education and sport demands that we not only recognise social and cultural differences but also value how they enrich societies. To promote equity, policies and practices need to regard individual differences in a positive framework. Celebrating and valuing difference is at the heart of the concern for equity. As sociologists Evans and Davies point out, 'the issue must not be whether differences can be dissolved . . . but how they can be celebrated in ways which negate **prejudice** and **stereotyping** and at the same time respect individual cultural identity' (1993, p. 19).

Promoting equity in physical education and sport in Australia therefore necessitates that we value all people in Australian society and appreciate their differences. When we address equity in relation to participation in physical activity and sport, we must consider not only whether opportunities are distributed equally and fairly among the population but also whether individual interests, values and life circumstances are taken into account.

You are probably aware of the pressures that many people feel to be a particular shape or size, particularly if they wish to become involved in physical activity. Society deems some body types to be more acceptable and desirable than others are. It portrays some body shapes and sizes as having a rightful place in sporting arenas but does not represent others this way. Greater value is assigned to participation and performance in certain favoured sports, or to the performances of men as compared with those of women. Many inequities remain in Australian society, both in schools and in sport. The media plays a critical role in promoting particular values and interests, and especially in portraying certain body images as acceptable and desirable. We should never set ourselves apart from these issues; we all have a part to play in challenging inequity.

PROMOTING EQUITY: A FRAMEWORK FOR UNDERSTANDING AND ACTION

Equity is a complex and challenging concept. It has many dimensions and far-reaching implications for policies and practices in physical education and sport. A framework developed by Figueroa (1993) is useful in exploring these dimensions and their implications at various levels of provision for physical education and sport. The framework consists of five levels that link together—individual, interpersonal, institutional, structural and cultural. The relationship between the levels works both ways; each level is shaped to some extent by the ones above and below it. The interaction of levels shows that we all play an active part in either creating and reinforcing inequities or challenging them.

Individual Level

Figueroa's first level directly concerns us as individuals. The individual level considers the attitudes and beliefs that we hold about other people, about desirable and undesirable behaviours in sport, about body shape, about forms of participation and about achievement in sport. These attitudes and beliefs contribute to the creation of inequitable situations if they mean that we value some people more than others or judge people on the basis of stereotypes.

Becoming more aware of our own attitudes and beliefs is an important first step if we are to achieve equity in physical education and sporting contexts. Our experiences as members of particular families, clubs, schools, societies and cultural groups shape our attitudes and beliefs. However, as members of these various groups, we actively contribute to the attitudes and beliefs that they instil in others.

Interpersonal Level

The dynamics between ourselves and others create the next level in this framework for equity, the interpersonal level. This level concerns the ways in which we interact with one another. It covers all forms of communication, including both oral communication and body language. In the context of physical education and sport, what people say to one another is an important consideration. However, there are also many non-verbal interactions. As a member of a team you might not say anything to anyone, either on your own team or the opposing one. However, you contribute to the creation of either an equitable or inequitable environment by how you play, how you interact with other players, to whom you pass or do not pass, and how you react to an aggressive tackle or an unfavourable decision.

Valuing differences promotes inclusiveness in physical education and sport. How children treat one another can influence how they feel about themselves, particularly in physical education at school. Unfortunately many young people may leave school with no desire to participate further in physical activity and sport because of the way other pupils have treated them. Teachers and coaches can influence individual feelings of competence and can be key people in encouraging involvement. Developing personalised programs and goals to suit individual abilities and interests is critical to ensuring that everyone benefits from participation in an activity and feels a sense of personal value and accomplishment. To promote equity, teachers and coaches need to develop appropriate practices and set realistic goals for everyone in a class, team or club. Ultimately, everyone contributes to equitable interpersonal relations in particular institutional, social and cultural contexts.

Institutional Level

At the institutional level we are concerned with the way routine practices in society and its institutions (such as schools, sports clubs and organisations) advantage or disadvantage particular groups of people. Institutions and organisations often have firmly established regulations and procedures. People typically do not question the established ways of operating. Rather, they accept them uncritically as the way things have always been done or the only way for things to be. They rarely pause to consider the implications of regulations or procedures. However, routine practices in contexts of physical education and sport have many implications for participation, especially for the degree to which different groups of people can become active participants and improve their performance.

Earlier, we mentioned barriers to participation. In some instances, institutional practices create significant barriers to the involvement of various individuals. For example, because of their religious beliefs, some girls and women may not be able to participate in swimming unless lessons are single-sex or take place in a facility where it will not be possible for other people to view the session. If clubs and facility managers are seriously committed to equity and inclusiveness in sport, they need to consider such issues when they make decisions about the timetabling of sessions and the design of facilities.

Managers must also consider who has priority use of sport facilities, particularly at peak times. Is it recreational groups or competitive teams? Are the arrangements fair to everyone who wants to use the facilities? Decisions on these matters are not impartial. Inevitably, some people's needs and interests are advantaged over others. In part, decisions reflect commercial interests and pressures, but in the timetabling of some facilities, particular types of participation and standards of performance are privileged above others.

Most sports clubs and schools also have rules and regulations about suitable clothing and equipment for participation in physical activities. Some rules clearly relate to safety and protect the best interests of everyone. Other rules, such as dress and equipment regulations, may reflect long-standing traditions of a sport or an institution. Whatever the origins of such regulations, they can sometimes restrict participation. This restriction occurs because owning or being able to borrow or hire clothing and equipment is a prerequisite to participating.

The exclusion of lower-income youth from particular sports is still evident in Australia. Some effort has been made to reduce obvious costs associated with sports by measures such as reducing club membership fees or subsidising the purchase or loan of equipment. However, the hidden costs associated with regular participation in sport remain a barrier to involvement for many people. The location and timing of many sports club sessions in the community mean that participation is only possible for people who have access to a car for transport. This obstacle is particularly a problem for young people who wish to train hard to reach higher levels of performance. Without supportive parents who own at least one car, pursuing such ambitions may be quite difficult. Therefore, routine arrangements for access to sports clubs and facilities have both direct and indirect effects on equity.

Structural Level

resources:
A term that may refer to both physical and human assets linked to providing opportunities for participation and performance. Resources include funding for development, facilities, equipment and coaching.

The next level in the framework concerns what factors underlie some of the inequities we can observe in the policies and practices of institutions. The structural level relates to matters such as the uneven distribution of **resources** and **rewards** within sport and in society. It relates to the different social position and status that is accorded to various people, sports and levels of participation. Media coverage of sport provides clear evidence of the different status (and resources) accorded to particular sports and to certain participants or performers in sport (to men as compared with women or to elite rather than recreational participants).

Cultural Level

rewards:
Direct or indirect incentives or benefits for participation in sport. Rewards include direct payment opportunities to gain sponsorship and support for training.

Media coverage of sport also reflects dominant beliefs, values and behavioural norms that feature in society and sport. Analysis at the cultural level is concerned with our shared assumptions, beliefs and values, particularly as they relate to matters such as gender, ability and ethnicity. Sometimes these assumptions or beliefs are misguided or simplify complex issues. For example, many sports are still regarded as men's or women's sports, and particular abilities or behaviours are still seen as inherently masculine or feminine. Assumptions and beliefs about the capabilities of each sex and about the types of participation appropriate for men as opposed to women deny the diversity among men and women.

Inequity operating at this cultural level often means that significant differences in abilities, interests and values are overlooked or denied. Implications then become explicit at other levels in the framework. Comparative studies are particularly useful in drawing attention to inequity at the cultural level. Different practices in other countries can point to assumptions about cultural values and norms and to the ways in which differences are reflected in, and actively reinforced by, society and its institutions. For example, in the United Kingdom men's sports, elite performances in sport and elite level men's soccer in particular dominate the sports pages of national newspapers. Sports that feature regularly in the Australian press, such as swimming, do not have the same cultural significance or social standing there.

Sport and physical education are arenas in which the reinforcement of social and cultural norms, beliefs and values is at times obvious and at other times quite subtle. Often we remain unaware of these processes of social and cultural reinforcement and of our own part in sustaining inequities in sport, schools and society. We can celebrate the good things sport has to offer to many people in society. At the same time, we must not forget to ask who is marginalised or excluded from the enjoyment and sense of achievement that sport participation can provide. We must always look critically at the values being promoted by the events and achievements that we are celebrating. Major international events, such as the Olympic Games, provide a useful focus for reflection. We can question whose values and interests are reflected in the modern Olympics, which groups in society benefit from such events, and what social values the Olympic Games promote.

Interaction Between Levels

People's attitudes and beliefs can influence their interpersonal behaviour in physical activity and sport settings. Interpersonal behaviour in turn can shape how institutions develop. Figueroa's framework enables us to understand better the transmission of inequity through the various levels of society. It also prepares us to challenge inequity at each level. For example, in relation to the social construction of masculinity and femininity, a tendency exists in many sporting arenas to marginalise boys who are not aggressive or assertive. Consider whether boys are free to show an individual interest in aesthetic activities such as dance or gymnastics. Think about how we can address the barriers that boys with such an interest might face at cultural, structural, institutional and at interpersonal levels, and about the ways in which changes at one level may generate changes at other levels.

••• Focus Activity —

EQUITY IN PHYSICAL EDUCATION CLASSES

Purpose

To identify instances of discrimination or exclusion in the physical education experiences of students.

Procedure

Reflect on your own experiences as a learner in physical education classes or in a sports club and share these reflections with a small group of classmates. Make notes on the following issues:

- What instances showed that discrimination or exclusion occurred?
- Whom did these behaviours disadvantage?
- Why do you think inequities occurred?
- What were some instances of equitable interpersonal interactions?

Written Task

Summarise the main points from the group discussion. Indicate whether your experiences of inequity in physical education were typical or atypical for this class. Identify some strategies that could minimise or eliminate the occurrence of inequity and enhance equitable relationships in physical education classes.

EXTENSION ACTIVITY

EXPLORING THE LEVELS OF INEQUITY

Purpose

To develop a fuller understanding of how inequity is reinforced and how we can challenge it in our schools, clubs, communities and society.

Procedure

Reflect on each of the points below, make notes and compare them with a classmate's notes:

- What are your beliefs about desirable and undesirable behaviours in sport, whose involvement matters most and what sort of participation is most important?

- In your physical education lessons, how do these beliefs influence your interactions with classmates? Are there situations in which your own actions have caused other children to leave the lesson feeling that they have failed? Identify ways in which you and others can behave differently to ensure that everyone enjoys physical education and feels they have achieved something.

- Think about the arrangements for participation and coaching in your school and local clubs, including rules that govern participation. Can you identify arrangements or rules that resonate with your own beliefs written under the first question?

- What are the intrinsic and extrinsic rewards associated with participation and performance in one of the sports that you have studied in senior physical education? What status do this sport and particular athletes who perform in it have in Australia? How and where is that status evident?

Written Task

Summarise the similarities and differences between your reflections and those of your classmate. Emphasise how your thoughts relate to the various levels within Figueroa's framework.

1. List some examples of how each of the following factors may influence participation in sport. Consider access, opportunity and equity in your answers: (a) age, (b) ability level, (c) body shape or size, (d) sex, (e) religious beliefs, (f) disabilities, (g) income and (h) culture. Which ones have affected you personally?

2. Explain the ways in which differences between individuals are viewed (a) from an equality perspective and (b) from an equity perspective.

3. List the five levels in which issues of equity operate, as identified by Figueroa, and explain the two-way connections between the various levels.

Body, Culture and Physical Activity

Chapter Overview

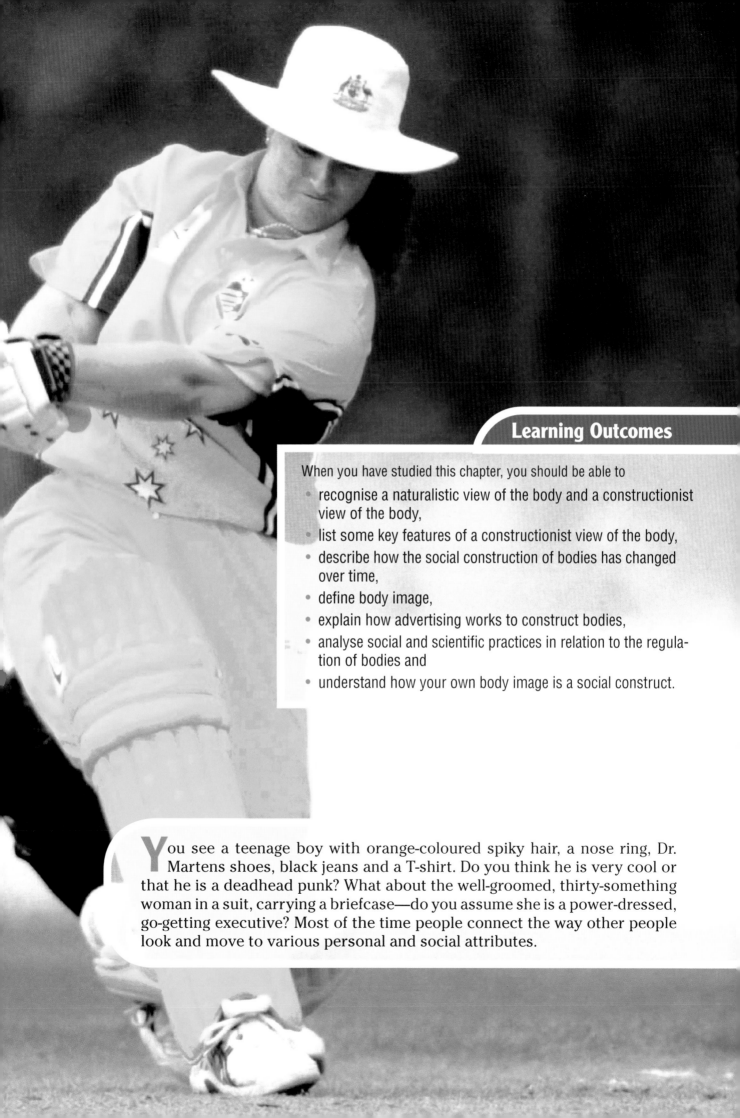

You see a teenage boy with orange-coloured spiky hair, a nose ring, Dr. Martens shoes, black jeans and a T-shirt. Do you think he is very cool or that he is a deadhead punk? What about the well-groomed, thirty-something woman in a suit, carrying a briefcase—do you assume she is a power-dressed, go-getting executive? Most of the time people connect the way other people look and move to various personal and social attributes.

SOCIAL CONSTRUCTION OF BODIES

social construction of bodies:
A process of attaching social values to particular body shapes and sizes.

The process of connecting how people look or how they move with a personality trait or social value is described as the **social construction of bodies.** It can be quite a complex process. Your personal life experiences and the values and attitudes you share with your friends play a big part in how you look at the bodies of others. Your own body image and those of your friends affect how you connect other people's body shapes, movements and clothing styles with personal and social values.

The process of socially constructing bodies makes connections between the physical features of bodies and the social values that are either shared or prominent among groups in Australian society. The gender of a person greatly influences whether we think of another person's body as normal or ideal. For instance, we may judge the shape and size of a woman's body by social values that are different from the ones we use for men. We may view a large woman negatively, as mannish or unfeminine, but a large man as strong and manly—a more positive assessment (see figure 9.1).

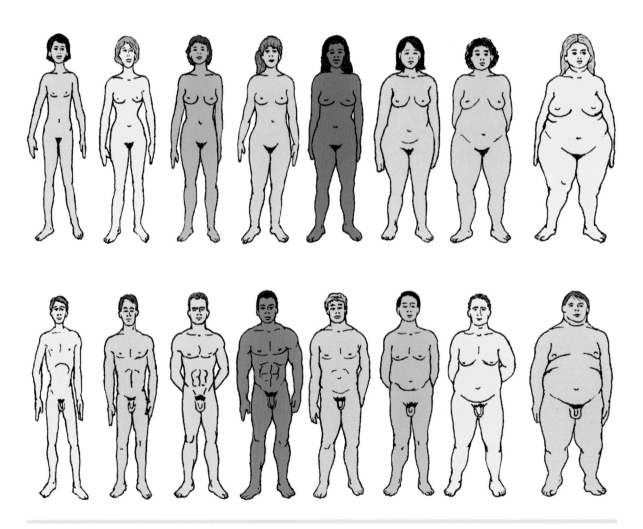

Figure 9.1   Select the figure that best represents your body type. In a survey conducted by the *Herald Sun,* 27 June 1992, subjects were asked to select their own body type from figures similar to those above. Ninety-five percent of women selected a body type that was fatter than they actually were, but men consistently selected body types slimmer and more muscular than their own.

••• *Focus Activity* —

SPORT AND THE IDEAL BODY

Purpose

To show that body shapes and sizes vary according to a performer's sport and role in their sport.

Materials

Photographs from magazines of the following sports participants: Rugby Union prop forward, netball goal attack, soccer goalkeeper, downhill skier, surf life-saver, golfer and gymnast.

Procedure

1. Collect photographs of the sports performers listed under materials.

2. In a small group, discuss and write down the body shapes of each performer and how their body shapes relate to their roles in their sport. Note differences and similarities between the sports performers.

3. Discuss the idea that there is an ideal body for each sport and note the main points that arise in your discussion.

Written Tasks

- Use your notes from the group discussion to evaluate the relationship between body shapes and sports. Is there an ideal body shape for sports participation in general? Justify your response. Write a short comment on whether the sex of the sports performer makes any difference to your views on the ideal body for each sport.

- If you wish, add your own favourite sport to the list. Then discuss the similarities and differences you have identified for performers in your list of sports. In a paragraph, write down what your results tell us about the social construction of bodies.

NATURALISTIC AND CONSTRUCTIONIST VIEWS OF THE BODY

The human body was a neglected topic in the social sciences until recently. Many social scientists acknowledged the individual within society, but relatively few extended their analyses to include the part people's bodies played in producing and reproducing social practices.

Part of the reason for this neglect was the success of the biological sciences in providing explanations for the body's structure and function. People tended to take for granted that bodies are flesh, blood and bones and the relevance of biological explanations of the body seemed self-evident.

On the occasions when social scientists did turn their attention to the body, their theories tended to reflect the **naturalistic view of the body,** which sees

naturalistic view of the body:
A view that the body is to be understood only in terms of muscle, bone and other tissue.

the human body as a primarily biological entity. This view led to claims that differences in sport performance between men and women can be explained solely in terms of biological factors such as strength (men are stronger) and psychological factors such as motivation (men are more aggressive). It produced similar arguments to explain racial differences in sport performance. Social scientists who still subscribe to a naturalistic view of the body assume that these differences explain variations in behaviour and in a wide range of social practices. In other words, they see differences in sex, colour, size and other physical attributes as the cause of how people behave and what they believe.

A problem with the naturalistic view is that it is too deterministic. An example of determinism is the notion that a social behaviour, such as behaving in ways typically associated with being masculine, is dependent on and determined by biological factors such as muscularity and physical size. However, recent work of sociologists, historians and cultural theorists challenges the naturalistic view of the body. Many social scientists have advanced the view that people develop an understanding of their bodies in large part because of the society in which they live. The social scientists claim that bodies are socially constructed at the same time that they are biologically constructed. In other words, they argue that the body is in nature and in culture simultaneously.

A **constructionist view of the body** suggests that biology does not determine social behaviour. In the case of **masculinity,** social constructionists point out that there are different forms of masculinity and a variety of social behaviours that people associate with being masculine. Some groups in society may consider a large, muscular physique to be an essential quality of masculinity. Other groups, however, may consider men who are not physically large or muscular to be just as masculine.

A social constructionist view suggests that how people communicate with their bodies is important to understanding how and why people, both as individuals and in groups, behave in the ways they do. People use their bodies to transmit messages, which are sometimes called **body language.** People also receive messages from the bodies of others, such as the appropriate ways for males to dress. This is why, with only a few specific exceptions, boys and men in Australian society do not wear skirts or dresses.

People's bodies reflect dominant social norms and values. Individuals do have some choices in relation to these norms. However, if a male chooses to wear some kind of skirt or dress, he is still sending messages about either his ethnicity or his personal identity.

Social and biological factors interact in all of these examples of how people perceive bodies and relate them to behaviours. A naturalistic view of the body stresses only one side of the process and presents social behaviour as inherently connected to biology. A social constructionist view of the body, in contrast, allows social scientists to analyse

- how bodies are constructed at different times in history,
- how body image interacts with self-esteem,
- how the media play a part in attributing social values to bodies and
- how bodies are involved in the regulation of behaviour.

constructionist view of the body:
A view that the body is both biological and social.

masculinity:
Qualities that society values as being characteristic of males, such as physical strength and aggression.

body language:
A term that describes the use of the body to communicate information, either consciously or unconsciously.

EXTENSION ACTIVITY

SOCIAL CONSTRUCTS

Consider This

Consider how the question of the social construction of the body might apply to the physical activity you are currently studying. To what extent have changes over the years, to the uniform and other clothing used in this activity, been due to biological and social factors?

Think and Write

- Think about the designs of the uniforms used in a wide range of sports.
- To what extent do the designs of the uniforms meet the particular requirements of the sport?
- To what extent do the designs exaggerate body shape and size?
- How might you link these factors to the social construction of feminine and masculine bodies?

Compare and Contrast

Are there any differences between the uniforms worn by women and men in this physical activity? Compare your current activity with others you have studied or participated in. Were there differences in men's and women's uniforms? Why do you think these differences exist or do not exist? Are the differences due to the biology of women and men or to issues of femininity and masculinity?

CHANGING CONCEPTIONS OF THE BODY AND PHYSICAL ACTIVITY

When you think about what might be a normal or ideal body, you will realise that deciding what is ideal is a more complex issue than it may appear at first. A body type that is ideal for one sport may be ill suited for various others. The fact that not all sports require the same type of body is just one example of how we can consider many different shapes and sizes of bodies to be normal or ideal.

Many other factors influence our social constructions of bodies. We have already mentioned the gender of the person as a factor. Age and stage of development, as shown in figure 9.2, are other key elements, as is lifestyle.

A naturalistic view of the body encourages the idea that the human body has remained constant over time—that bodies were much the same in the past as they are now. If you consider the process of evolution, however, you can see that this conjecture has not been proven. People of different races have developed physical differences such as skin colour, facial features, length of limbs, and so on. Even within racial groups like Caucasians, there have been important developments over time, such as changes in height. The knights in shining armour of the fourteenth and fifteenth centuries were often no more than five feet tall. More recently, in the latter part of the twentieth century, evidence suggests that people in western nations such as Australia are becoming taller and heavier.

Figure 9.2   Did you know that Michael Jordan did not make his sophomore year (year 10) basketball team? At 178 cm, he was considered too small. He was what is known as a late bloomer. He is now 198 cm tall. If he had undergone Australia's current talent identification test, it would have led him to believe that he would never be any good at basketball.

© SportsChrome

The changes in bodies over time have been more than just physical. The ways in which people have socially constructed bodies have also changed. Changes in the shared values of groups in society cause these changes in people's social constructions of bodies. One obvious example is the history of fashion. At various times in recent Australian history, women and men have worn different kinds of clothes than we wear today. Changes in the styles of sports attire over the last one hundred years or so, such as the alterations in women's tennis outfits (see figure 9.3) or the evolution of swimming costumes, provide clear examples of changes in the social constructions of bodies.

a

b

c

Figure 9.3   Female tennis players: *(a)* 1905, *(b)* 1970 and *(c)* 1990s.
© Sport The Library

••• *Focus Activity —*

WOMEN'S SPORTS CLOTHING AND CHANGING SOCIAL VALUES

Purpose

To show how changing social values are evident in changing styles of female tennis players' clothing.

Procedure

1. Examine the photographs of female tennis players in figure 9.3.
2. In a small group, discuss how their clothing has changed and what these changes might suggest about developing social values.

- Describe the changes that have taken place in women's tennis attire. Write down the transformations in social values that may have allowed the alterations in female tennis players' clothing to take place.

- Think of examples that illustrate the range of ways in which bodies are constructed by finding examples of what people in different cultures consider to be attractive or beautiful.

SAMPLE LEARNING EXPERIENCE

Social Construction and Swimming

Sally was doing an assignment about social construction of the body as part of her swimming unit. The assignment proved to be particularly interesting to Sally, since it forced her to re-evaluate her perceptions about her own body and to examine more closely the social behaviour of other students in her swimming class.

Sally's assignment was to research the history of the swimsuit in Australia. She had to explain how changes to swimsuit design might be an outcome of, and perhaps a contributor to, changing attitudes toward the body. She then had to relate her findings to social interactions she observed among students during her swimming classes.

Sally's analysis of a variety of pictures in both historical texts and recent magazines revealed that swimsuits have changed considerably over the past 100 years. Early swimsuits for both men and women were full-length costumes so that only the hands, feet and head were exposed. Sally thought that the women's suits looked coquettish and ultra-feminine, whereas suits for men were generally plain. During the first 50 years of the twentieth century, swimwear gradually became briefer, revealing more and more of the body.

Sally discovered, to her surprise, that the first appearance of the two-piece bikini in the late 1950s caused a sensation and much public outcry. Far from provoking a backlash and a return to the older styles of swimsuit, however, the bikini initiated a trend for both men and women to wear increasingly skimpy and more revealing swimsuits. This trend continued through the 1960s, 1970s and 1980s.

Sally found that in the 1990s there appeared to be a growing market for swimsuits that covered and protected much of the body. She wondered whether concerns about the relationship between exposure to the sun and skin cancer might have been responsible for persuading swimsuit manufacturers to introduce a more protective style.

Sally noted that the ideal bodies displayed in swimwear had changed over time. These changes had affected both men and women. From the early 1900s to the 1930s, for example, she noted that the ideal male body looked like what we might now think of as a circus strong man. Sally came across several pictures of heavily muscled, relatively short men with moustaches, in classical Greek poses. She recorded the differences between this ideal body and the currently dominant ideal. She noted that today men are still required to display good musculature, but they are also required to be taller, with broad shoulders, tight washboard abdominals and narrow hips.

The ideal body for women had also changed, perhaps even more dramatically than that for men. The pictures that Sally found of women in swimsuits at the end of the nineteenth century showed a softer and rounder ideal than subsequent ideals. Swimsuits were modest and discreet, revealing very little of the female body. For the period spanning the 1920s to the 1950s, Sally thought she could distinguish at least two ideals.

The first ideal female body was the outdoor, athletic woman in a plain, practical swimsuit. These women looked healthy and physically capable, and Sally thought they looked the same as an average woman in the 1990s, except for the styles of their swimsuits. She discovered that the second ideal body was more explicitly feminine. This ideal grew increasingly curvaceous as swimsuits began to reveal more of the female body, from the 1950s onward. Sally concluded that the 1990s ideal, the tall woman with broad shoulders, long legs and slim hips, was almost the complete opposite of the earliest photographs she discovered. The high-cut, one-piece suits of the 1980s and 1990s seemed to have been designed for this slender kind of body, rather than bodies like hers and those of most of the females she knew.

Explanation

Sally's class had been studying the social regulation of body image in relation to physical activity, in this case swimming. Central to Sally's interpretation of the history and current status of swimsuit design was her understanding of a constructionist view of the body. She explained in her assignment that over time the change in the notion of an ideal body is difficult to justify using a naturalistic argument. A naturalistic view would suggest that changes in swimsuit design and corresponding changes in the ideal body for men and women were due to biological changes in each new generation. However, Sally argued that a period of 100 years was too short for biology to be the main factor.

Instead, Sally argued from the social constructionist point of view that social circumstances brought about alterations in what people perceived to be the ideal body. She stated that in the current age of mass visual media, it is possible to use bodies very effectively to sell products and ideas associated with the products. Television and video make it easier to view the body voyeuristically. Since Sally believed that everyone lives in a patriarchal society dominated by masculine interests, she decided that women's bodies in particular come under voyeuristic scrutiny. She suggested that these scenarios affected all females and males, not just the people who model swimsuits.

When Sally began to apply these insights to social interactions between students in her swimming class, she highlighted the following points:

- Most girls wore T-shirts over their one-piece swimming costumes. Most tried to get into the water as quickly as possible. Any comments made by boys or teachers about their bodies were extremely embarrassing for the girls and sometimes caused them to make up excuses to avoid swimming.

- These actions were evidence of the girls' self-consciousness about their bodies. This self-consciousness was a symptom of voyeuristic scrutiny of female bodies in general, which was encouraged by media representations of ideal bodies.
- Most boys wore board shorts rather than swimming trunks. The majority seemed not to mind that their bodies were on view, and some seemed to enjoy it. The boys frequently made derogatory comments to some girls about their bodies. The boys also made derogatory comments to some other boys about their bodies.

Sally considered these points carefully, because she realised that the boys in her class were also affected by the factors that caused the girls to behave the way they did. It seemed that boys, for the most part, were allowed to display their bodies without being made to feel self-conscious. Perhaps this difference occurred because they were being judged by different standards than the girls. Sally was aware that some of the less physically mature or less developed boys in her class showed behaviour more like that of the majority of girls than that of the other boys.

Sally found it interesting that no one in her class, either boys or girls, wore trendy swimsuits, even though they sometimes wore them at the beach. She concluded that the places and the circumstances in which people wear swimsuits influence the ways that the body is constructed. This realisation helped Sally to see that although there were dominant constructions of bodies, alternative social values could challenge them.

BODY IMAGE AND PHYSICAL ACTIVITY

An image is something that portrays, reflects or mirrors an idea or a way of thinking. **Body image** is a combination of the pictures people have of their own bodies and the values that they attribute to body shape and size. Although body image is unique to each individual, people reveal something of their body images in the ways they move, dress and decorate themselves (for example, with make-up and jewellery). Therefore body image, though personal to each of us, reflects our values and the values of people around us.

body image:
A combination of the picture people have of their own bodies and the values that they and others attach to various body shapes and sizes.

Body image influences how people construct other people's bodies. Just as constructions of bodies differ and change across time and across culture, body images change as people grow older and see their bodies change over time.

Recent research links body image to self-esteem. The findings of this research suggest that poor body image is likely to be a major contributing factor to low self-esteem among adolescents. The combination of poor body image and low self-esteem can make people reluctant to participate in physical activities. Thus they deny themselves access to a healthy and active lifestyle. However, a poor body image is often based on incorrect assumptions about normal body shape and size.

••• *Focus Activity —*

USING MEASUREMENTS TO MAKE JUDGEMENTS

Purpose

To question the validity of using physical measurements (anthropometry) to make judgements about the moral and social worth of children.

Procedure

Read the following text: At the beginning of the twentieth century, Australian researchers in a field called anthropometry were interested in measuring and comparing the bodies of children from different races. Hans-Christian Bjelke-Petersen, an eminent Australian physical culturist, undertook one of the first anthropometric studies in Australia in 1902. His intention was to obtain measurements of the physical development of Tasmanian boys and compare them to measurements of boys from other countries and races. Bjelke-Petersen and an assistant examined over 500 Hobart schoolboys. They collected data on the racial origins of the boys and a range of measures of their physical dimensions. Bjelke-Petersen concluded from his study that 'the bright pupil has fewest physical irregularities of growth, the dull pupils score slightly higher, while the criminal boys are leading by a long way. These lines indicate that the normal boy is likely to be the best boy morally'. Consistent with the long line of anthropometric research that preceded him, Bjelke-Petersen drew conclusions about the social and moral value of the boys in his study from their physical size.

Written Task

Is Bjelke-Petersen's study a valid use of anthropometry? Justify your answer.

MEDIA REPRESENTATIONS OF THE BODY

Research suggests that a major factor contributing to incorrect assumptions about normal and ideal bodies is media representations of the body. If you open just about any magazine or turn on the television, what confronts you? Bodies are on display, usually in clothing that shows off the model's body shape to best effect.

Connecting Values With the Body

Much of the time, images of bodies appear in advertisements as a means of selling a product. Sometimes the body that appears on the television screen has some obvious connection with the product being sold, as in ads for sports clothing or shoes, or for a cosmetic or health product. Often, however, there is no obvious connection between the image and the product, and the bodies in these cases are used to attract our attention to the ad. They also link the values associated with particular body shapes to the product. An example is the image of a fit and muscular athlete in an advertisement for an insurance company. In this case, the advertisers might be trying to connect the insurance company to the values you associate with a fit, successful, powerful and talented body.

Something happens to bodies when they appear as a means of selling a product. All of the familiar social values that people connect with various shapes and sizes of bodies are mixed together and repackaged, or reconstructed, in order to sell the product. **Representation** is this process of making new associations between bodies and social values.

In consumer societies, our sense of ourselves in relation to society is only possible through continuously making choices and decisions. Researchers argue that a lack of fixed traditional roles compels us into active self-formation. The acts of acquiring, consuming and throwing away are at the centre of a complex process of self-formation. Advertising is in a crucial position to give substance to this process, since it stimulates desire and offers apparent alternative personae and lifestyles from which to choose.

The material that the media supply is not absorbed passively. Each of us actively appropriates this material to make sense of ourselves and of our place in the social world. The media also manufacture our hopes and expectations of the future and provide a means of expressing our experiences. Media in consumer culture play a crucial role in the formation of our self-identities. Visual representations of the body offer important resources in the process of self-formation. Advertising in particular not only establishes bodily norms, it also stimulates desire around these norms for the ways of life that it uses the body to signify.

Advertisements accomplish ideological work at a submerged or implicit level through linking otherwise unrelated ideas. Through their more obvious function of selling products, advertisements also create structures of meaning. They reassemble or reconstruct already existing pieces of information into new combinations. By attaching a series of already meaningful elements to other already meaningful elements, advertisements create new chains of meaning.

Each of us can interpret an advertisement differently. However, if the advertisement is to be effective at selling products, consumers must interpret it in a particular way. The image is a puzzle that needs to be decoded before it can be understood. The creators of advertisements attempt to reduce the possibility of someone misunderstanding their intentions by targeting the advertisement at a specific group of readers or viewers. Moreover, for advertisements to work, they must not be taken literally. You do not really have to believe that *Persil washes whiter* or that *Coke is the real thing*. Advertisements work instead at the level researchers call the signifier—the meeting point of associations of already established chains of meaning.

Framing is the term advertisers use to describe their arrangement of material in an advertisement—what to include and what to leave out. It refers to what they intentionally include, which could be associated with the images they are presenting, and what they intentionally omit—the non-favoured information. Advertisements are put together in this calculated way so that they target particular groups of people who are potential customers for the product. Advertising can have a powerful influence on a person's body image, because advertisers can gain the attention of specific groups of people by including in the advertisement information, ideas and images they know will appeal to that group of people.

Media representations of bodies manage to reconstruct bodies, in a sense, by repackaging the associations between body types and values that people hold in their everyday lives. Researchers who subscribe to a naturalistic view of the body might argue that repackaging the associations makes the new constructions artificial. Social constructionists say that the representation of body types in the media is only one source among many through which bodies are socially constructed; the ideas about bodies that are prominent in Australian society result from the interaction of many sources.

representation:
A process of displaying the body that encourages people to make associations between the body and particular social values.

framing:
The inclusion of selected material within an advertisement and the exclusion of other appropriate but non-favoured material.

••• *Focus Activity* —

ANALYSING ADVERTISING

Purpose

To show how the body is socially constructed through advertising that uses images of bodies to sell products.

Procedure

1. From a contemporary magazine of your choice, select an advertisement that features the body as a means of selling a product. Try to select an advertisement that makes interesting or novel links between body shape or size and the product.

2. Analyse the advertisement by answering the following questions:
   - Who is in the advertisement?
   - What are they doing, how are they dressed and how are they posing?
   - What else is in the advertisement?
   - Where did the advertisement appear?
   - What is the target group for this advertisement?
   - What is the message of the advertisement?
   - How is it conveyed to you?
   - How does it work?

Written Task

Complete the same procedure with a second advertisement. In addition, write down answers to these questions:

- How does the message make you feel?
- Can you associate yourself with the message?
- How does the message intend to make a member of the target group feel?
- What values are linked to the body through its association with the product?

Commodification of the Body

When the body is used as a means of selling products through advertisements, it is drawn into the process of commodification. The social consequences of body commodification take at least two forms. Both forms turn the body into an object.

The first form of commodification involves a concern for body maintenance, in the sense that bodies require regular care and attention to preserve their efficiency and look. In this respect, bodies become sites of consumption in themselves, particularly consumption of the products and services of the beauty, cosmetics, clothing, exercise and leisure industries. Researchers suggest that this process has led to an increasingly widespread view of the body as a project. The commodified body is considered an object to be worked on according to the lifestyle choices you make, including what you eat and how you exercise.

In the second form, bodies are a focal point of the commercial process. The everyday meanings attached to bodies are reconstructed to create new associations with commercial products. Bodies are used to sell products by linking these products to particular values, such as connecting muscularity and slenderness (seen as symbols of fitness), along with health and social success, to a product such as low-fat milk.

SOCIAL REGULATION OF THE BODY THROUGH PHYSICAL ACTIVITY

Anthropologists have provided evidence of **social regulation** of the body through their research into different cultures. In some cases, people are able to do things as a matter of course that most Australians could not, such as climbing trees to collect fruit or holding their breath underwater for extraordinary lengths of time to collect oysters. On the other hand, some of the things Australians learn to do, such as swim in surf, are unknown in other cultures. These techniques of the body (as one anthropologist has named them), such as walking, running, climbing, sleeping and sexual activity, have to be learnt.

social regulation: A process of controlling bodies that involves acquiring skills and competencies that allow some bodily practices and disallow others.

The biological and biomechanical structure of the human body sets some clear limits on how the body can move. Within these constraints, some movements are reflexes, such as the reflex that occurs when the doctor taps the patellar tendon with a rubber hammer, and the knee involuntarily extends. However, within the constraints that the musculoskeletal system provides, most movements are voluntary and learnt. The process of acquiring physical competencies through learning contributes to the social construction of the body and to the regulation of social behaviour (see figure 9.4).

Physical competencies and skills that people regard as basic to a normal existence are body movements that particular groups within Australian society value. Most people are not aware of when they learnt to move in some ways and not in others. They are unaware because they learnt many of the basic movements, such as how to walk and run, how to wash and clean their teeth and even how to use the toilet, in the course of their everyday lives as children. Some activities are more complex to learn, such as the specialised skills of operating a car or machinery or specific skills for playing a sport. Usually we need help to master these physical competencies.

Regardless of the movements people master, they are engaging in the social regulation of their bodies. Learning to play a game such as basketball is a good example of this process. All games are rule-bound activities, and their rules create their characteristic forms. As soon as people agree to abide by the rules, they immediately accept the regulation of their behaviour. For instance, they agree to certain rules about where and how their bodies may move in space. They can play the game only inside the boundary lines of the court, and they must control the ways they move in relation to other players. People also learn where to move on court to their advantage—for example, how to get into a good position to shoot.

Learning the skills of basketball is another part of the social regulation process. People learn to dribble, pass and shoot the ball in particular ways because the majority of people consider those ways to be the most effective within the context of the rules and strategies of basketball.

Figure 9.4   Mastery of a physical activity can cause a person to move in the same style automatically, like the cowboy who walks bow-legged from riding his horse.

© Sport The Library

Any activity in which we learn to move in prescribed ways is a form of social regulation of the body, or corporeal regulation. Sometimes people resent corporeal regulation. Children often protest when told to walk, not run, around the side of a pool. In most cases, submitting yourself in order to learn to move in particular ways is necessary for achieving certain goals, like being a good basketball player. All of these activities contribute to the social construction of the body. The values of groups in Australian society shape the ways in which people learn to move.

People regulate their bodies by a whole array of social factors, such as media images, peer pressure, self-identity and self-esteem. In current Australian society, these social factors combine to encourage some females and males to participate in activities that maintain a slender body shape. Eating a sensible diet and taking regular exercise helps most people maintain an appropriate and healthy body weight and shape. However, when a person's pursuit of slenderness involves eating and vomiting, or not eating at all, the person may be bulimic or anorexic. Other practices that people might use to reduce their weight or produce a slender body include using diuretics and even surgical techniques such as liposuction.

Rather than trying to achieve slenderness, young men and women may try to alter their body shape, size, weight and muscularity by working out with weights. Reports indicate that some people take this practice to dangerous extremes, trying to supplement their weight-lifting exercises by taking drugs like anabolic steroids. In these cases, they are regulating their bodies through scientific developments and related social practices, such as commercial pressure on elite athletes to succeed in their sport.

SCIENTIFIC REGULATION OF THE BODY

Bodies are regulated whenever scientific processes or knowledge shape the ways that people behave. In this respect, it is hard to imagine a situation in contemporary Australian society in which science or technology does not regulate bodies to some extent. Even the simple act of crossing the road is predicated on the existence of motor vehicles, and on the knowledge of what can happen if they collide with the human body. People adapt their movements to the use of technological innovations in all aspects of everyday life. This adaptation is also true of the effect of science and technology on sport.

The scientific regulation of bodies is a highly specialised dimension of the broader process of corporeal regulation. One way that corporeal regulation takes place in sport is through the various training regimes that players or athletes participate in to prepare themselves for competition. Some sociologists and historians point out that these regimes are increasingly reliant on scientific information derived from biological, neurological and biomechanical research on the body.

You can also include recreational exercisers amongst people who engage in the scientific regulation of their bodies. Treadmill machines, now common in gyms, compute the exerciser's weight and provide information on heart rate, walking or running speed, and the amount of calories the person uses in a session. If you want to improve your cardiorespiratory endurance, knowledge derived from scientific research on the effects of training on the body suggests you should

- run, row, cycle or swim;

- move at a particular speed appropriate to your current level of fitness; and

- exercise for a set period of time.

You could reasonably describe this entire process as the scientific regulation of the body, since information obtained from scientific research shapes your movements.

This notion of the scientific regulation of bodies sounds reasonable and indeed essential to the improvement of sport performance or health enhancement through exercise. However, is there a more sinister connotation of the idea that science regulates the body? Perhaps there is if you consider the use of drugs as a means of improving performance in sport. Once again, the body and its capacities are shaped to some extent by scientific research, but this time in ways that may meet with social disapproval.

You should also consider other illustrations of a sinister side to the scientific regulation of the human body. Examples are surgical techniques that reduce body fat, such as liposuction, and perhaps the ever diminishing fractions of time used to measure performance in some sports such as track running and speed skating.

There are, without question, misuses of scientific information that may shape and regulate the body and its movements. It seems that some degree of regulation is unavoidable. Some people see regulation as desirable and necessary to the conduct of everyday life, and in particular to leading an active and healthy life. Social regulation of bodies is a key dimension of the social construction of bodies and an inevitable consequence of living with other people in both groups and communities.

REGULATING THE BODY THROUGH DRUG USE

Purpose

To question whether the use of drugs in sport is a legitimate form of the scientific regulation of the body.

Procedure

Read the following story: Lee is a very promising sprinter. For the last three years, he has been the best youth and junior male athlete in his country over both the 100 and 200 metres. Each year he has set national age group records for his events. Now he has run second in the World Junior Championships. Lee, his family and his coach are delighted. Lee thinks he is lucky to have such a good coach and access to excellent training facilities. He also has support from three major sponsors, which relieves the financial pressure on his parents, who supported him at their own expense until two years ago. For years his parents had saved and scraped together all the money they could to help him get to some of the big competitions. He is keen to be able to repay them some day.

Lee has been widely tipped to win a place in the senior nationals next year. If he does, he is assured of a trip to the World Championships. To win a place in the seniors, however, he needs to improve his time by about three-tenths of a second.

At the training track after the junior championships, an older athlete who retired from competition a year ago approached Lee. This man is still a national hero, and Lee has a lot of respect for him. The former athlete said that he thought Lee could go all the way to gold in the World Championships the following year. However, he also said that Lee was being naïve if he thought he could do it without some extra help from performance-enhancing drugs. The athlete said the use of drugs among top athletes was widespread and widely accepted, and he put forward his case very persuasively. He said he could help Lee out, and that his help would be an investment for the future. He also said Lee's coach had been approached about the drugs and was in. He said that Lee simply would not make it to the top unless he accepted the help that was on offer. Lee had always thought that taking drugs to enhance sports performance was wrong, and now he was extremely confused.

Procedure

1. Use the case study as the basis for a class debate with this topic: Is the use of drugs in sport a legitimate means of regulating the body scientifically?
2. Form teams to take the affirmative and negative sides.

Written Tasks

- Write a brief summary of the main points of each side of the debate.
- Use this information to defend your view about whether the use of drugs is a legitimate form of scientific regulation of the body.

1. What does the *social construction of bodies* mean? Use figure 9.1 to answer the survey question described in the figure caption, selecting a match for your body type. Did your result agree or disagree with what the survey found?

2. What key assumption do social scientists who subscribe to the naturalistic view of the body make? Have you ever experienced this assumption? If so, explain. How does this assumption affect your current sport?

3. The human body has been socially constructed in different ways at various periods in history. List at least two points to support this view. Is there a socially constructed body that best supports your current sport?

4. What links exist between body image and self-esteem? How will this impact upon sports such as aquatics, aerobics, touch and your current sport?

5. Select a current advertisement or write a sentence to explain how the media manipulate social values in order to sell products.

6. Write a sentence to explain the role the media play in the social construction of our bodies.

7. What does the *social regulation of the body* mean? Does this notion affect your current physical activity? If so, what impact does it have?

Lifestyle, Leisure and Physical Recreation

Chapter Overview

Learning Outcomes

When you have studied this chapter, you should be able to

- describe changing conceptions of lifestyle, leisure and recreation;
- explain the concept of the commodification of lifestyle;
- identify patterns of participation in recreational physical activities and sport;
- analyse the social factors affecting participation; and
- recall and comprehend issues relating to spectatorship in sport.

The terms *leisure* and *recreation* have a long history, but until about 50 years ago they were terms that many people associated mainly with the privileged and wealthy minority of Australians. Leisure and recreation, along with the idea of lifestyle, are notions that have come to prominence for the general public only since the 1950s. This attention has come about because these concepts are related to innovations in work patterns, the result of increasingly sophisticated technology. As we will see in this chapter, researchers have examined closely the impact that lifestyle and leisure have on patterns of participation as well as on the creation of social barriers.

CHANGING CONCEPTIONS OF LIFESTYLE, LEISURE AND RECREATION

A bewildering array of so-called labour-saving devices, items that we now regard as commonplace and essential, were just beginning to make an impact on the home and the workplace 20 or 30 years ago. For example, as recently as the early 1960s it was not unusual for women to do the family wash by hand, with the aid of a scrubbing board and a mangle. Washing machines became household items that were taken for granted only by people born since the late 1950s. The same is true of electrical appliances such as the vacuum cleaner, refrigerator, electric heater and fan. Recent innovations, including the microwave oven and the tumble dryer, also seem always to have been around, even though these appliances were not common in homes until at least the mid-1980s.

At work, increasing mechanisation and automation of labour-intensive tasks have had an enormous effect on work practices. Technological innovations have reduced working hours and required workers to develop new skills. The downside has been that as the existing skills of some workers have become obsolete (for instance, the trade of making moulds for products in the steel industry), these workers have become unemployed. In general, over the 30-year period from the end of the Second World War to the end of the 1970s, working hours have fallen, as shown in table 10.1. These developments provided ordinary people with more time for **leisure** than previous generations had possessed, and with more money to enjoy it.

leisure:
The time that is available to people when they are not engaged in work.

Other products of the technological revolution, such as the television set (introduced during the 1960s) and the video recorder (a more recent innovation) have influenced our ideas about leisure, recreation and lifestyle. By the end of the 1960s, social theorists had yet to realise the extent to which television would affect the use of leisure time. They confidently predicted that Australians would have much more leisure time than they had ever enjoyed before. This pronouncement prompted physical educators to claim that people should occupy their free time with physical, recreational activities. At the same time, state and federal governments developed policies for sport and recreation that primarily focused on providing facilities for people to play both competitive team and individual sports. During the 1960s and 1970s, people began to construct their current understanding of notions such as leisure, recreation and lifestyle.

Recreation was the earliest of these notions to have an effect on everyday life. Recreation refers to your ability to re-create or regenerate yourself through activities that are alternatives to work, whether the domestic work of running the home or wage labour. The first national campaign to promote recreational physical activity in Australia occurred in 1938 and 1939. It led to the successful passage through Federal Parliament of the National Fitness Act in 1941. The National Fitness Act provided federal government with money for a national coordinator and State Councils for National Fitness. The state councils were responsible for generating policies and for providing facilities and instruction for physical recreation. Newly formed government departments of sport, recreation and youth absorbed the State Councils' work in the 1970s.

TABLE 10.1 Standard Weekly Work Hours for Adults, 1914-1986

Year	Males	Females
1914	48.93	49.08
1920	47.07	46.47
1930	45.93	45.48
1940	44.84	44.15
1950	39.96	40.00
1960	39.96	39.67
1970	39.91	39.67
1980	39.79	39.67
1986	38.52	38.61

Reprinted from W. Vamplew, 1987, Standard weekly work hours for male and female adults, 1914-1986. In *Australians Historical Statistics 1987* (Fairfax, Australia: Syme & Weldon). By permission of the author.

recreation:
Activities that are undertaken for pleasure and relaxation.

The notion of leisure was the next to have an effect on everyday life, becoming prominent during the late 1960s and early 1970s. Although recreation can refer to a broader range of activities than sport and exercise, people generally understand that leisure refers to all of their available time when they are not working. Leisure is a broader notion than recreation, but it lacks the connotation of healthy regeneration of energy that recreation suggests. If anything, leisure suggests non-vigorous forms of activity, such as going to the cinema, hobbies and just about anything else that does not relate to work.

Lifestyle is the most recent of these three concepts to have an effect on everyday life, appearing in the late 1970s. The notion of lifestyle assumes that people have some degree of freedom from the responsibilities to work, family and other commitments. It also assumes that they possess the time, self-discipline and money to shape their lives in particular ways. Implied in the notion of lifestyle is the idea that people can be in control of their lives, and that they have a range of alternatives to choose from. Therefore, it should be possible for most people to choose to lead an active lifestyle or a sedentary lifestyle. This idea of lifestyle choice has been a key assumption that has underpinned many health promotion campaigns in Australia.

lifestyle:
The ways in which we conduct our lives, a concept that suggests that everyday practices can be consciously styled.

Recent research by social scientists suggests that some of the assumptions connected with the notion of lifestyle are too simplistic, much like the theories and predictions in the 1960s about the leisure society. Evidently, people are a long way from having not only abundant leisure time in which to engage in physical recreation but also the freedom, time and money to choose an ideal lifestyle from a range of alternatives. The reality is that people today may have less freedom because of an assortment of new social pressures. In many cases, they might have even less leisure time than their parents and grandparents did.

COMMODIFICATION OF LIFESTYLE

In contemporary Australian society the notion of lifestyle subsumes leisure and recreation as well as work and other everyday activities. One of the helpful things about lifestyle as a concept is that it allows us to talk about all of the aspects of everyday life in relation to each other. Therefore, you often hear references to leading a balanced or an active lifestyle. For instance, the choice of an active lifestyle determines your use of leisure time, the amount of regular exercise you do, your diet, the quality of your work or school environment, and a host of other everyday matters.

Useful though it may be, the notion of lifestyle can be misleading and even dangerous. It is easy to slip from a point of view that quite correctly says we have some control over our everyday lives and are responsible for our choices to the mistaken view that assumes we can choose whichever way of life we wish. The commodification of lifestyle encourages the latter view. **Commodities** are items or objects that can be bought and sold. Cars, computers, foodstuffs, household appliances, furniture and houses themselves are all commodities, because people produce them with the primary intention of selling them in a commercial transaction. The **commodification of lifestyle** occurs when the commodities and services we buy sell us the idea that they can construct particular ways of life along with a corresponding self-identity.

commodity:
A product that exists in order to generate profit.

commodification of lifestyle:
The process by which people are sold the idea that particular ways of life can be bought.

Usually the process of commodifying a lifestyle involves acquiring items such as cars, boats and backyard tennis courts, or sports goods and services. Typically, vendors attempt to convince you that having a particular item automatically provides you with the way of life you want. For example, vendors might target busy, well-to-do businesspersons as a group likely to buy a boat or yacht so that they can escape from it all on weekends. Other vendors might target older men as people susceptible to the idea that a holiday home close to good fishing will provide the tranquillity they are looking for in retirement. Advertisers tell young people that they need to buy all manner of brand-name sports gear so that they will feel good about themselves or be acceptable to their friends.

••• Focus Activity —

BRAND NAMES AND SPORT

Purpose

To identify the relationships between the use of brand names on sports clothing and equipment and the commodification of young people's lifestyles.

Equipment and Materials

Photographs of performers in the sports listed, advertising materials for these sports and items of clothing and equipment associated with these sports: surfing, basketball, mountain biking, tennis and aerobics.

Procedure

1. In a small group, share the collection of photographs, advertising, clothing, equipment and other products associated with the sports in the list.
2. Make a list of the brand names. Discuss why you think these brands are popular.

Written Task

Evaluate the effects of brand names on leisure and sports clothing, shoes and equipment in relation to the commodification of the lifestyles of young people. Make particular references to

- the most popular brand names among the members of your group;
- the reasons these brands are popular, including the values young people associate with each brand; and
- the effect that wearing or using brand name products has on young people's lifestyles, in your opinion.

EXTENSION ACTIVITY

BRAND NAMES AND SPORT

Examine some of your favourite sports that are not included in the list above. Make a list of the brand names associated with these sports. If there are no brand names readily associated with these sports, write down why you think there are none.

The idea that we can buy a particular way of life and a ready-made identity to go along with it draws heavily on leisure activities. Leisure activity is one area in people's lives in which they are most likely to have at least some freedom to choose between alternatives.

Studies show that the lifestyles people form through leisure pursuits can spill over into other aspects of their everyday lives. They begin to form self-identities in relation to the activities they engage in. For example, recreational sports such as surfing and snow skiing show how the commodification process can construct particular lifestyles around leisure activities. Advertisements for brand-name clothing and equipment and other products and services accentuate the already existing cultural activities, forms of dress and behaviours that people associate with these activities. It is somewhat ironic that the culture of surfing, once non-conventional in relation to mainstream society, has become highly commodified and marketable. Surfing brand names that were once specialised are now highly visible beyond the surfing community.

Few areas of recreational physical activity remain in which commodification is not already well advanced. You need only think of bungee jumping, whitewater rafting and parasailing to see how far the commodification process has penetrated the leisure market and manufactured novel forms of activities to attract consumers.

Sociologists of leisure and sport argue that the assumption that most people have the freedom and means to construct their own lifestyles oversimplifies a complex process. Since the commodification of lifestyle requires that people can pay for products and services, there are financial barriers to constructing a lifestyle of their choice. Nevertheless, people often work and save to buy what they want. It seems obvious that not everyone can afford regular snow-skiing holidays, a tennis court in the backyard, a private swimming pool or a yacht. Yet within their own financial circumstances, many people participate in and contribute to the commodification of their lifestyles.

Most Australians construct their lifestyles partly through their own efforts and partly through commitments to work, family, home and friends. However, these factors, in addition to finances, life circumstances and social forces (such as gender, race, disability and health), can constrain an individual's freedom to choose a particular lifestyle. These limitations cause a tension or dynamic interplay between freedom of choice and life circumstances, between work and play, and between self and others.

Young adults are a large target group for manufacturers and advertisers of leisure and recreation products and services. Businesses perceive young adults to have fewer constraints operating on them in terms of relationships, responsibilities for children or other family members, and careers. They are also likely to be relatively healthy and to have a higher proportion of disposable income than other groups. Compared to other members of Australian society, young adults are more involved in constructing their lifestyles and their emerging self-identities through participation in commodified leisure and recreational pursuits.

Although you may recognise that constraints operate on a person's ability to construct an ideal lifestyle, it is a mistake to believe that the same constraints act in the same way on all Australians. Before you consider some of the factors that affect lifestyle and participation in recreational physical activity, you need to know something about participation levels and the kinds of recreational physical activities people typically engage in during their leisure time.

SAMPLE LEARNING EXPERIENCE

The Commodification of Physical Activity and Surfing

Surfing was a popular pastime for Kevin and his friends, whose homes and school were within walking distance of a prominent surfing beach. Kevin's uncle was also a surfer, and he had often told Kevin that surfing was not always the popular sport that it is today. In fact, other members of the community once regarded surfers as lazy, non-working social misfits who had nothing better to do with their time than to ride the waves on makeshift boards.

Back in those days, the gear that surfers wore was generally second-hand and fitted poorly. Surfers had little coordinated dress sense, and looking different from non-surfers was valued highly. A surfer used the way he looked to make a social statement. Kevin's uncle felt that nowadays surfing had become too popular. People who were more interested in looking like a surfer than actually being one had taken it over. Kevin had a chance to understand more about the changes to surfing that his uncle had talked about when his physical education class began to study the commodification of sport in relation to surfing.

Kevin and the rest of the class assembled at the beach with their equipment ready to begin their surfing lesson. Before they entered the water, the teacher asked the students to examine and make a list of the equipment and specialised clothing that they were using, all of which they owned. The students made the following observations and recorded them for future discussion:

- Almost all of the students were wearing some kind of clothing created by a surf clothing company.
- All of the equipment students were using was branded with the logos of popular surfing merchandise companies.
- Some of the equipment advertised names of champion surfers and the titles that they had won.

Kevin and his classmates listed all of the brand names and the names of endorsing surfers. In class the next day, the teacher produced some surfing magazines for scrutiny. The class perused the periodicals and listed all of the surfing brand names they could find. They also listed other major brand-name companies that advertised in the magazines, along with the manner in which they advertised.

The teacher asked the class to discuss, in groups, some key points that explained the forces behind the prominence of brand names and celebrities in surfing. They then had to report to the whole class. The teacher directed the groups to some reading about the commodification of sport and asked them to use this material in their explanation.

Explanation

As the groups reported on their discussions, it became clear to the class that surfing merchandise was big business. It was also clear that the equipment and clothing brands they themselves owned were prominently advertised in the magazines. It was obvious to them that they had been influenced to purchase certain brands of equipment and clothing in order to dress and equip themselves in keeping with the surf culture. Recalling his uncle's comments, Kevin mentioned in his group discussion that there seemed to be an increasing number of people who wore the same brands of clothing as surfers but were not surfers, and were not even regular beach-goers. Some others in the group said they had seen people wearing surf clothing in towns and cities that were many kilometres away from a beach.

By examining the lists of their own possessions on the beach, Kevin and his classmates recognised that they were party to a process of commodification of surfing. They all wore clothing that was clearly identifiable as popular brand-name surf wear. It was loose fitting and had a particular style—exactly what Kevin and his surfing friends wanted. The T-shirts, shorts and caps might have been styled to look like the clothes Kevin's uncle would have worn, but Kevin's clothes were brand named and brand new, not second-hand cast-offs. Similarly, the equipment he and his mates owned was no longer makeshift; it was state-of-the-art, scientifically designed, and very expensive.

Kevin's class listened while the teacher explained that a commodity is something produced primarily for the purpose of selling and buying. Surfing was gradually commodified as it was increasingly drawn into a profit-making process primarily centred on merchandising and sponsorship. Before long, elite-level surfers were able to make a living on the professional circuit and to supplement their income through their endorsements of surf clothing and equipment.

This notion of the commodification of surfing helped Kevin to understand more clearly what his uncle had been talking about. These days, surfing was marketed to appeal to a wider population than serious surfers alone. Kevin realised that surf wear was increasingly becoming a fashion industry. What attracted non-surfers to buy surf clothing was the image that went along with it. The clothing provided people with the image of a surfer or at least a beach-goer, without them ever having to climb on a board. Kevin's teacher asked the class to note that this process of commodification is not restricted to surfing but is now commonplace in a wide range of sports.

The teacher also commented that commodification had brought many changes to surfing, and that not all of them were bad. With increased media exposure, it had become possible for athletes to earn a living from surfing. It had provided avenues for travel and for product endorsements that until recently had been available only to mainstream sports. The sport in general now enjoyed a better public profile because of commodification. Champions promoted healthy lifestyles and positive work ethics, qualities not traditionally associated with surfing. People now recognised the sport for its technical aspects and accepted surfers as athletes in the sporting fraternity.

EXTENSION ACTIVITY

RESULTS OF COMMODIFICATION

Consider This

Consider how the commodification of sport in general has affected the physical activity you are currently studying. Make a list of the changes to the activity that you think have taken place as a result of the commodification of sport in terms of rules, styles of play, uniform design and so on. Consider also how the commodification of sport in general has affected the lifestyles of you and your friends.

Think and Write

Think about the overall effect of commodification on physical activity and how it influences the ways in which physical activity fits into the lifestyles of you and your friends. Think also about the desirable and less desirable consequences of the commodification of physical activity and lifestyle. Explain the effects of commodification from your point of view.

(continued)

PATTERNS OF PARTICIPATION IN RECREATIONAL PHYSICAL ACTIVITY

Since the mid-1980s, Australians have participated in regular surveys of their participation in recreational physical activities. The surveys generally involve self-reporting, in which people respond to a series of questions on a questionnaire. This commonly used research technique depends heavily on the clarity of questions in the questionnaire, the honesty of people's responses, their ability to understand the questions and their motivation to complete the questionnaire as well as they can. An additional issue that researchers often raise about this form of survey in physical recreation is its completeness. The questionnaires most often collect information on the type of activity and frequency of participation, but less often about the duration of activity, and almost never about the intensity of activity. This deficiency is due to difficulties in developing consistent terminology for use in all surveys.

Some researchers believe that the omission of intensity and duration measures is a significant shortcoming, since it means they cannot say whether the activity is having a training effect. Recently exercise physiologists began to question some of the assumptions that they had previously made about the relationship between training effects and the health benefits of exercise. Now the consensus is that the intensity of exercise need not be as high as they formerly thought in order for individuals to gain health benefits. Even so, the problem created by the omission of intensity and duration measures in questionnaires remains, and you need to look at the survey data with this shortcoming in mind.

Studies conducted over a 10-year period between 1984 and 1993 show that from 60% to 70% of the Australian population over the age of 14 participate in physical activities on a regular basis. Table 10.2 lists these studies.

TABLE 10.2   **Studies Reporting Percentages of Physically Active Adults and Adolescents**

Study and date	Location	Age range	Sample #	% Participating		
				Female	Male	Total
DASETT, 1988	National	14+	3500	68.1	73.7	70.9
DASETT, 1992	National	18+	2289	76.0	78.0	77.0
ASC, 1991	National	13-18	1700	65.0	63.0	64.0
ABS, 1994	Queensland	15+	2,299,900	61.1	65.2	63.1

The most popular physical recreational activity for both females and males and across all age groups is walking, as shown in figure 10.1. Recreational swimming, fishing, aerobics, weight training, tennis, jogging and golf are the most popular activities overall.

Differences are evident in the types of activities preferred by females and males. As you can see in figure 10.2, more women than men walk and do aerobics, whereas more men than women jog, work out in the gym and play team sports. Roughly equal numbers of men and women swim.

Notable differences also exist in the popularity of activities across age groups. A study conducted by the Department of the Arts, Sport, the Environment,

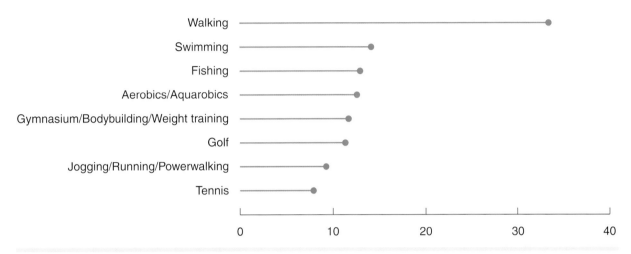

Figure 10.1   Participation rates in various activities.

Reprinted from Australian Bureau of Statistics, 1994, Participation rates in various activities. In *Participation in sporting and physical recreational activities, Queensland, October 1993* (Belconnen, Australia: Australian Bureau of Statistics). Data used with permission from the Australian Bureau of Statistics. www.abs.gov.au

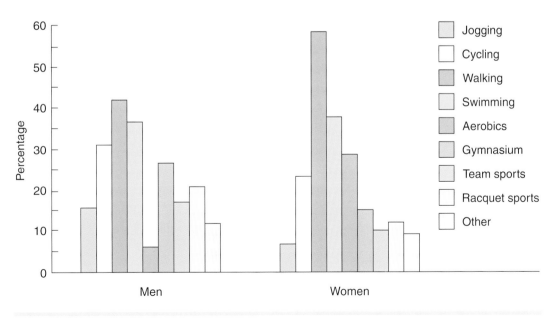

Figure 10.2   Female and male activity preferences.

Reprinted from Australians Department of Arts, Sport, the Environment, Tourism and Territories, 1992, Summary of the pilot survey of the fitness of Australians (Canberra, Australia: Australian Government Department of Communications, Information Technology and the Arts). Copyright Commonwealth of Australia reproduced by permission.

TABLE 10.3   Participation in Activity by Activity Type and Age (Percentages of Active Respondents)

Activity type	Age group (years)			
	14-24	25-34	35-49	50+
Walking	48	53	57	75
Swimming	30	25	24	12
Callisthenics/aerobics	30	26	17	9
Jogging/running	27	19	14	3
Bicycling	25	15	14	7
Cricket/football	29	16	8	1
Tennis	13	11	13	5
Golf	8	10	10	12
Squash	10	10	6	1
Sailing/boating	7	7	7	4
Table tennis	7	5	5	2
Netball/basketball	10	5	2	*
Lawn bowls	*	*	1	10
Athletics	5	1	1	*

* Less than 1%

Tourism and Territories (DASETT) between 1984 and 1988, shown in table 10.3, reveals that walking grows in popularity as people get older; golf and tennis remain about the same across all adolescent and adult age groups; and lawn bowls increases markedly as people get older.

We know less about activity preferences and participation levels among younger Australians. For school-age children and adolescents, the sport and physical education programs at their schools seem to dominate participation in physical activity. The few surveys conducted within this age group show that competitive team sports tend to be the dominant activity for children and adolescents up to about 13 or 14 years of age and tend to be most popular among boys. Adolescents over age 15, particularly girls, begin to show a greater preference for individual exercise activities.

You may think that the relatively high percentages of the adult population that participate in regular physical recreational activity are healthy, but some researchers question the amount of benefit people gain from their exercise. These researchers persistently claim that only a minority, around 15% of the 60% to 70% of active Australians, perform an activity vigorously enough and often enough to reap health benefits. They claim that, as a result, Australians are highly susceptible to so-called lifestyle diseases such as heart disease and cancer. Few surveys have collected evidence of the intensity levels of activity. For this reason, and because the intensity of activity required to have a health benefit is not only in dispute but also probably varies from individual to individual, you must approach these claims with caution—even though they are espoused by many health promoters.

Little evidence of commodification of lifestyle is found in these surveys, except perhaps for the popularity among both women and men of working out in commercially operated gyms. More compelling forms of evidence about the widespread effects of commodification are

- the extent to which people participate in physical activity because they believe it is a part of a healthy lifestyle and
- the belief of many people that they must buy the accepted clothing and equipment and have the right look before they can participate.

SOCIAL FACTORS AFFECTING PARTICIPATION IN PHYSICAL RECREATION

How can you explain that the surveys' findings show over one-third of adult and adolescent Australians have **sedentary lifestyles?** One explanation is that people are sedentary because they are either lazy or ignorant; if they knew the facts about the health and other lifestyle benefits of exercise, then they would become more active. According to this theory, sedentary people are more likely to eat poor diets, smoke and consume unhealthy levels of alcohol. Armed with the facts, they would choose to eat better, stop smoking and reduce their alcohol consumption. Most health and exercise promotion campaigns are based on the assumption that if people only knew what was good for them, they would act on the information.

sedentary lifestyle: Participating in little or no regular physical activity in the course of everyday life.

Although laziness and ignorance may be factors that affect participation, research suggests that they are influential in only a minority of cases. The findings of these studies support other explanations, showing that many reasons other than being lazy influence people's participation in recreational physical activity. The 1992 DASETT study shown in figure 10.3 reveals that the reasons men and women give for not exercising vary considerably according to the sex of the individual.

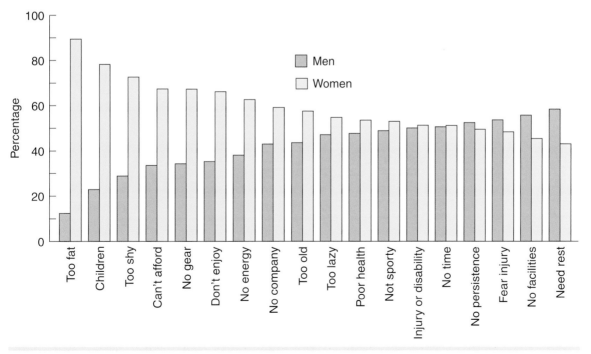

Figure 10.3   Reasons given by men and women for not exercising.

For women, the perception that they were too fat, mentioned by almost 90% of respondents, is overwhelming evidence of the social pressures women feel to look right. It confirms the concept discussed at length in chapter 9, that bodies are socially constructed. If many women and some men feel self-conscious about exposing their body shape to the gaze of others, health promotion campaigns that present the facts about exercise are likely to cause even higher levels of guilt than those women and men feel already.

Just under 80% of women in this survey reported that the main reason they did not exercise was caring for children, whereas children were a factor for less than 30% of men. This finding provides evidence of the structure of Australian families and of the considerably larger role women play in caring for children compared to men. This disparity is a significant factor in reducing the opportunities for women to be physically active. It cannot be resolved merely by informing women of the health benefits of exercise or giving them motivational talks.

These two factors alone suggest there is more to the issue of participation than people's desire to be active or their knowledge about exercise and health. Many of the other reasons for inactivity listed in figure 10.3, such as *can't afford, don't enjoy, not sporty* and *no time,* suggest that many complex social, structural and educational factors influence people's failure to exercise, rather than just the individual inclination not to be active.

Another factor influencing participation that has far-reaching implications for a country such as Australia is its multicultural population. In 1994, the Australian Bureau of Statistics (ABS) reported the findings of its national survey of participation in sporting and recreational activities (see table 10.4). It found that Australians born in Australia, New Zealand, other Oceanian countries, Britain and Ireland are more likely to participate in recreational physical activity than are Australians born in Asian countries or European countries other than Britain.

The figures suggest that the cultural norms that people bring with them to Australia from some European and Asian countries have considerable impact on the likelihood of their participation in physical activity. For a Muslim girl, to take one example, participation in physical activity is limited by factors that may not affect non-Muslims, such as the requirement that she keep her body covered in public, avoid activities considered to be masculine, and participate in physical activity only with other females.

TABLE 10.4 **Participation Rates According to Country of Birth**

Country of birth	Participated		Did not participate	
	Number	%	Number	%
Australia	1,169,000	64	647,000	36
NZ/Oceania	68,000	67	32,000	33
UK and Ireland	113,000	63	67,000	37
Other European countries	47,000	45	57,000	55
Asia	26,000	44	33,000	56
Other	28,000	71	11,000	29

Reprinted from Australian Bureau of Statistics, 1994, Participation rates in various activities. In *Participation in sporting and physical recreational activities, Queensland, October 1993* (Belconnen, Australia: Australian Bureau of Statistics). Data used with permission from the Australian Bureau of Statistics. www.abs.gov.au

Age is another important factor influencing participation. Survey research between 1984 and 1993, shown in figure 10.4, reveals that participation levels fall as people get older. You might expect this finding, since as people get older they become less physically able to be active and more likely to suffer from illness. However, at the same time that these things are happening to people in their fifties, they also begin to have more time to themselves—usually because of less responsibility for small children. They might even have retired. Therefore, health promotion campaigns might be more effective in persuading people in the over-fifty age group that there are benefits to their health and general well-being from regular exercise.

There is little evidence in the survey research to show a relationship between socioeconomic status and the likelihood of participation in physical activity. This finding is somewhat surprising, when you consider that access to some activities requires higher levels of wealth than others (figure 10.5). For example, the cost of membership of golf clubs varies, but most of these

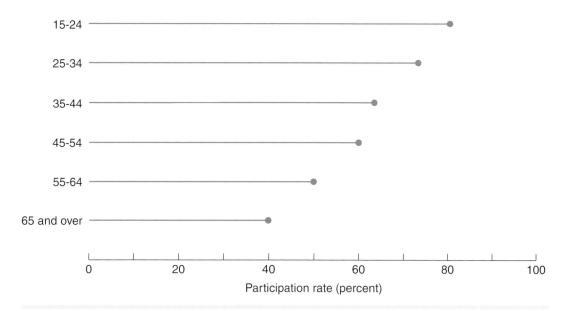

Figure 10.4 Participation rates in physical activities by age group.

Reprinted from Australian Bureau of Statistics, 1994, Participation rates in various activities. In *Participation in sporting and physical recreational activities, Queensland, October 1993* (Belconnen, Australia: Australian Bureau of Statistics). Data used with permission from the Australian Bureau of Statistics. www.abs.gov.au

Triathlon

Equipment

Bike

Safety equipment

Clothing

Goggles

Shoes

Coaching fees

Nomination fees

Travel accommodation

Cricket

Equipment

Uniform

Protective equipment

Bats, balls

Club fees

Travel accommodation

Gymnastics

Club fees

Coaching fees

Uniform

Nomination fees

Travel accommodation

Figure 10.5 The costs of children playing sport.

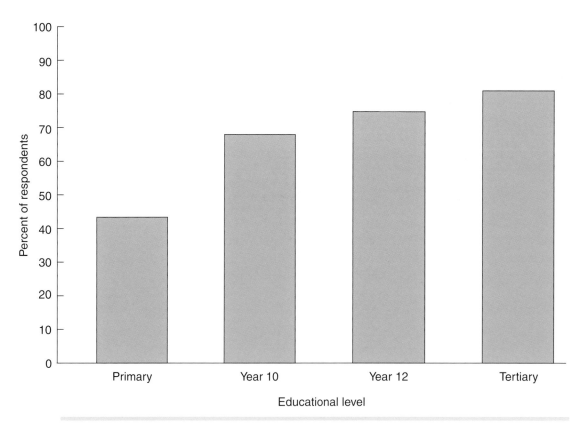

Figure 10.6   Participation rates in physical activities by educational attainment.

Reprinted from Australians Department of Arts, Sport, the Environment, Tourism and Territories, 1988, Physical activity levels of Australians (Canberra, Australia: Australian Government Department of Communications, Information Technology and the Arts). Copyright Commonwealth of Australia reproduced by permission.

costs are normally out of reach for many Australians. Owning and caring for a horse is usually beyond the means of most suburban families but is probably more realistic for country people. Any activity that requires highly specialised equipment or facilities has cost implications for the user. Lack of evidence of a relationship between activity levels and socioeconomic status may be due to survey sampling techniques or the questions asked of respondents.

The 1988 DASETT study, shown in figure 10.6, did report that a relationship exists between people's level of education and their participation in activities. Sociologists have solidly established that people's socioeconomic backgrounds are important in determining what level of education they attain. This evidence may be an indirect indicator that wealth and social class have some influence on the type and level of participation in physical activity.

PATTERNS OF PARTICIPATION IN SPORT

From the findings of surveys of physical recreation (shown in table 10.3) you can see that there is a significant decline in levels of participation in sport from around the age of 15, with only a very small minority of Australians playing sport at any level beyond their mid-thirties. Even though in the last decade there has been an upsurge of interest in veterans or masters sport, the number of participants over 40 years of age currently remains very small. We can conclude from these findings that only young people play sport in significant numbers, with the exceptions of golf, tennis and lawn bowls.

Participation in sport by young people under the age of 15 is dominated by the traditional team games of football (Rugby Union, Rugby League, Australian Rules and soccer) and cricket for boys and hockey, softball and netball for girls. In the last decade, opportunities for children as young as 6 years of age to play organised sports in community settings in contrast to school settings have grown.

A study sponsored by the Australian Sports Commission showed that up to 80% of the children who play a club sport come from middle-class families. This imbalance occurs because there are a range of significant direct and indirect costs of participation, including fees, equipment, clothing, transportation to training and competition venues, and parents' time. These findings suggest that schools remain the major provider of sport for many Australian children. At the same time, we must note that not all children have the same quality of experience in school sport and physical education. Significant differences may exist in the facilities, equipment and teaching expertise that different schools offer.

Since the 1980s, the range of sports available to children has grown considerably. Although the traditional team games still dominate participation, it is now commonplace to find boys playing field hockey and girls playing soccer. Individual sports such as squash and new sports such as triathlons and competitive aerobics are also appearing in schools. Most organising bodies of sports have junior policies and sections.

The quality of children's participation in sport has become an issue of major significance, and the current proliferation of junior sport policies is the result of the National Junior Sport Policy released in 1994, which lays down guidelines for the provision of junior sport. Queensland was one of the first states to produce its own policy, the Queensland Junior Sport Action Plan, based on the national guidelines.

The national policy was developed in response to increasing perceptions, from the mid-1980s onward, that the rate at which adolescents were dropping out from sport was increasing. In the late 1980s and early 1990s, research studies suggested that dropout from sport was highest among adolescent girls, and this finding stimulated a campaign to encourage girls to stay in sport. These studies also found that although some adolescents dropped out of a particular sport, they also dropped back in again later or took up another sport. This evidence suggested that the problem of dropout was less serious than some organising bodies had feared.

Another study found that what the majority of young people actively participating in sport disliked most was their parents or coach forcing them to take their participation too seriously. Many ranked fun as the major reason for participating in sport and cited pressure to win at all costs as the factor most likely to cause them to give up the sport. This study suggested that sport is highly valued by young sports participants; most said they would spend more time playing sport if they could, as long as it remained fun.

SPECTATORSHIP IN SPORT

Researchers who claim that too few people are physically active also suggest that Australians would prefer to watch sport rather than play it. It is certainly the case that some professional sports attract large crowds of spectators, with the Australian Football League being the most popular competition in terms of spectator numbers. Australian Rules football was one of the first games to attract substantial numbers of spectators during the last decade of the nineteenth century, when the introduction of the five-and-a-half-day working week allowed workers a Saturday afternoon off to attend the local football match.

Spectatorship at sports competitions grew from the notion of sport as entertainment. Modern Australian sports such as cricket, football and netball were not, of course, the first to attract spectators. In ancient Greece and Rome, the free citizens among the population strongly supported sports contests.

As the notion of sport as entertainment began to catch on in Australia, sports began to change. The earliest forms of organised cricket and football were played in open spaces and parkland. When these and other sports began to grow as forms of popular entertainment, it became necessary for clubs to enclose the playing area. The entrance fee, at least in part, enabled clubs to control entry and cover the cost of providing both special facilities for spectators and players' wages.

By the beginning of the twentieth century, sports such as cricket, football, boxing and horseracing were attracting large crowds. During the 1920s and 1930s, the Heads of the River boat race between elite private schools in Melbourne and Geelong attracted tens of thousands of spectators. Since the 1930s spectatorship has played a key role in the emergence of modern sport, and with the invention of **media sport,** some sports rules were actually changed in order to make them even more appealing to spectators.

media sport:
Novel or modified forms of traditional sports or the invention of new sports to suit television broadcasting.

Sports contests have been televised since the 1950s, when television first began to find a mass market. By the end of the 1960s many Australians owned a television set, although these could only broadcast black-and-white pictures—not an ideal medium for sport as entertainment. Kerry Packer's promotion of one-day cricket in the late 1970s is generally acknowledged as the beginning of media sport. Media sport refers to modified or novel forms of traditional sports, or the invention of new sports to suit television broadcasting. Rugby Union and Australian Rules football are good examples of traditional sports that changed their rules significantly over a 10-year period to increase the attractiveness of their sport on television. Shows based on pseudo-sports, like *Gladiators,* are an example of sports produced specifically for television.

The opportunities available to people to watch sport as entertainment have increased considerably because of television. However, media sport has not led to a decrease in the number of spectators attending sports venues, suggesting that the experience of being a member of the crowd remains important to many Australians. In many sports, such as football, local loyalty to a team is an important reason why people spectate at sports competitions.

You might think that the emergence of media sport would cause people to spend more time watching sport instead of playing it as they used to, but this assumption is not quite accurate. People now have more opportunities to watch sport on television, but there is little evidence to show that this form of spectatorship has taken the place of people playing sport themselves. Sport as entertainment clearly remains a popular leisure-time pursuit with many Australians, and television and sophisticated marketing have produced large revenues for players, owners and the media.

••• *Focus Activity* —

THE COST OF SPORT PARTICIPATION

Purpose

To investigate and compare the costs of participating in selected sports.

Materials

Sports good catalogues, club handbooks.

Procedure

1. Select a sport you are familiar with. Find out and note the annual costs in that sport (for someone about your age) for equipment, uniform, club membership, coaching fees, travel and accommodation.

2. Based on this data, what is the direct cost to a family for one person to participate in the sport at club level? Compare your data with those of at least four other classmates who have investigated other sports.

Written Tasks

- Identify differences and similarities among the sports in terms of direct costs. Explain any major differences and similarities.

- Identify some of the other factors, in addition to direct financial costs, that affect participation in the sports you have already examined. Explain any major differences and similarities among the sports for each of these factors.

• • • Test Yourself —

1. Explain how the increase in mechanisation has affected your parents' current lifestyle compared to their childhood lifestyle.

2. Explain (a) leisure, (b) recreation and (c) lifestyle as they apply to you.

3. What does the term *commodification of lifestyle* mean? Give examples of the impact of commodification on your lifestyle.

4. Commercial agencies have focused on young Australian adults as their largest target group. In one or two sentences, explain why they have done so.

5. Why should you view survey results about patterns of participation in recreational physical activity with an open mind?

6. List some of the major differences in preferred types of physical activities for males and females and for different age groups. Do you fit the male and female role model?

7. Knowledge of the long-term benefits fails to motivate people to volunteer for physical activity. Explain how the following social factors influence participation in physical activity: (a) sex of the individual, (b) culture and (c) age. Give specific examples of the impact of these social factors from your family, friends and class group.

8. How can economic or financial factors influence a person's lifestyle?

Money, Media and Power in Sport, Recreation and Exercise

Chapter Overview

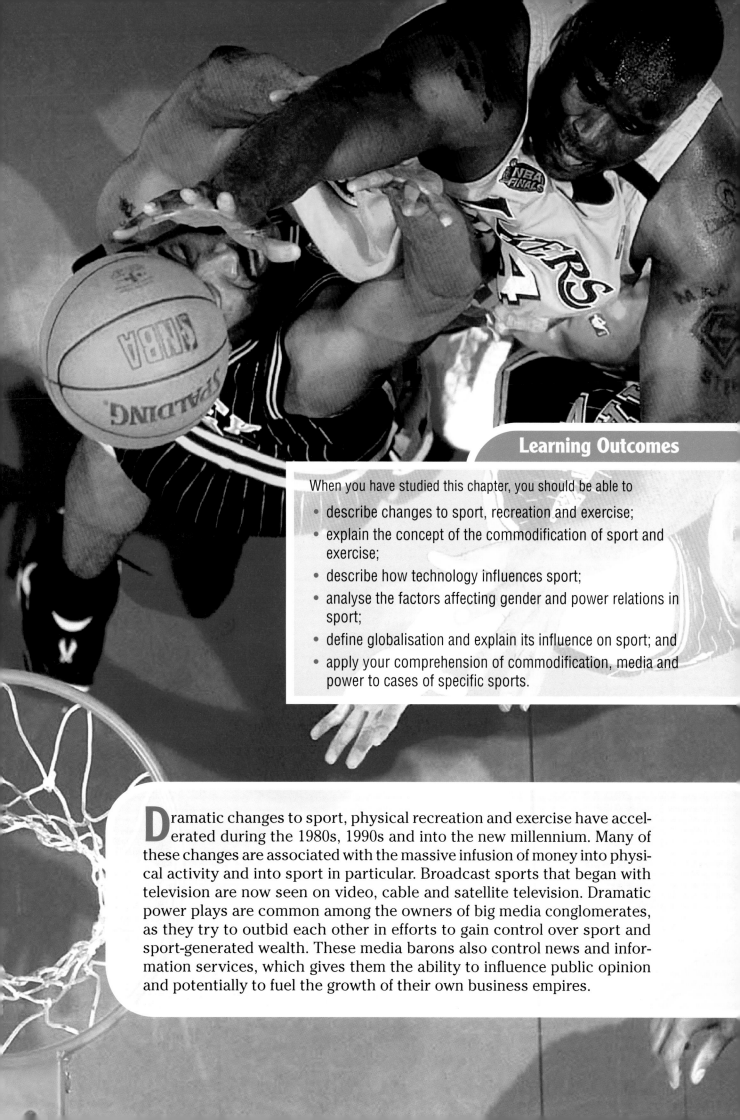

When you have studied this chapter, you should be able to

* describe changes to sport, recreation and exercise;
* explain the concept of the commodification of sport and exercise;
* describe how technology influences sport;
* analyse the factors affecting gender and power relations in sport;
* define globalisation and explain its influence on sport; and
* apply your comprehension of commodification, media and power to cases of specific sports.

Dramatic changes to sport, physical recreation and exercise have accelerated during the 1980s, 1990s and into the new millennium. Many of these changes are associated with the massive infusion of money into physical activity and into sport in particular. Broadcast sports that began with television are now seen on video, cable and satellite television. Dramatic power plays are common among the owners of big media conglomerates, as they try to outbid each other in efforts to gain control over sport and sport-generated wealth. These media barons also control news and information services, which gives them the ability to influence public opinion and potentially to fuel the growth of their own business empires.

CHANGES TO SPORT, RECREATION AND EXERCISE

We must not underestimate the extent to which money, media and power are essential considerations in understanding sport in contemporary Australia. Sport has become a commodity, an item to buy and sell, but sport is not the only arena of physical activity affected by commodification. This process also influences leisure, physical recreation, and exercise for health and fitness, as you will discover later in the chapter.

In order to understand how these recent and sweeping media changes affect sport, recreation and exercise, you need to consider the commodification of sport and exercise. Consider in what ways the following statements are true:

- Sport and exercise are two industries primarily concerned with wealth generation and profit-taking.
- Technological developments are part of the commodification process.
- Gender and politics are issues closely associated with various forms of physical activity.
- People use the process of globalisation to link changes in Australia to changes in other parts of the world.

We will begin our investigation of these issues by looking more closely at sport as the area of physical activity most obviously changed by the influence of money, media and power.

COMMODIFICATION OF SPORT

Sports such as cricket, the various forms of football, and track-and-field athletics have been spectator sports for over one hundred years and have served as a form of entertainment for many Australians. Sport on television began in earnest in Australia with the televising of the 1956 Melbourne Olympic Games. With the mass availability of television sets a decade later, televised sport became a regular feature of everyday life. Before the 1950s, if you had not seen an event live, you could see it replayed in cinema newsreels. Initially the televising of sport as entertainment had little direct effect on the sports themselves, and most continued to exist in the same forms that they had in the late nineteenth century. Minor modifications to rules and styles of play came mainly from within the sports; only in a few cases were changes influenced by considerations for spectators.

The introduction of one-day cricket to Australians in the late 1970s marked a profound change in the nature of sport as entertainment. Here was a sport modified from its original format and designed specifically for television. Players wore brightly coloured uniforms rather than traditional whites, and the technological development of powerful floodlights made it possible for play to continue into the night. One-day cricket was based on the idea of limited overs that could be packaged in a form more accessible for a television audience than the five-day match. Broadcasts during peak viewing times meant that additional revenue could be generated through advertising, which was screened during the time it took to change overs. The result of these changes arguably turned cricket into a faster, more aggressive and more entertaining sport.

The example of one-day cricket shows that media sport is different from traditional forms of sport in several respects. One important difference is that sports organizations change the key aspects of the rules and the styles of playing the game in order to enhance its entertainment value for a television audience. Another important difference is that television makes an event accessible to many thousands (perhaps millions) more people than is normally possible. The larger audience opens up the potential for advertising agencies to generate huge revenue through selling advertising space during the broadcast. It generates an entire secondary industry in sports goods and other memorabilia and paraphernalia, which also makes a huge profit. For example, the profit made from selling Chicago Bulls merchandise is many times larger than the revenue generated by the basketball matches themselves.

Media sport marks a crucial departure from traditional notions of sport as entertainment. The process of transforming a regular sport into a media sport affects only some sports to the same extent that it has affected cricket. However, all sports that feature regularly on television have now begun to alter rules, uniforms and styles of play in order to retain their share of the entertainment market. Figure 11.1 shows some of these changes. Nevertheless, only some sports have been able to persuade the owners and operators of television companies that they have a high enough public profile to warrant the televising of the sport in the first place.

It is no accident that the sports that have claimed the lion's share of television exposure are the traditional male team sports. Sports played predominantly by women, such as netball, tend to receive much less media attention, a matter we will return to later in this chapter when we discuss the question of sport and gender.

You can view media sport as a part of the broader process of the commodification of sport. Sports other than the ones that are televised have been commodified, although media sport has been the primary example of this process at work. Commodification affects all levels and all kinds of sport—in some cases indirectly, but never without some social and cultural significance. What does it mean, therefore, to suggest that sport has been caught up in the process of commodification?

As chapter 10 explained, commodities are items or objects that one can buy and sell. The process of exchange from producer to buyer does not mean that the items have no other uses than making money for the producer. However, commodities are items that would probably never have been produced, certainly never on a mass scale, unless they were capable of generating wealth.

Basketball rule changes

30-second shot clock

3-point arc

No zone defence under 12

6 individual fouls

Must dribble before drive to basket

Baseball technological changes

Carbon fibre bats add 10 m to long hits

Increased pressure in the cork centres of the balls, advanced stitching and tighter yarn improve the ball's life and compactness

Improved style and shape of gloves

Cricket marketability changes

1-day cricket introduced

Coloured uniforms, white ball

Day/night matches in primetime television

Player theme songs

Interstate and international competitions

Limited over games

Heroes and villains on teams

Figure 11.1   Changes have been made to rules, equipment and marketing of sport in order to sell it to the media and to spectators.

commodification:
The process of turning something into a commodity that can be bought and sold.

Commodification is a process through which items or objects become commodities. Typically, these items or objects did not start out as commodities and only became commodities over the course of their existence. Usually the commodification process changes the nature of the item or object. In what sense might we describe sport as a commodity? Sport becomes a commodity when its primary purpose—the main reason for its existence—is to produce wealth for owners.

A good example of the process of the commodification of sport is Super League, which we can regard as a version of the traditional game of Rugby League. Rugby League did not start out as a commodity. It developed as a separate game from Rugby Union after a split in the code towards the end of the first decade of the twentieth century. From its beginning, Rugby League developed as a professional sport. It was strongly supported by the working classes, the Australian Labour Party and the Irish Catholics of Sydney and Brisbane; whereas Rugby Union remained amateur, middle-class and Protestant in its affiliations.

Rugby League initially paid players on a part-time basis and quickly became a popular form of entertainment. These two features of the sport, professionalism and entertainment, suggested that the game was in the early stages of commodification during the first few decades of the twentieth century. Nevertheless, it lacked both the mass exposure that television now offers and the intensive marketing that characterised Super League before the reunification of the game.

Super League was created specifically for television. It was the outcome of a battle between media barons Kerry Packer and Rupert Murdoch to control the television rights to the sport (see figure 11.2). Super League would not have existed if not for the combined influence of money, media and power. Particular sports become commodities when their existence depends on their profitability; when teams can be bought, sold and relocated (from state to state and from city to city); and when success or failure depends on the ability of a team or club to buy talented players.

The commodification of sport affects all levels of sport to some extent. For example, sponsorship of competitions and teams is now commonplace, even in school and junior sport. Merchandise for sport, particularly equipment and uniforms worn by teams, is a multi-billion dollar business that operates on a global scale. Talented young sports performers, particularly those in the most prominent sports, might realistically expect to earn large sums of money

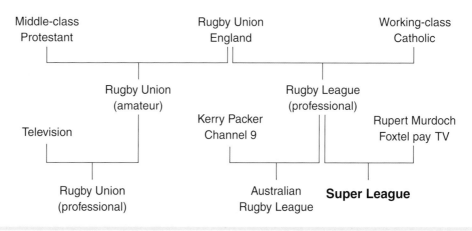

Figure 11.2   The Super League family tree.

from their sport and from associated merchandising. The process may soon reach the stage at which participation in some sports becomes too expensive without sponsorship.

••• *Focus Activity* —

SPORT AND THE MEDIA

Purpose

To understand the effects of the media on sport.

Materials

Newspaper articles, books, magazines, segments of television sports shows.

Procedure

1. Select a sport you are familiar with.
2. Collect materials from newspapers, books, magazines and television sports shows that provide information on how the sport has changed to increase its media and spectator appeal.

Written Task

List the specific strategies employed by the sport you have selected to increase its media and spectator appeal. Do you think the changes are desirable or undesirable? Justify your answer.

COMMODIFICATION OF EXERCISE

The specific ways in which money, media and power have affected exercise are in some respects different from the ways they have affected sport. However, you can see the influence of the process of commodification, particularly through the emergence of an exercise industry in Australia since the mid-1970s. The existence of an industry presupposes that a number of conditions exist, including

- a service or product that people will buy,
- a group of paid workers who claim to have specialised skills and knowledge and
- a reasonable prospect of making a profit for the owners of the businesses.

The existence of exercise gyms is not as recent as you might think. Professional **physical culturists** ran commercial gymnasiums in Melbourne and Sydney from at least the 1850s, where the public could pay to receive a massage or instruction in callisthenics, weight-lifting, swimming or Indian clubs. Some exercise gyms or clubs catered solely for women and were popular among sections of the middle classes in the major cities.

physical culturists: A term used to describe professionals who ran gyms between the 1850s and 1930s.

However, the mid-1970s marked a new point in the history of commercial gymnasiums. One important difference between the old and new forms of gym was that the latter were intended to appeal to a mass market rather than to a small cross-section of wealthy Australians. This intention, fuelled by the need to maximise profits, affected the ways in which the gyms presented their services.

In the early days of the modern exercise industry in Australia, many gyms were set up as small businesses, and they (like many other small businesses) struggled to survive. In some cases, the closure of a gym left people who had bought services in advance, such as a 12-month membership, without their money and without the service. People also were concerned that some gym owners and instructors might lack the necessary expertise to deliver the services they claimed to offer, such as fitness assessment and exercise prescription. No regulation of these gyms had been established, and virtually anyone could set up an exercise business, regardless of qualifications. Accusations of **charlatanism** were common.

charlatanism:
Pretending to be someone or something one is not.

The early experiences of the exercise industry caused some damage to its public credibility. One of the ways in which the industry responded was by beginning to regulate who was qualified to offer services such as exercise instruction. Since the 1980s, a number of organisations have offered fitness instructor courses. Now that confidence in the industry has returned, universities are offering degree-level courses that equip professionals to make fitness assessments using scientific techniques. These courses also train them to offer advice and counselling on how to develop an exercise program.

Weight control or weight loss has been, and still is, a predominant theme of gymnasiums. It reflects sociocultural pressures relating to media representations of bodies and body image. Another feature of the new wave of commercial gyms is their emphasis on the use of technology such as computerised treadmills and other sophisticated exercise equipment. The technology includes scientific equipment for measuring and monitoring the important physiological and anthropometric effects of exercise on the body. A more recent difference is the claim that some of the services offered by workers in exercise gyms require extensive training in the exercise sciences.

The exercise industry is based on the idea that exercise is a commodity, a product that can be exchanged through a financial transaction. The existence of the industry presupposes that people will pay for services that improve their appearance and health through exercise. It also assumes that most people lack the knowledge or motivation to work at looking and feeling better on their own. As with any other commodity, the exercise industry must make people aware that it exists and persuade people that they need the services it offers. In order to exist, the exercise industry must sell the message that the best and most effective way to become fit is to buy the services and expertise it supplies.

Critics question some of these assumptions about people in general. They suggest that the level of knowledge people require to exercise safely and effectively is not especially complex. Most people with a sound physical education can identify their own needs and, if they are in sound health, exercise to meet those needs. Critics also point out that it is in the business interests of the exercise industry to persuade Australians that they need the services the industry sells.

mesomorphic bodies:
Muscular and lean bodies with slim hips, trim waist and broad shoulders.

Some of the exercise industry's advertising and marketing strategies may exacerbate the problems they claim to solve. A good example of this problem is using images of **mesomorphic bodies** of male and female models in advertisements for a gym that emphasises weight loss. Critics argue that this advertising technique is widespread in the exercise industry; it may contribute to anxiety and unrealistic ideas about normal body shapes among many women and girls (and among some men and boys). They also point out that the cost of membership for a commercial gym is beyond the means of many Australians. If the services these gyms offer are essential, according to their own claims, then why should the many people who cannot afford to buy a membership miss out on the health benefits of regular exercise instruction and advice?

The commodification of exercise is part of the broader process of the commodification and construction of lifestyle. For some people, exercise plays a major role in the process of styling their lives. Exercise is a way in which they can work on their bodies. As one sociologist puts it, the body becomes a project. Part of the project is to shape the body in the particular ways that a person desires. This shaped and maintained body then comes to represent that person's preferred view of him or herself. Of course, many people embark on this body project using exercise as a major tool but do not achieve their aims.

••• Focus Activity —

THE COMMERCIALISATION OF THE EXERCISE INDUSTRY

Purpose

To analyse the ways in which the exercise industry sells its products and services.

Materials

Brochures and advertising materials.

Procedure

1. Visit a local exercise facility.
2. Note the services and products the facility provides and the ways in which the facility advertises them.

Written Task

Analyse the notes and materials you have collected. What messages do they communicate? Whom do the messages target? How do they portray exercise? Do you think this portrayal is desirable or undesirable? Justify your answers.

TECHNOLOGY AND SPORT

We have already noted the ways in which technology, from floodlights to the computerised exercise treadmill, has had an impact on sport and exercise. Because so many technological innovations surround sport, it is easy to form the impression that the entry of technology into sport is relatively recent; but it is a mistaken impression. The invention of the wheel not only made a valuable contribution to transportation, it also made possible sports such as chariot racing. Much later, around the end of the nineteenth century, the same technological innovation, with some additions like the rubberised pneumatic tyre, was responsible for the emergence of cycling as a sport.

The ability to time foot races has also been developing since the emergence of reliable clocks, towards the end of the seventeenth century. The earliest clocks could time races to within half a minute—which was fine, perhaps, for the longer distances, but not good for the shorter sprints. Over a period of 200 years, clocks became precise and reliable enough to time a race to within one-quarter of a second and, by the early decades of the twentieth century, to one-tenth of a second. It was not until the 1980s that sprint races were timed to one-hundredth of a second. The replacement of manual timing with electronic timing made this precision possible.

The technological refinement of clocks has had a critical effect on how we think about the measurement and recording of human performance in sports such as running, cycling, swimming, downhill skiing and speed skating. As clocks have become more sophisticated, it has seemed appropriate to measure performance in increasingly minute fractions of time. Before the 1980s, in sports such as track and field and swimming, people were prepared to accept the dead heat and the widespread use of the photograph finish linked to electronic timing. Now, in running events, horse racing, swimming and other sports, every effort seems to be made to separate the winner from the also-rans.

Only occasionally have sociologists of sport questioned the appropriateness of the use of technology in timing. Even though a particular technology exists (such as electronic timing to one-hundredth of a second), they question whether it is appropriate to use it in, for example, track events. Does one-hundredth of a second indicate a significant difference in performance over a short distance such as 100 metres? What about the marathon? If it is not possible to separate runners with the naked eye, is the small difference between them, measurable only by technology, important enough to require that they be separated into winner and also-ran? Some sociologists also wonder where this process might stop. If it becomes possible to measure performance in terms of one-thousandth of a second, will we use this technological development next?

The use of increasingly sophisticated technology to time races is just one case in which sociologists question the appropriateness of the relationship between sport and technology. The idea that using technology somehow makes sport less natural and more artificial often underlies their questions. Sociologists cite as one such case the use of video playbacks in cricket and Rugby League to help umpires and referees make decisions. The surfaces of hockey and gridiron football fields are often referred to explicitly as artificial turf. The switch to AstroTurf in field hockey has resulted in significant changes to the rules and techniques of the game. Technological developments that have had an effect on the design and manufacture of equipment for sports such as kayaking (as shown in figure 11.3), provide yet another area of controversy about the denaturalising impact of technology.

Craft material

Bark
Timber
Aluminum
Fibreglass
Plastic
Fibreglass/carbon

Craft shape

Banana—manoeuvrability
Sprint—speed and stability
Slalom—improved turning

Paddle material

Timber
Aluminum
Fibreglass
Plastic
Fibreglass/carbon

Paddle shape

Flat
Asymmetrical
Propeller
Energy
Crank

Figure 11.3   The changing face of kayaking.

Advocates for the anti-technology position sometimes overlook the fact that all sports are social creations or constructions and thus hardly qualify as natural activities in the first place. The decisive factor in moving these activities away from their folk origins and from any kind of natural state was when the rules and methods of play of many major games and sports were formalised in the late nineteenth and early twentieth centuries. It is also true, as we have already noted, that technology has had an intimate relationship with sport since the invention of the wheel. Players and the manufacturers of sports equipment and facilities have constantly searched for superior materials and better designs. They have done so in the belief that better materials will prove more reliable, durable and effective and that a new design will improve some aspect of the game. Some examples are the change from wood to metal golf clubs and the alterations to the head of the hockey stick that allow players to use the reverse stick dribble and to hit the ball harder.

EXTENSION ACTIVITY

TECHNOLOGY AND SPORT

Consider This

Consider the physical activity you are currently studying. Is it an activity for women, men or both sexes? In what ways has technology affected it? How has it been politicised or otherwise drawn into power relations in society?

Compare and Contrast

- Compare and contrast the ways in which women and men actually participate in the activity, including techniques, strategies and levels of aggression; and note any significant differences and similarities.

- Compare and contrast the effects of technology on the activity today in relation to 20 years ago and 50 years ago.

- Compare and contrast the activity with other activities, in relation to the effects of politics and power. Note any differences or similarities.

PHYSICAL ACTIVITY, GENDER AND POWER

In any discussion of gender and sport, you must define the two basic terms—sex and gender—and note the differences between them. **Sex** refers to biological characteristics that distinguish females and males. **Gender** is the socially constructed pattern of behaviour people recognise as feminine or masculine. Since people socially construct gender, it is dynamic and responds to social change. Therefore gender differs across social classes, ethnic groups and cultural groups, both within the same society and among different societies.

Sport, physical recreation and exercise involve work on the body. The body is important to the construction of self-identity (who we think we are) and to a sense of self-worth. We socially construct gendered bodies, since we attribute different social values to female and male bodies. The stereotype of the homosexual who has a limp wrist and walks with a hand on his hip provides a vivid, if wildly inaccurate, example of the ways in which people use basic movement, posture and comportment to denote appropriate or inappropriate gendered behaviour.

sex:
The biological characteristics that distinguish females and males.

gender:
Socially constructed patterns of behaviour recognized as feminine or masculine.

The naturalistic perspective on the body invariably reduces matters of gender that involve social values to matters of sex or biology. A social constructionist view of the body, in contrast, suggests that biology and social values interact to construct forms of femininity and masculinity. You cannot reduce one to the other. The distinctions between sex (in terms of femaleness and maleness) and gender (in terms of femininity and masculinity) are significant to any discussion of gender and sport. Arguments that people use to exclude females from sports or treat them differently from men are often forms of gender discrimination in the guise of biological arguments about sex differences.

Femininity and Masculinity in Sport

Even a superficial examination quickly makes it obvious that many sports were originally developed either for males only or for females only. Netball, a sport that continues to be played almost exclusively by women and girls, was developed as a modification of basketball. For many years it was known as *women's basketball,* until women began to play the male version of basketball, forcing the name change. Middle-class women in Australia, Britain, New Zealand and North America developed netball's rules and styles of play at the end of the nineteenth century. The rules clearly demonstrate their ideas about appropriate behaviour for young ladies, such as the absolute prohibition against physical contact.

Netball stands in stark contrast to a game such as Rugby Union, in which the game rules accommodate and actually require rough physical contact, including knocking other players over. Figure 11.4 shows other contrasts. Historians have noted that the explicit educational goals for Rugby Union were the development of character, which demanded that a boy who had been knocked down would get up and rejoin the fray; and manliness, which required that players show appropriate levels of controlled aggression and competitiveness.

Male characteristics	Female characteristics
Physical	Delicate
Aggressive	Fragile
Non-emotional	Helpful
Competitive	Emotional
Skilful	Cooperative
Strong	Less skilled
Dynamic	Weak
Sweaty and dirty	Clean and tidy
Rough	Pretty

Sport characteristics	Sport characteristics
Physical contact	Non-contact
Violence	1m rule
Tackling	Limited running spaces
Speed	Set positional areas
Agility	No running with the ball
Strength	Strict dress requirements
Risk taking	
Open field	

Figure 11.4   Socially and culturally traditional values are reflected in the gender-specific sports of football and netball.

Whereas games such as netball and hockey emphasise physical dexterity over strength, speed and force, the rules of rugby and other football codes often advantage the fast and strong player over the skilful one.

When team games that remain major sports in contemporary Australian society were emerging in the late nineteenth century, they were firmly and explicitly designed to emphasise the social characteristics of femininity and masculinity valued at that time. Throughout its modern history, therefore, sport has been an important means of stressing differences between men and women and of maintaining those differences. Nowadays, women play rugby and men play netball. Does this reversal mean that we have made progress and eliminated gender as a factor in the conduct of sport?

The fact that some women now play traditionally male sports and some men now play traditionally female sports owes much to women's long struggle and steady perseverance, in the face of extreme hostility from male organisers and administrators of sports. Even so, women cannot be full members of golf clubs in many parts of Australia. The best female performers in sports such as soccer, running, golf, swimming and tennis are not allowed to enter the same competitions as men. Therefore, women do not gain access to the same levels of prize money as men do in sport. They do not receive the same media attention, and they get fewer benefits (such as sponsorship). Sport does not exist outside of society, but instead actively contributes to the social construction of gender in other spheres of life. The inequalities and injustices between females and males that sports demonstrate are also present, to a greater or lesser extent, in general Australian society.

One of the arguments people commonly use to justify the continuing use of sport as a means of constructing power relations based on gender is that females and males are naturally different, both biologically and emotionally. Men, so the argument goes, will always be bigger, stronger and more aggressive than women will. We see the naturalistic view of the body resurfacing in such a viewpoint.

Elite-level performers in sports such as rugby may provide some evidence to support this claim. The point is not as strong as it seems, however, when we recall that the rules of rugby were originally drafted with particular characteristics in mind—characteristics that were attributed to manliness, such as strength, speed and aggression. Putting elite athletes aside and taking figure 11.5

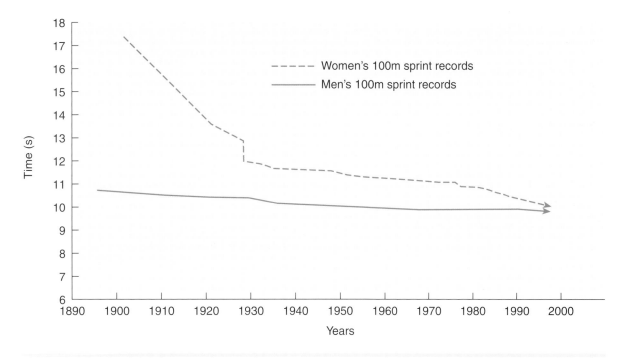

Figure 11.5   The gap narrows, but will it ever close?

Figure 11.6   While men traditionally wear baggy uniforms, women wear figure-hugging bodysuits. Is this caused by market pressures?
© Sport The Library

into consideration, does the argument that female performers are inevitably inferior to male performers hold true for other levels of ability?

The media play a key role in maintaining the view that women's participation in sport is of inferior quality to men's. Surveys of media coverage of sport, on television and in print, show that sport involving women receives only a fraction of the coverage of the major team sports involving men. In defence of their selective coverage, representatives of the media argue that ratings and audience approval drive the process; and that their viewers and readers find women's performances in sport less entertaining than men's performances. The problem with this argument, as sport sociologists have noted, is the classic chicken and egg dilemma: Which came first, media coverage or lack of popularity of some sports? Thinking back to our discussion of media sport earlier in this chapter, there can be no question that the media actively market and promote sport; they do not act as a neutral relay of sport to the television audience.

When women's participation in sport does receive media coverage, it often places an emphasis on the attractiveness of women's bodies and their revealing costumes or uniforms, with less attention paid to physical performance (figure 11.6). One magazine article written by a male journalist in the early 1990s questioned whether netball would need to get sexier before it could hope to attract sponsorship and media attention. His view of sexier netball involved the players wearing high-cut leotards. Few articles have appeared posing the same question for the football codes or men's cricket.

Some sport administrators cite the unequal treatment of women in sport, based on gender, as a major factor causing adolescent girls to drop out of sport in larger numbers relative to boys. They argue in support of girl-friendly sport. Since the mid-1980s, this advocacy has influenced the development of a number of government-funded initiatives aimed at increasing the sport participation of girls.

SAMPLE LEARNING EXPERIENCE

Body Image and Sexualisation of Women's Sport

Stacey is a regional representative in touch. She has been studying touch in her physical education class. The unit she was concentrating on was the relationship between body image and physical activity. The topic was of great interest to Stacey, because she was aware that many of her team-mates in the regional team were sensitive about their body images in relation to the team uniform they had to wear. Stacey herself felt unhappy about wearing the uniform, which was a tight-fitting Lycra leotard, even though she felt quite comfortable most of the time with her own body shape. She did not really know how to express these sensitivities about the uniform until she began to study body image and gender in sport in her physical education class.

Stacey's physical education teacher had acquired a video of men's and women's touch matches between Australia and New Zealand. The class was to view the video and make notes on two topics. The first task was to note specific game strategies that the elite players used and to assess the effectiveness of their decision-making on the field. On a separate page students were to make some notes of the social construction of gender and how it might relate to the body, by comparing aspects of the men's and women's games.

The first task seemed relatively straightforward, since the class members were able to identify strategies that they were already using in the game of touch during physical education classes. They noted these tactics along with some of the more advanced strategies that the elite players were able to employ. The class decided that the higher skill and fitness levels of the players allowed them to use these more complicated strategies. It was also clear that there was a match plan and that the tactics used were implementing this plan. Stacey's class agreed that there was little difference between the standard of play or the skills used by men as opposed to women.

The second task produced less agreement. First, some of the girls in the class objected to the uniforms that the women were wearing. Whereas the men were dressed in loose-fitting shorts and T-shirts, the women wore a tight-fitting Lycra uniform similar to a leotard. The majority of the class believed that the women were not very comfortable with the uniform, as evidenced by the regular adjustments they kept making.

During the class discussion of the videos, Stacey argued that the players should not have to worry about how they looked in a uniform that seemed more suited for the gym or the beach than for playing a game like touch. Some students in the class disagreed, saying that the uniform looked good and added to the enjoyment of watching the women play. Needless to say, this group consisted almost entirely of male students.

Stacey justified her position on these issues in an essay that each class member had to write. She reflected on her own experiences in touch and related her perceptions to the issues that arose from the video analysis.

Explanation

Stacey said that she and many of her team-mates felt embarrassed to wear the leotard-type uniform. It was the standard uniform for the regional representative team, however, and they were required to wear it. Stacey always felt preoccupied with her body shape when she wore this uniform. She raised the question of why her team could not wear shorts and shirts as the men did.

In physical education she had learned about the social construction of the body and the sexualisation of women's sport. It seemed to her that these topics, taken together, might throw some light on why players in her touch team were required to wear such revealing uniforms. They might also indicate some of the consequences for women's sport and for women's welfare generally.

Stacey had read that some sports played by women had been sexualised in the sense that the players' bodies were displayed in a revealing way in order to attract sponsorship and media attention. Her teacher had given the class a short article from *Woman's Day* magazine which asked whether netball should become sexier in order to promote the sport. Although Stacey agreed with the comments of an international player quoted in this article, saying that Australian netballers deserved more attention from the media and sponsors, she had misgivings about attracting attention by making the players' bodies and sexuality the selling point for the game.

Stacey argued that the women's touch game risked being devalued for its skill component and marketed instead on its sex appeal. The contention raised by some in her class, that the way the women looked in the uniforms added to the spectacle of the game, only proved that this process was already taking place. Stacey was anxious about this trend, because she aspired to be an athlete, not a model. She argued that it was unfair and exploitative to treat sportswomen in this way. If spectators and the media were so concerned about portrayals of body image, would having a socially acceptable, attractive body eventually become part of the selection criteria for making a team?

Stacey was troubled that the images portrayed in the touch video added weight to already dominant but questionable values. She was primarily concerned with the idea that men's sport can be appreciated for skill alone, whereas women's sport needs to be boosted with sex appeal to make up for the relatively slower pace and lower level of aggression. Perhaps it was reasonable to acknowledge that some women found this attention to body image flattering. It was equally understandable, however, that many of Stacey's team-mates found the attention to their bodies to be intimidating and embarrassing.

In her essay, Stacey argued that stereotypical forms of being masculine and feminine were supported through the sexualisation of women's sport. She observed that whereas women's sport was marketed on looks and body image, men's sport was marketed on aggression and violence. She suggested that although the media and spectators would typically accept that aggressive behaviour complimented men's touch and made it more exciting, the same audience might condemn aggressive or violent behaviour in the women's game; such behaviour would be labelled as unladylike or butch. Stacey concluded, therefore, that not only did the female players have to look good and display their bodies, they also had to behave in a manner consistent with stereotypical ideas about femininity and masculinity.

Ideological Hegemony and Hegemonic Masculinity

The focus on girls within debates about sport and gender has also diverted attention away from two other situations:

- The role sport plays in constructing masculinity among boys
- The role sport plays in maintaining dominant forms of masculinity that celebrate extreme behaviours such as aggression, competitiveness and physical violence

The concept of *ideological hegemony* is sometimes used to help explain why masculinity is often overlooked in debates about gender.

The theory of ideological hegemony was first expressed in the writings of the Italian Marxist Antonio Gramsci in the 1920s. Sociologists sometimes use it to explain how power operates in society. Gramsci claimed that in advanced capitalist democracies, it is not brute force or coercion that maintains inequitable power relations, but most often the willing compliance of the oppressed with their own subordination. Compliance is achieved by denying that inequalities are problematic and viewing them as part of the fixed, natural order of things. Gramsci argued that power is never absolute; it is constantly contested and negotiated.

The notion of hegemony is particularly useful for understanding why it appears to be so hard to change some aspects of the gender order in relation to sport and other activities. An Australian sociologist, R.W. Connell, has identified the key characteristics of hegemonic masculinity as specific combinations of force, skill and the occupation of space. He suggested that sport is by definition centrally connected with these characteristics. Bodily prowess and physical size, generalised beyond sport into work, sexual activity and fatherhood, form the key ingredients of hegemonic masculinity for many adult males.

This version of masculinity becomes ideological and value-laden when linking its various elements appears to be natural and inevitable; whereas what is actually happening is social construction, an arbitrary forging of associations that have no necessary relationship with each other. Hegemonic masculinity acts as a framework for both boys' experiences of school physical education and people's expectations of normal behaviour for boys in this setting. A feature worth noting is the absence of health issues from this privileged definition of masculinity. Indeed, boys' participation in many of the physical activities informed by hegemonic masculinity may actually threaten their health; expectations for masculine behaviour often endorse physical violence, leading to serious injury.

Researchers argue that society must question and reform hegemonic masculinity in order to tackle gender discrimination and equal opportunities. The overriding concern for girls in debates about sport and gender tends to divert attention away from the part sport plays in constructing masculinity among boys. Sport may nurture styles of masculinity that emphasise dominance and celebrate extreme behaviours such as aggression, competitiveness and physical violence. Some feminist researchers suggest that gender-equity interventions in education on behalf of girls have left hegemonic masculinity intact and that a great deal of work must be done with both boys and girls, concerning the problematic aspects of masculinity. Not only girls and women are underprivileged by hegemonic masculinity. Boys and men who do not wish to conform to aggressive and competitive behaviours on the sports field and in other areas of their lives may be disadvantaged or discriminated against. Researchers suggest that men and women who feel such behaviour is inappropriate need to work together to bring about acceptance of a variety of models of femininity and masculinity that can find expression in and through sport.

• • • *Focus Activity* —

SPORT AND THE SOCIAL CONSTRUCTION OF GENDER

Purpose

To examine the ways in which sport contributes to the social construction of gender.

Procedure

1. In a small group, discuss and note which of the listed sports segregate females and males on the basis of sex differences (biological factors), and which sports segregate on the basis of gender differences (social and cultural factors)?

(continued)

2. Think of all levels of participation, not only the elite level, for the following sports: golf, Rugby League, sailboarding, snooker, basketball, artistic gymnastics, tennis, soccer, synchronised swimming, netball and freestyle skiing.

Written Task

Summarise briefly the arguments for segregation in sports in which the basis is biological differences and sociocultural differences. Explain how sport contributes to the social construction of gender.

POLITICS AND POWER IN SPORT

The relationship between sport and politics is a highly controversial issue. One powerful viewpoint (which was until recently the dominant position and continues to allure some television commentators, sports administrators and politicians) is that sport is above or outside of politics. From this point of view, sport provides a common language across cultures and nations that otherwise share little in common. Since powerful international bodies standardise the rules of sports, sports can be a means of bringing nations together. If nations must be in conflict, sport is at least a relatively harmless and much less drastic way to compete, compared with warfare. Advocates of this perspective hold that sport at its best can be ennobling—the finest expression of the human spirit.

A second perspective, now on the ascendancy, is highly critical of the first viewpoint. Advocates for this position suggest that sport never has been and never will be above politics. On the contrary, since modern sport emerged along with the nation-state in the late nineteenth century, it has always been interwoven with politics. One can put forth at least three arguments in support of this view.

The first argument is that sport is political in that it contributes to making the alleged inferiority of women relative to men appear natural. The previous section of this chapter discusses in detail arguments both for and against this view. Attempts to use sport as part of gender politics, so the argument goes, show that politics and sport are inseparable.

A second argument is that sport contributes to the maintenance and naturalisation of social class divisions in society, particularly through the distinction between amateur and professional athletes. Towards the end of the nineteenth century, middle-class men who wished to protect their sport from working-class participation declared the sport amateur. This pronouncement meant that unless an individual could afford to play without earning money from the sport, they were effectively excluded. Two sports that adopted this strategy in earnest were track-and-field athletics and Rugby Union, and they were among the last to let it go. Although the distinction between amateurs and professionals is no longer effective in maintaining class divisions, sociologists and historians suggest that sport continues to contribute to class politics. Some sports are accessible only to the wealthy, and many ordinary Australians cannot afford to participate in any sports or physical recreational activities.

The third argument claims that sport is political because people use it explicitly to advance the causes of political parties and nations. Critics of the perspective that sport is above politics point to how the former prime minister, Bob Hawke, used his association with successful sports performers to reflect glory back on himself. Examples include his association with the America's Cup yachting success of 1983 and with high-profile Australian sports performers such as Greg Norman. The existence of the Australian Institute of Sport and its continuing sponsorship by governments from both sides of politics suggest that Australia's political parties are keenly aware that the glory reflected from gold medallists may be a means of winning votes and retaining power. The increased funding for elite sport in the period leading up to the Sydney Olympics is further evidence that sporting success is important in party politics.

Successive boycotts of the Olympic Games throughout the 1970s and 1980s serve as further evidence for the view that sport and politics are inseparable. For instance, the United States' boycott of the Soviet Union's 1980 Moscow Olympics was considered to have more to do with hostile international relations between the countries than with America's claim that it was expressing disapproval at the invasion of Afghanistan by the Soviet Union (as the country was then called).

Politics also agitated earlier Olympics. The most notorious example was the Nazis' use of the Berlin Olympic Games of 1936 to promote their ideology of the supremacy of the Aryan race—a message that was significantly undermined when the black American, Jesse Owens, gave stunning performances in sprinting and the long jump. Even though from their inception the Games were supposed to promote internationalism over nationalism, no one could compete unless selected for a national team, and league tables of medal winners were kept, beginning early in the twentieth century.

Proponents of the perspective that sport is political suggest that the Olympics are just one example of the ways in which particular nations use international sport to promote their political ideologies on the international stage and to promote the fortunes of governments at home (when their teams or individuals win). They claim that sport is an ideal political tool because of the relative ease with which people can distinguish winners and losers. Politicians and other power brokers can use the characteristics of sport as metaphors for their own spheres of activity. Many of these metaphors find their way into everyday language, ranging from the now archaic *it's just not cricket, old boy* to *making the hard yards* or *levelling the playing field.*

GLOBALISATION OF SPORT

The term **globalisation** refers to the ways in which technological developments have made it possible for people, manufactured goods, information and ideas to travel to what were once diverse and distant cultures. For instance, airline travel and sophisticated telecommunications, commonplace features of our everyday lives, compress time and space. Therefore the world is much smaller today than it was 100, 40 and even 20 years ago. Since it takes much less time to cover distances, places become closer than they once were, making it easier for ideas, customs and practices to travel.

Because of the compression of time and space, a practice that is local to a particular area for a time globalises when other people in other places take it up. In the process of being adopted by people in the new place, the practice is altered in some way. An example of the globalisation of dietary practices is the spread of the McDonald's chain of fast-food restaurants from the United States to other parts of the world. Fried potato chips and hamburgers now form part of the diet of people in countries where this kind of food might otherwise never have been consumed.

The McDonald's example provides some clues to the key features of globalisation. One feature is uniformity. Regardless of where in the world the McDonald's hamburger is served, the customer can be sure that it will look and taste the

globalisation:
The ways in which technological developments disseminate information, people and products around the world.

same. Another characteristic is that practices that globalise tend to emanate from only a small number of very powerful countries. The dietary practices of people in the so-called Third World tend not to become globalised. A third feature is that globalisation is strongly dependent on televised communications and advertising. This dependence means that globalisation is in part a result of the commodification of various aspects of culture, including sport.

The previous sections of this chapter discussed how sport is a commodity and how television and advertising have influenced the commodification of sport. This discussion shows how the marriage of advertising and business with televised communications can lead to the globalisation of practices in sport. The razzmatazz that has surrounded sports such as gridiron football and basketball in the United States is now evident in many parts of the world and in other sports, such as Rugby League in Australia.

One important issue the globalisation of sport raises is how the transfer of practices from one country to another alters local culture. An example of cultural change connected with globalisation is the way in which some young people in Australia have taken up the forms of dress and codes of behaviour associated with basketball in the United States, such as wearing baseball caps, baggy trousers and basketball boots as everyday forms of dress. Globalisation is most profound when it influences aspects of everyday life that we typically remain unaware of. Cultural transformation through globalisation takes place when people forget that the styles of dress and ways of behaving associated with basketball originated in the United States and begin to believe that these practices are their own.

The basketball example of cultural alteration prompts us to remember that the globalisation of sport has been going on for a very long time, since many of the sports that we now regard as Australian emanated from Britain, from the middle to the end of the nineteenth century. Historians have argued that sport was one strategy among others used by the British to colonise many parts of the world. The imposition of British systems of law, commerce and other aspects of culture on colonised people is called **cultural imperialism.**

cultural imperialism:
A process of imposing systems of government, law, customs and culture that originated in another society.

The progressive compression of time and space greatly accelerated the globalisation of sport towards the end of the twentieth century. Some sociologists argue that the United States has now superseded Britain as the source of cultural imperialism. They argue that the practices in sport and everyday life that originate in the United States have now taken root in other places, including Australia. Although there is evidence to support this argument, we should bear in mind that one hundred years of globalisation has not necessarily erased local culture and practices. Australian Rules football remains the dominant spectator activity, despite the fact that football games such as soccer are played in many other countries. Australian football has taken on many of the practices of commodified, professional sport in the United States. However, with the exception of a similar game in Ireland, it remains well-established in, and unique to, Australia. Netball remains the sport with the largest number of participants in Australia, yet this game does not have a high profile in the United States.

1. The marketing of sport as entertainment has resulted in major changes to sports. Explain three changes made to cricket in the late 1970s to suit a television audience. Then note some of the possible positive and negative consequences of the commodification of sport for players, consumers and administrators.

2. What effect might the commodification of sport have on schools?

3. Explain briefly how modern commercial gyms use sociocultural pressures related to body image and technology to sell the product of fitness.

4. List some of the technological changes that have had a major effect on your current physical activity.

5. Does society treat men and women equally in sport? How does this treatment affect your physical activity level in sport?

6. What impact has the emergence of sport as entertainment had on the presentation of women's sport? Can you think of specific examples?

7. Apply the hegemonic theory to your current physical activity to explain inequities in performance and participation.

8. In a short sentence, list three points to support the argument that sport can be used as a political tool. Provide current examples in which politics influence sports nationally.

9. Define globalisation.

10. In a sentence, explain how the globalisation of American basketball has affected Australian culture.

11. Is globalisation a new phenomenon or part of a historical process?

Test Yourself Answers

CHAPTER 1

1. Traditional theories suggest that learners are like mirrors or sponges, mimicking the teacher's actions or absorbing information as a sponge absorbs water. Neither analogy fully explains how learning takes place in terms of individual development, personal differences, prior experiences, maturity, rates at which people learn, or learners' needs and interests.

2. Applied to your physical activity, you should include the areas you are in for the (a) perceiving phase: identifying relevant information; (b) deciding phase: decide on the best course of action; and (c) acting phase: muscle stimulation for execution of movement.

3. As an athlete you gather information for the feedback loop by using visual perceptions of your environment, visual perceptions of your limbs, kinaesthetic information (how a movement feels), auditory information, verbal information (from a coach or teacher) and sources such as video analysis of performance or analysis of the result of performance.

4. Kinaesthetic feedback would assist in all visual input into your skills.

5. The schema theory is based on the theory that a set of movements is controlled by a single generalised motor program that initiates different phases when reproduced at varying speeds.

6. The constructivist approach also includes active, developmental and multi-dimensional learning.

7. Learning is active because learners actively attempt to make sense of specific tasks within a set of environmental conditions and in relation to what they know they can already do.

8. Developmental changes as a teenager will affect your learning because your expectation of how your body will perform a skill that in the past seemed automatic was based on a smaller frame. Your skill performances will have to adjust to your changing shape (such as the growing length and width of your limbs).

9. Learning first involves the cognitive phase, in which you grasp the basic demands of the task. Next is the associative phase whereby you improve your ability to cope with more information about both the task and the environment through practice and experience. Finally, you move into the autonomous phase where the physical skill becomes so automatic you will not have to consciously think of the actions to perform the skill.

10. The term *automatic* assumes that the performer does not think. In active learning, however, the person is continually dealing with the processes of perceiving, deciding and acting, hence thinking takes place all the time.

11. The autonomous phase refers to the fact that the learner's highly proficient performance is continually being fine-tuned, even though it is difficult for an observer to detect the changes.

12. Multi-dimensional learning highlights the complexity of acquiring all skills. You acquire information not only through conscious effort but also by gathering a wide range of multi-dimensional input.

13. As a facilitator of learning, your teacher or coach creates opportunities for you and your team-mates to learn through a diverse range of experiences or instructional methods and through providing different types of feedback. Give your own example.

14. As a student or player, you gain independence and responsibility through task-based learning and independence through reciprocal learning. You also find additional information through your own abilities in guided discovery.

CHAPTER 2

1. Motivation is the effort and persistence we put into the activities we choose to do. Arousal refers to the level of psychological and physiological activation, ranging from deep sleep to high excitement. Cognitive anxiety refers to feelings of nervousness and worry associated with changes in arousal. Somatic anxiety refers to physiological responses such as a faster heart rate and sweaty palms associated with increased arousal. Self-confidence is the realistic belief that you have the ability to achieve your goals. Self-talk is the things that we say to ourselves. Social cohesion refers to how much team members like each other and enjoy each other's company. Task cohesion refers to the degree to which team members work together to achieve a specific goal. Task orientation is a focus on learning new skills and comparing performance with personal standards. Ego orientation is a focus on beating others and comparing your performance with those of other people.

2. Mental climate may be different for each student, but you should mention something about your levels of motivation, arousal, confidence and concentration. For example, my mental climate when I perform best is one in which I feel highly motivated (motivation), view the competition as a challenge (arousal, motivation), feel excited with a few butterflies (arousal), feel positive about meeting the challenge (confidence) and focus on what I have to do (concentration).

   Strategies may also be different for each student, but might include (a) goal setting to adjust your motivation and make sure that you are focusing on the task instead of the outcome (helps with arousal and concentration); (b) relaxation or breathing techniques and stretching, if you need to calm down (arousal down); (c) loud music or jumping on the spot, if you need to wake up (arousal up); (d) positive thoughts to replace negative thoughts (for confidence and cognitive anxiety); (e) a pregame or preshot routine (helps concentration and arousal management); (f) cue words to focus your concentration; and (g) employing positive imagery (confidence, arousal, motivation).

3. If you attribute success or failure to stable causes, you will expect to succeed or fail again in the future. Therefore, if you have succeeded, you expect to succeed again and participate in the future. If you have failed, you expect to fail again, and future participation is less likely. If you attribute success to internal factors (elements within your control—e.g., ability or effort), you experience greater pride and satisfaction than if you attributed suc-

cess to external factors (elements that are out of your control—e.g., task difficulty or luck). Therefore, you are more likely to participate again in the future. If you attribute failure to internal factors, you experience greater shame than if you attribute failure to external factors. Therefore, you are less likely to participate in the future.

4. Task orientation is motivationally adaptive because it provides greater personal control. You are focusing on what you can do and how well you can do it, and not on how well someone else performs (which you can't control).

5. Goal setting may help because (a) it sets out smaller steps (goals) on the way to the ultimate goal so that you can see where you have come from and what improvements you are making; (b) it helps identify strengths and weaknesses which can be worked on to make sure you get to your ultimate goal in the best state of preparation; and (c) it gives you a sense of purpose and direction—you know what you are working on and why.

   Steps in effective goal setting include (1) set specific goals, (2) set challenging goals, (3) set long-term and short-term goals, (4) set performance goals, (5) identify strategies that will help you achieve your goal, (6) write down your goals and (7) evaluate your goals regularly.

6. The catastrophe model is the best explanation. It suggests that when cognitive anxiety is low, increases in somatic arousal will follow the inverted-U (i.e., there will be gradual decreases in performance beyond optimal levels of somatic arousal). If cognitive anxiety is high, the model suggests that once somatic arousal passes optimal levels there will be a sudden and dramatic decline in performance. Robert, on days when he is not bothered by feeling physically tight (somatic arousal), has low cognitive anxiety; therefore, the tightness does not affect performance. On days when he worries about the tightness (increased cognitive anxiety), the tightness (increased somatic arousal) affects performance.

7. Arousal and concentration are linked. If arousal is high, you may not be concentrating on the right things (because you are too busy worrying), or your focus may be too narrow. You may miss vital cues, and therefore your performance decreases. If arousal is optimal, you are free to concentrate on appropriate things, and performance is also optimal. If your arousal is low, your mind tends to wander off to irrelevant details; therefore, concentration is lower and performance decreases.

8. To lower somatic arousal, you would use physical techniques such as stretching, deep breathing and physical relaxation techniques. You would use physical techniques because you are trying to change physical arousal.

   To lower cognitive anxiety, you would employ cognitive techniques such as thought stoppage, positive imagery and cue words, which concentrate the mind on positive things and therefore reduce the capacity for worrying (cognitive anxiety).

9. To use tennis as an example, the familiarity of a consistent mental and physical preparation routine means that you are more likely to focus appropriately when you actually serve (i.e., you are concentrating on the moment and thinking positively). A regular routine can also maintain your arousal at appropriate levels, because of the relationship between arousal and concentration.

An example of a pre-serve routine for tennis might include (1) check stance, (2) decide on the serve, (3) imagine the serve going in, (4) bounce the ball twice and take a deep breath in and out, (5) visualise the target, (6) think of the cue word *target* and (7) serve.

10. Use positive thoughts. Be aware of the negative things you say to yourself. Come up with positive statements to counter these negative thoughts. Positive thoughts should be task oriented (i.e., focused on what to do), concentrated on the present and encouraging. When you have negative thoughts in the future, replace them by repeating the positive statements to yourself—say them as if you mean them. Focus on challenging but achievable task goals (rather than outcome goals). When you concentrate on things you can control, you are likely to feel more confident.

11. If a sport requires a high degree of mutual interaction (e.g., basketball, in which passing and both offensive and defensive patterns are required), task cohesion is more important than it is in sports that require little or no interaction among team members during the event (e.g., archery or team triathlon). The degree of interaction determines the importance of task cohesion; the greater the interaction, the more important the task cohesion.

12. Arrange for some easy games early on to ensure early team success; have a team T-shirt or uniform that identifies members; have a team goal; or focus on performance, not outcome, as a measure of success.

CHAPTER 3

1. Biomechanics can be applied to improve physical performance and prevent injury.

2. Both linear and angular motion refer to movement of the body. However, linear motion relates to a straight line and angular motion relates to rotation.

3. The axis would be inside when swinging around a high bar and outside when in a pike somersault off a vault box.

4. The combined value of linear and angular distances, displacements, speed, velocity and acceleration is known as <u>kinematics</u>.

5. Linear speed—b; linear acceleration—c; linear distance—e; linear velocity—d; linear displacement—a.

6. The correct measurements are (a) metres (m), (b) seconds (s), (c) metres/second (m/s), (d) metres/second (m/s) and (e) metres/second/second (m/s^2).

7. Car racing, speed skating, sprinting or long-distance running would improve through analysis by linear kinematics.

8. Angular displacement is the <u>angular</u> change that occurs during a <u>time period</u> and is measured in <u>degrees</u>. One complete rotation equals <u>360°</u>, but if an object has rotated back to its initial orientation, then the <u>angular displacement</u> is zero, whereas the <u>angular distance</u> is the distance the object has rotated through during the time interval, in this case, <u>360°</u>. <u>Angular velocity</u> refers to the rate and direction of change in angular displacement of a body in a time period, whereas angular speed is the <u>angular distance</u> divided by <u>time</u>.

9. Newton's law of inertia states that the velocity of a body remains constant unless a force acts on it (e.g., hitting a pool ball with a cue).

10. A basketball released from the hands of a player at the free throw line has maximum velocity. This velocity gradually decreases because of the effect of gravity. Finally, the ball will reach zero velocity and will then start its downward flight to the ring because of gravity.

11. Objects of regular shape have a centre of mass at the centre of the object, and objects of irregular shape may have the centre of mass further away from the object's centre.

12. The parabola of an object is influenced by the initial velocity of the object, the initial position and the acceleration caused by gravity. By the performer lowering two arms, the centre of gravity will be lowered and the speed of the rotation will be increased. By the performer raising two arms, the centre of gravity will be raised, therefore slowing the body down in its rotations.

13. The centre of gravity is changed by the arrangement of the body's mass. By lowering the legs in a jump such as a volleyball block or basketball jump shot, the centre of gravity is lowered; hence it appears that the body hangs in flight.

CHAPTER 4

1. Force is measured by Newtons (N).

2. Gravity, air resistance, muscles on bones, and contact between objects may influence the performance of physical activity.

3. (a) Action—body jumping forwards; reaction—canoe moving backwards

   (b) Action—soccer ball's change of direction; reaction—velocity of foot slowed

   (c) Action—cricket ball's change of direction; reaction—cricket bat reduction of velocity

4. (a) The open angle of the golf club at impact, (b) connection of the ball with the top of the softball bat and (c) connection of the hand with the top of the volleyball.

5. The torque of a force is equal to the magnitude of the force multiplied by the moment arm: torque = force × moment arm.

6. The rotation of the forearm during the forehand swing at contact causes the racquet to connect with the side of the tennis ball and spin the ball. This spin results in a turning effect or torque.

7. Force = mass × acceleration or acceleration = force ÷ mass.

8. The moment of inertia is when <u>angular acceleration</u> caused by a given <u>torque</u> is dependent on the <u>resistance</u> of the object to turning around the axis of rotation.

9. The greater the mass, the greater the linear acceleration. The smaller the mass, the less resistance to turning; therefore, the greater the angular acceleration.

10. (a) Impulse = force × time and (b) momentum = mass × velocity.

11. When force is applied to an object for a specified period, the impulse is equal to the change in momentum that results.

12. Cricket backstop catching, bowling, vaulting in gymnastics and catching a fly ball are some skills that could utilise an understanding of impulse and momentum to improve performance.

13. (a) Angular impulse = torque × time and (b) angular momentum = angular velocity × moment of inertia.

14. Newton's law of inertia states that momentum remains constant when no resultant forces or torques are acting.

15. Gymnasts maximise their angular momentum by increasing their angular velocity. First they complete a tumbling run along the mat and then they increase the moment of inertia by tucking the body. The tucked position minimises air resistance, and the impulse of the torque increases because of the increase in the change of angular momentum.

16. (a) Work = force × displacement and (b) power = mass × gravity × displacement.

17. Energy is found as chemical energy stored in the body, mechanical energy and thermal energy.

18. Skills that gravitational potential energy influences include springing off a dive board, long jumping and downhill skiing.

19. The rebound of the ball is a result of the coefficient of restitution. The rebound height is influenced by the nature of the rebound surface and by the temperature and nature of the ball.

20. The sweet spot is important because it is the exact spot on the racquet or ball where the striker's hands can apply the least amount of force for maximum output to resist the acceleration.

21. Drag is the force applied by air or water to an object passing through it in an opposite direction. Lift is force applied by air or water to an object passing through it at right angles.

22. An example is cycling: helmet, shaved legs, wheel frame and Lycra® spandex clothing designed to minimise drag from air. Another example is speed skating: clothing and helmet designed to minimise drag from air. A third example is swimming: caps or shaved heads, rounded goggles, tight-fitting clothing designed to minimise drag from water.

23. To maximise lift, swimmers use sideways movement in strokes. Volleyball players use a topspin on a spike and a force on the side of the ball with lower pressure to maximise lift. A spin bowl in cricket also creates topspin. The topspin causes one side of the ball to oppose the direction of motion, thereby increasing the fluid pressure on that side. Thus, the lift force acts on the side of lower pressure.

CHAPTER 5

1. The energy source that muscle fibres use comes from the change of a molecule called <u>adenosine triphosphate</u>, or <u>ATP</u> for short, into <u>adenosine diphosphate</u>, or <u>ADP</u>. ATP is stored within the <u>muscle fibres</u> in sufficient quantities for one explosive action such as a <u>volleyball spike</u> or <u>golf swing</u>. Once this action has occurred, the muscle cell must resynthesise <u>adenosine diphosphate</u> back into <u>adenosine triphosphate</u> by using other sources from within the cell or bodily systems. The cycle will continue as long as <u>energy</u> is available to turn ADP back into ATP.

2.

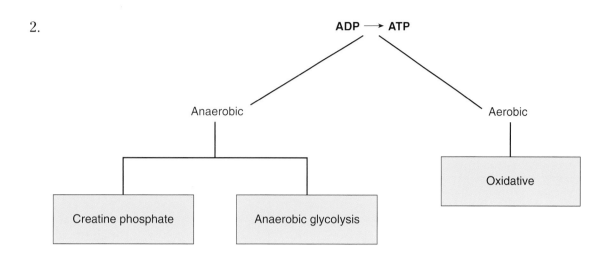

3.

Energy source for ADP → ATP resynthesis	Creatine phosphate	Anaerobic glycolysis	Aerobic (oxidative)
Is oxygen used?	No	No	Yes
Source	Creatine phosphate	Glycogen	Glycogen (carbohydrates), fats, protein
Storage of source	Cell	Cell Muscles Liver	Muscles Liver Fat stores
Length of source	10-15 s	3 min	Unlimited after 3 mins
Resynthesis length	5-6 min	20-60 min	—
By-products	Phosphates	Pyruvic acid Lactic acid	Water, CO_2
Is fatigue developed?	No	Yes	No
Intensity of physical activities	Maximum effort	Maximum effort	Sub-maximum effort

4. The utilization of energy is reflected in the performer's changes in time for each 100 m. The first 100 m predominately uses the creatine phosphate stores. In the second 100 m, the creatine phosphate cuts out and anaerobic glycolysis provides the ATP required, resulting in a slightly slower 100 m. With each of the following segments, the by-product of anaerobic glycolysis (lactic acid) will build in the cell. This build-up creates fatigue as the aerobic system slowly starts working; thus each 100 m is slowing down.

5. Energy sources are (a) lactic acid and creatine phosphate; (b) the aerobic system; (c) creatine phosphate, anaerobic glycolysis and the aerobic system; and (d) the aerobic system and creatine phosphate.

6. Your answer should include the approximate percentages of the three energy systems used: creatine phosphate, anaerobic glycolysis and aerobic.

7.

Food source	Carbohydrates	Fats	Proteins
Fuel source	Glycogen	Fatty acids	Amino acids
Utilised aerobically or anaerobically	→ ATP	→ ATP	→ ATP
Storage of fuel source	Muscles, liver	Adipose tissue	Muscles
Level of exercise intensity	Moderate to high	Rest and low	Low when all else has run out

8.

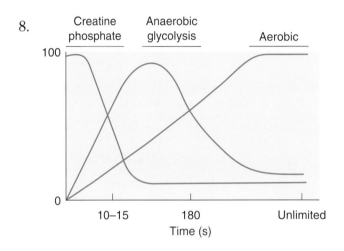

9. *Hitting the wall* is the stage in energy production at which glycogen stores are depleted. The athlete must reduce her exercise intensity to allow the increased oxygen consumption to meet her body's needs.

10. Dietary guidelines are (a) a normal balanced diet to provide sufficient energy for the body's needs; (b) a high carbohydrate diet to increase the amount of glycogen available, in preparation for exercise; (c) 500 ml of water to prevent dehydration; and (d) 250 ml of water per 15 min of exercise to prevent dehydration.

CHAPTER 6

1.

Energy stored	Creatine phosphates	Anaerobic glycolysis	Aerobic
Training: intensity level	High	Moderate to high	Moderate to low
Training: duration	Short	Medium	Long
The body's physical adaptation	Increased • ATP, CP storage in the muscle • ability to generate large amounts of energy quickly	Increased • glycogen storage in muscle • activity of enzymes • lactic acid tolerance	Increased • activity of enzyme to liberate energy • ability to utilize aerobic energy

2. $\dot{V}O_2$max is the rate of oxygen consumed by the muscles, or maximum O_2 consumption. The higher the level of $\dot{V}O_2$max, the greater the fitness level because of the way the body physically adapts to increase its ability to utilise aerobic energy.

3. Lactic acid threshold is the exercise intensity below which muscles can metabolise pyruvic acid. When lactic acid starts to accumulate, fatigue sets in. Trained athletes have increased their ability to store muscle glycogen and utilise this energy source for maximum performance output with the least amount of lactic acid production.

4. Oxygen consumption and heart rate remain elevated after exercise to replace the stores of creatine phosphate and glycogen used during exercise, to return the body temperature to normal and to clear carbon dioxide from the blood. Some students will return faster because of better fitness levels.

5. $\dot{V}O_2$max enables you to select an appropriate level of intensity for training, which will vary from that of your classmates.

6. Minute ventilation is the volume of air brought into the lungs each minute. Increased maximum minute ventilation enhances the body's capacity to excrete carbon dioxide.

7. (a) Stroke volume is the volume of blood pumped by the heart during each beat, (b) cardiac output is the volume of blood pumped by the muscles each minute and (c) maximum heart rate is the highest rate at which the heart is capable of beating, usually expressed as beats per minute.

8. Cardiac output at rest is low because of the low demands on the body. Cardiac output during exercise increases according to the intensity levels of the exercise.

9. To calculate your maximum heart rate, use this formula: 220 beats/min – your age. The equation for a 60-year-old is 220 – 60 = 160. Therefore a 60-year-old's heart rate during exercise must be lower.

10. With increased age, the heart rate potential decreases and so does the potential exercise intensity.

11. Impacts of high-endurance training are (a) maximum heart rate is not affected, (b) heart size increases, (c) stroke volume increases, (d) cardiac output at rest is not affected, (e) resting heart rate decreases and (f) cardiac output during exercise increases.

12. From rest to activity the circulatory, respiratory and muscular systems redirect the blood to the muscles and skin; narrow the arteries to the internal organs; widen the arteries to the muscles involved; carry O_2 to muscles and remove carbon dioxide, lactic acid and heat; and extract up to 85% of the oxygen from the blood.

13. $\dot{V}O_2$max and the lactic acid threshold determine the intensity level that your body can maintain for prolonged periods without fatigue occurring.

14.

Muscle fibres	Types	Main energy source	Fatigue rate	Rate of contraction	Type of movement
Slow twitch	I	Aerobic glycolysis	Low	Slow	Balance and endurance
Fast twitch	IIA	Aerobic glycolysis and glycogen	Moderate to high	Fast	Sprinting
	IIB	Glycogen	High	Fast	Weight-lifting

15. Different muscles within the body and between <u>people</u> have different combinations of <u>fast-</u> and <u>slow-</u>twitch fibres. Explosive physical activity requires <u>fast-twitch</u> fibres, whereas <u>low-force</u> activities require slow-twitch fibres. Elite athletes such as endurance runners have a high predominance of <u>slow-twitch</u> fibres, whereas <u>sprinters</u> and <u>weight-lifters</u> have larger portions of type II fibres.

16. Responses to training include increased number of capillaries, changes in the function of the nervous system and increased size (muscular hypertrophy) or number (muscular hyperplasia) of fibres.

17. Capacity for physical activity increases through childhood to early adulthood and then decreases after about 30 years of age.

18. Changes that occur after 30 years of age are the decline of $\dot{V}O_2$max due to lower maximum heart rate, reduced maximum cardiac output, decreased number of capillaries and less vascular ability to redirect blood to working muscles.

19. Training can reduce the rate and amount of reduction in the $\dot{V}O_2$max.

20. (a) $\dot{V}O_2$max is slightly higher for males and (b) there is no difference in strength.

21. Exercise restricts the hormonal disruption that causes the reduction of bone density.

CHAPTER 7

1. Specificity—c; progressive overload—a; reversibility—e; individuality—d; overtraining—b.

2. Definitions: (a) static force—a force that is exerted without movement; (b) dynamic force—a force that is exerted with movement; (c) repetitions—the number of times an exercise is performed; (d) sets—the number of blocks of each group of repetitions; (e) maximum load—the greatest amount a person can lift; (f) eccentric training—muscle is lengthening; and (g) concentric training—muscle is shortening.

3.

Purpose	Maximum strength	Health-related strength
Weights	80%-100%	Lower load
Reps	1-8	Higher
Sets	3-6	3-6
Speed	Slow	Slow

4. Plyometrics is the prestretching of the relevant muscles before exerting rapid explosive movements.

5. Interval training is high-intensity exercise interspersed with periods of rest.

6.

Purpose	Creatine phosphate	Anaerobic glycolysis	Aerobic system
Intensity	95%-100%	60%-80%	50%-90% of $\dot{V}O_2$max
Duration	Up to 30 s	30 s to 2 min	Over 3 min
Recovery time	5 min	1 to 4 min	Equal or less than duration
Recovery type	Rest	Active	Rest

7. Continuous training involves relatively low-intensity activity performed for relatively long duration to improve the ability to utilise energy derived from the aerobic system.

8.

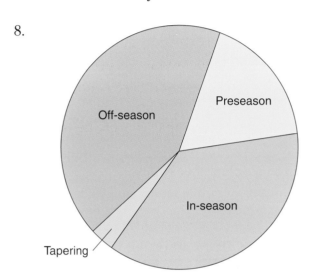

9. Warm-up starts with low-intensity aerobic activity and stretching, followed by the training program, then a cool-down of low-intensity aerobic exercises.

10. The benefits of a warm-up include an increase in flexibility, reduction of injury and preparation of the body for work. The benefit of a cool-down is that it speeds up the process of removing lactic acid.

11. Training for health reduces the risk of obesity, osteoporosis, heart disease and diabetes.

CHAPTER 8

1. Some examples of how participation in sport may be influenced by each of the following factors are

   a. limited opportunities for participation or coaching in masters sports and the lower status of masters competitions in comparison to elite senior level competitions;

   b. the tendency for quality coaching to be provided primarily to elite performers; the tendency for children to avoid passing the ball to lower-ability players in team game situations;

    c. sports clothing manufacturers producing clothes to suit a limited range of sizes, or to emphasise particular shapes (such as tight-fitting clothing for female performers); people of particular shapes or sizes feeling self-conscious about their bodies in sport settings;

    d. varying prize or appearance money being paid to male as compared with female athletes in the same sport;

    e. dress codes for Muslim women participating in sport and restrictions on the settings in which they are able to participate (relating particularly to whether or not they may be seen by men when they are participating);

    f. the high cost of modified wheelchairs for specific athletic events, meaning that only some people with disabilities can perform at the highest levels;

    g. the indirect costs associated with accessing participation opportunities, including childcare and travel to training sessions, that prevent some people with limited income from participating; and

    h. continuation of the myth that certain sports are an exclusively male or an exclusively female domain.

2. Differences between individuals and in society: (a) From an equality perspective difference is viewed as deficiency. Some people are regarded as lacking in comparison to others, and this lack is seen as a problem to be addressed. (b) From an equity perspective difference is viewed as a resource to be valued and celebrated as a richness of society.

3. Figueroa's framework for equity covers five levels, and dynamic relationships exist between the levels. For example, actions at the individual level are shaped by those at the interpersonal level; at the same time, actions at the individual level act to shape those at the interpersonal level. The cultural level refers to the shared assumptions, beliefs and values that are so embedded that they are regarded as the norm within particular societies. The structural level relates to the distribution of resources within sport and within society. The institutional level is concerned with routine practices, rules and procedures within organisations. The interpersonal level addresses our interactions with others. The individual level relates to our own attitudes and beliefs.

CHAPTER 9

1. The social construction of bodies refers to the process of making links between social values and body shape, movement and dress.

2. A naturalistic view assumes that the biological functioning of bodies determines how people behave, what they believe and how they feel.

3. The social construction of our bodies has changed over time. Examples include changes in the shapes, sizes and appearances of bodies in relation to what we believe is beautiful; how we dress; who can wear body decorations such as tattoos, make-up, jewellery and so on; and how we think about head, facial and body hair. Examples of socially constructed bodies include the ideal gymnast (a petite female) and the ideal weight-lifter (a large muscular male).

4. Body image is a major contributing factor to self-esteem. Poor body image and poor self-esteem are especially linked among adolescents. Aquatics pressures students to wear togs, aerobics to wear a leotard, and touch to wear the high-cut body suit for girls.

5. The media target specific groups of people (for example, adolescents) with a particular message they know will appeal to the group. They link such messages to their products by means of careful advertising, with a view to selling the products.

6. Through the media, advertising uses bodies to sell products by linking the product to social values that are associated with the way particular bodies look or are shaped.

7. Social regulation of the body refers to activities developed within society that people master in order to control their movements. These activities vary from one society to another.

CHAPTER 10

1. Mechanisation has led to an increase in their potential leisure time, a decrease in physical activity performed in everyday work and home practices, an increase in diseases related to sedentary lifestyles and an increase in unemployment.

2. Definitions: (a) Leisure is the time available that is not associated with work, be it domestic work or wage labour; (b) recreation is the ability to re-create or regenerate through a broad range of activities that are alternatives to work and (c) lifestyle is shaping or controlling a range of everyday practices.

3. The commodification of lifestyle involves thinking about everyday life as if it were a commodity created for buying and selling.

4. As a young person, you have fewer constraints compared with older adults, fewer commitments to family and a larger disposable income. Advertisers know that it is important to most young people to purchase popular goods, because young people often view such goods as indicators of position or status in relation to peers and others.

5. Surveys depend on people's honesty, the clarity of questions, people's ability to understand the questions and their motivation to complete the questionnaire as well as they can. They also typically exclude questions relating to the intensity of physical activity; hence, the data collected may be inaccurate.

6. A difference between females and males is that more women walk and do aerobics, whereas more men jog, work out in the gym and play team sports. Some differences between age groups are that more adolescents get involved in team and individual sports than people aged 20 and older, and more people aged 20 and older tend to participate in exercise activities such as walking, swimming, golf and lawn bowls.

7. (a) Social factors relating to sex include body image and responsibilities such as caring for children. (b) Social factors relating to culture include expectations and values that are incompatible with sport. (c) Social factors relating to age include increased responsibilities of home and family.

8. The high cost of some sports prohibits some groups of people from participating.

CHAPTER 11

1. Changes to cricket include the following: One-day cricket, based on limited overs, made the game accessible for television because it introduced faster

results and more action in the game. Changing the cricket whites to colours made for more interesting television viewing, allowed for easier association with teams and boosted marketing potential. Changing the colour of the ball made it easier to see on television, especially during night games.

	Positive	Negative
Players	• increased salaries • professional athletes • professional coaches and support available • improved facilities	• greater pressure • loss of privacy • short professional careers • meeting commitments; e.g., promotions • sponsors unable to meet players' salary demands • inequity between players
Consumers	• entertainment value	• high cost of merchandise • cost of spectating
Administrators	• profits • prestige	• competitiveness between sports • salary negotiations of players • takeover bids

2. Your school might seek sponsorship for sporting competitions, award private scholarships, maintain a school of excellence or compete for prizes.

3. Commercial gyms sell knowledge and motivation to individuals who want to improve their appearance and health. They promote this product by advertising with images that promote the socioculturally acceptable body.

4. Technology has affected sport through enhanced timing, video playbacks and improved sporting equipment.

5. Society does not treat males and females equally in sport as evidenced by segregation of competitions, different levels of prize money and different levels of media coverage.

6. The impact of sport as entertainment on the presentation of women's sport has caused emphasis to be placed on the attractiveness of women's bodies. Uniforms or costumes (for example, high-cut leotards) have drawn spectators' attention primarily to women's appearance and not as much to their physical performance.

7. Hegemony means that some players in the team will be dominant and others submissive for some parts of your current physical activity.

8. Sport can be used as a political tool when it contributes to making inferiority of women relative to men appear natural. It can also contribute to the maintenance and naturalisation of social class divisions in society and advance the causes of both political parties and nations.

9. Globalisation refers to the ways in which technological developments have made it possible for people, manufactured goods, information and ideas to travel to what were once diverse and distant cultures.

10. Globalisation of basketball has resulted in cultural change as young Australians have adopted forms of dress and codes of behaviour associated with basketball in the United States.

11. Globalisation is not a new phenomenon, since Australians' historical sporting culture originated in Britain.

Bibliography and Suggested Readings

Chapter 1

Abernethy, B., V. Kippers, L.T. McKinnon, R.J. Neal and S. Hanrahan. 1996. *The biophysical foundations of human movement.* Melbourne: Macmillan.

Kirk, D., J. Nauright, S. Hanrahan, D. Macdonald and I. Jobling. 1996. *The socio-cultural foundations of human movement.* Melbourne: Macmillan.

Mosston, M. and S. Ashworth. 1994. *Teaching physical education.* 4th ed. New York: Macmillan.

Chapter 2

Kirk, D., J. Nauright, S. Hanrahan, D. Macdonald and I. Jobling. 1996. *The socio-cultural foundations of human movement.* Melbourne: Macmillan.

Kirk, D., D. Penney, R. Burgess-Limerick, T. Gorely, and C. Maynard. 2002. *A-level physical education: A reflective performer.* Champaign, IL: Human Kinetics.

Nideffer, R.N. 1976. *The inner athlete: Mind plus muscle for winning.* New York: Crowell.

Orlick, T. 1986. *Psyching for sport.* Champaign, IL: Human Kinetics.

———. 1986. *Psyching for sport coaches' training manual.* Champaign, IL: Human Kinetics.

Steiner, I.D. 1972. *Group processes and productivity.* New York: Academic Press.

Weinberg, R.S. and D. Gould. 1999. *Foundations of sport and exercise psychology.* 3rd ed. Champaign, IL: Human Kinetics.

Williams, J.M., ed. 1993. *Applied sport psychology: Personal growth to peak performance.* 2d ed. Palo Alto, CA: Mayfield.

Chapters 3 and 4

Abernethy, B., V. Kippers, L.T. McKinnon, R.J. Neal and S. Hanrahan. 1996. *The biophysical foundations of human movement.* Melbourne: Macmillan.

Carr, G. 1997. *Mechanics of sport.* Champaign, IL: Human Kinetics.

Enoka, R. 1994. *The neuromechanical basis of kinesiology.* Champaign, IL: Human Kinetics.

Hay, J.G. 1978. *The biomechanics of sports techniques.* Englewood Cliffs, NJ: Prentice Hall.

Chapters 5, 6 and 7

Abernethy, B., V. Kippers, L.T. McKinnon, R.J. Neal and S. Hanrahan. 1996. *The biophysical foundations of human movement.* Melbourne: Macmillan.

Wilmore, J.H. and D.L. Costill. 1994. *Physiology of sport and exercise.* Champaign, IL: Human Kinetics.

Chapters 8, 9, 10 and 11

Australian Bureau of Statistics. 1994. *Participation in sporting and physical recreational activities, Queensland, October 1993.* Brisbane: Australian Bureau of Statistics.

Australian Sports Commission. 1991. *Sport for young Australians: Widening the gateways to participation.* Canberra: Australian Sports Commission.

Department of the Arts, Sport, the Environment, Tourism and Territories. 1988. *Physical activity levels of Australians.* Canberra: Australian Government Publishing Service.

———. 1992. *Summary of the pilot survey of the fitness of Australians.* Canberra: Australian Government Publishing Service.

Evans, J. and B. Davies. 1993. Equality, equity and physical education. In *Equality, education and physical education,* edited by J. Evans, pp. 11-28. London: Falmer Press.

Figueroa, P. 1993. Equality, multiculturalism, antiracism and physical education in the National Curriculum. In *Equality, education and physical education,* edited by J. Evans, pp. 90-102. London: Falmer Press.

Goldlust, J. 1987. *Playing for keeps: Sport, the media and society.* Melbourne: Longman Cheshire.

Kirk, D., J. Nauright, S. Hanrahan, D. Macdonald and I. Jobling. 1996. *The sociocultural foundations of human movement.* Melbourne: Macmillan.

McKay, J. 1991. *No pain, no gain? Sport and Australian culture.* Sydney: Prentice Hall.

Vamplew, W., ed. 1987. *Australians: Historical statistics.* Sydney: Fairfax, Syme & Weldon.

Index

Note: The italicized *f* or *t* following a page number denotes a figure or table on that page. The italicized *ff* or *tt* following a page number denotes multiple figures or tables on that page.

About the Authors

David Kirk, PhD, has been a physical education teacher, an educator of physical education teachers and a researcher in physical education since 1979. He held the position of professor of human movement studies at the University of Queensland, Australia, from 1995 to 1998. He is now professor of physical education and youth sport at Loughborough University, England. Professor Kirk is recognised internationally for his research in physical education, having published many articles in academic and professional journals. He has authored or co-authored seven texts, including the critically acclaimed *Schooling Bodies: School Practice and Public Discourse, 1880-1950* (1998). Professor Kirk has worked extensively as an editor and reviewer for journals and publishers.

Professor Kirk earned his PhD from Loughborough University, England, in 1986. He was a founding member of the Queensland Junior Sport Council, a member of the HPE Advisory Committee of the Queensland Board of Senior Secondary School Studies, and coordinator of the Australian Council for Health, Physical Education and Recreation (ACHPER)/the Australian Association (AARE) Special Interest Group Research in Education. Professor Kirk was awarded the President's Prize of the International Olympic Committee in 2001 for his research and development work in physical education.

Robin Burgess-Limerick, PhD, is a lecturer in biomechanics in the department of human movement studies at the University of Queensland, Australia, where he earned his doctorate in biomechanics in 1994. Dr. Burgess-Limerick has conducted research on diverse topics including field hockey, locomotion and manual lifting. He has published many research articles in journals of biomechanics, motor behaviour and ergonomics. He is a member of the International Society of Biomechanics and the Ergonomics Society of Australia. In his spare time, Dr. Burgess-Limerick enjoys playing field hockey.

Michael Kiss graduated with a BHMS (Ed) from the University of Queensland in 1986. He taught health and physical education in high schools from 1987 to 2002. Mr. Kiss was the head of the department of physical education at Bundaberg North State High School from 1994 to 2002. He was appointed to the Queensland Board of Secondary School Studies in 1990 and performed review panellist duties at district and state levels before being appointed State Review Panel Chair–Physical Education with the newly formed Queensland Studies Authority in 2002. He has an advisory role for curriculum development in physical education through his position on the HPE Subject Advisory Committee. Mr. Kiss has maintained his commitment to physical education despite moving on to administrative duties at the school level. In this capacity, Mr. Kiss reviews school samples of work, advises schools on the maintenance of syllabus standards and provides assistance to schools regarding curriculum development.

In his spare time, Mr. Kiss enjoys playing golf, volleyball, tennis and all types of football, as well as listening to music and playing guitar.

Janine Lahey has been head of the department for health and physical education at Sunshine Beach State High School in Noosa since 2001. Ms. Lahey has been a high school physical education teacher since 1979. During that time, she has gained valuable experience in creating personalized content for high school students. She was involved in the pilot stage of the syllabus development.

Ms. Lahey has been a member of the District Review Panel for Health and Physical Education since 1992 and a member of the State Panel of Physical Education since 1996. She is a member of ACHPER. In her spare time, she enjoys bushwalking, snorkelling, scuba diving, Surflifesaving (ADD) and canoeing.

Since 1990, **Dawn Penney** has conducted research focusing on policy and curriculum development in physical education and junior sport in the United Kingdom and Australia. As a research scholar at the University of Southampton and subsequently a research fellow at Loughborough University, Dr. Penney was involved in research that tracked the development of the National Curriculum for Physical Education in England and Wales. In 1996 Ms. Penney took up a two-year appointment as a research fellow in the department of human movement studies at the University of Queensland. There she studied the implementation of the national statement and profile in health and physical education, evaluated the new senior school physical education syllabus in Queensland and studied the socio-economic determinants of participation in junior sport. In 1998 Dr. Penney returned to the United Kingdom as a senior research fellow in physical education at De Montfort University and subsequently Loughborough University. She has retained her interest in curriculum developments in physical education in England and internationally. In July 2003 Dr. Penney joined the staff at Edith Cowan University in Perth, Australia.

Dr. Penney earned her doctorate in education in 1994. She is a member of ACHPER and the Physical Education Association of the United Kingdom. In her spare time, she enjoys running, cycling and swimming.